Northwest Historical Series
VI

NARCISSA PRENTISS WHITMAN
From Nixon, *How Marcus Whitman
Saved Oregon,* 3rd edition.

MARY AUGUSTA DIX GRAY
From a photograph.

SARAH WHITE SMITH
From a miniature, about 1838, in the
Missionary Album, Honolulu, 1937.

SOUTH PASS, WYOMING, MONUMENT TO
FIRST WHITE WOMEN OVER THE ROCKIES
Photo by Dan W. Greenberg.
Courtesy, Oregon Historical Society.

For Mrs. Whitman, no picture made during her lifetime is known to be in existence.
The above, considered a good likeness, is reported to have been drawn under
the supervision of "a gentleman familiar with her appearance
and with suggestions from members of her family."

For Mrs. Spalding, there is no known picture in existence.

FIRST WHITE WOMEN OVER THE ROCKIES

Diaries, Letters, and Biographical Sketches
of the Six Women of the Oregon Mission
who made the Overland Journey
in 1836 and 1838

With Introductions and Editorial Notes by

CLIFFORD MERRILL DRURY
California Professor of Church History
San Francisco Theological Seminary

In Two Volumes

VOL. I

Mrs. Marcus Whitman, Mrs. Henry H. Spalding,
Mrs. William H. Gray, and Mrs. Asa B. Smith

THE ARTHUR H. CLARK COMPANY
Glendale, California
1963

To my mother

CHARITY MAE DELL DRURY
1864 - 1908

the first to give me a love for books

Contents of Volume I

Illustrations

Sources and Acknowledgments

An astonishing amount of original source material pertaining to the Oregon mission of the American Board is extant. Some of these manuscripts go back to 1833, almost one hundred thirty years ago. The diaries, letters, and reports written by one of the six couples connected with this Mission, Elkanah and Mary Walker, contain at least three hundred thousand words. The very existence of such a mass of original material written by these two people, who surely must have considered themselves to have been very ordinary folks, has added importance to their story and has set them apart as being extraordinary.

The following libraries or depositories, which contain original material used in the preparation of this work, have granted permission to the author to publish such documents or extracts of documents as he felt were important. The abbreviations used in the footnotes to identify the respective collections are indicated.

The American Board of Commissioners for Foreign Missions has in its archives, now on deposit in Houghton Libary, Harvard University, the original correspondence received from its missionaries in Oregon together with copies of letters sent to them totaling about one million words. (Coll. A.)

Coe Collection, Yale University Library, has about one hundred letters written by members of the Oregon Mission to one another, together with other source documents. (Coll. c.)

The Hawaiian Missionary Children's Society, Honolulu, has a collection of about twenty-five letters from all of the seven men of the Oregon Mission together with other related documents. For the most part this material has never before been used in any history of the Oregon Mission.

The Henry E. Huntington Library and Art Gallery, San Marino, California, purchased from the Rosenbach Company of New York in 1922 a collection of Oregoniana which had been assembled by the late Frederick W. Skiff of Portland, Oregon. This collection contains forty letters written by Elkanah or Mary Walker and eleven addressed to them during the years 1839-63. Also included are a number of notebooks containing Elkanah's diary for the following periods: March 7-May 15 and September 10-October 5, 1838; 1841; November 21-December 31, 1842; 1843-47 inclusive; January 1-April 30 and May 5-

October 13, 1848; and a series of sixteen notebooks containing Mary's diary from May 9, 1837, to November 11, 1848. For additional information about the Walker Collection in this depository see the *Huntington Library Bulletin,* May 1931. Mary's diary for June 10-December 21, 1838, with some omissions, appeared in the Montana *Frontier,* March 1931. This is the longest extract of either of the Walker diaries which has been published. (Coll. H.)

The Oregon Historical Society, Portland, Oregon, is rich in its holdings of original material dealing with the Oregon Mission of the American Board including the original Protestant Ladder painted by Mrs. Eliza Spalding; Elkanah Walker's diary for January 1-November 20, 1842; many original Whitman letters; and a wealth of collateral items. (Coll. o.)

The Presbyterian Historical Society, Philadelphia, Pennsylvania, owns a collection of eight Spalding letters including the earliest written by either Henry or Eliza Spalding; the original record book of the First Presbyterian Church of Oregon; and much collateral material.

Washington State University, Pullman, Washington, has a fine collection of Walker items including Mary's diary 1833-38, and 1848-90. After leaving the Mission, Mary was not as faithful in making regular entries in her diary. Also at Pullman are many of the letters written by Elkanah and Mary to each other, a number of books from the Mission library including some of Dr. Whitman's medical volumes, and other documents. (Coll. WN.)

Whitman College, Walla Walla, Washington, ranks with the Oregon Historical Society in the extent of its holdings of letters and diaries of the missionaries. This collection includes one of the two copies of Mrs. Whitman's diary; the diaries of both Henry and Eliza Spalding; and a wealth of other material. (Coll. w.)

The second copy of Narcissa Whitman's diary, July 18-October 18, 1836, is in the Bancroft Library, Berkeley, California, together with the Whitman letters listed as being a part of Collection u in the appendix of the author's *Marcus Whitman, M.D.* Caxton Printers, Caldwell, Idaho, owners of the copyright of the author's trilogy published by them, 1936-40, has granted permission to make quotations from these volumes.[1]

Permission to publish for the first time the diary of Mrs. William H. Gray has been granted by the owner, Miss Mary A. Gray, a granddaughter of William and Mary Gray, of Portland, Oregon. Location and acknowledgments of other source materials used in this work will be made in footnotes.

A complete transcript of Mary Walker's diary for the period March 5, 1838-July 3, 1848, made by the author from the original documents,

---

[1] *Henry Harmon Spalding, Pioneer of Old Oregon,* 1936; *Marcus Whitman, M.D., Pioneer and Martyr,* 1937; and *Elkanah and Mary Walker, Pioneers Among the Spokanes,* 1940.

has been deposited with the Eastern Washington State Historical Society, Spokane, Washington. Because of the limitations of space, about twenty thousand words of the diary were omitted in the present work. Much of the author's correspondence dealing with his researches extending back over more than twenty-five years together with his collection of pictures, pamphlets, and many of his notes, have likewise been turned over to this Society.

To all members of the staffs of the above-mentioned libraries or depositories who have so willingly assisted me, to the many who have granted me permission to use materials, and to the large company of historians and others to whom I have turned for counsel I wish to express my deepest appreciation.

CLIFFORD M. DRURY

Introduction

Introduction

This is the amazing story of the first six white American women to cross the Rocky Mountains. Here for the first time copies of their diaries and of some of their letters which tell of their travel experiences and which describe their pioneer life in Old Oregon are brought together in one published account. Much of the documentary material here given has never before been printed.

Two of these women, Mrs. Marcus Whitman and Mrs. Henry Harmon Spalding, crossed the continent from western New York with their husbands in 1836. They began their journey the middle of February and arrived at Fort Vancouver near the mouth of the Columbia River on September 12. The journey took about seven months. The first part of the three thousand mile trek was made by wagon to Pittsburgh and then by river boats via St. Louis to Liberty, Missouri. From that western extreme of the frontier, the party rode horseback about nineteen hundred miles to Fort Walla Walla on the Columbia River. Since it was then thought unbecoming for a woman to ride astride, Mrs. Whitman and Mrs. Spalding rode most of the entire distance on the old-fashioned sidesaddle. For a part of the journey the missionaries had with them a light wagon in which the women occasionally rode.

The party crossed the Continental Divide through South Pass, in what is now western Wyoming, on July 4, 1836. That was seven years before the first wagon train of Oregon-bound immigrants rolled through the same great Oregon gateway. The last part of their journey, from Fort Walla Walla to Fort Vancouver, was by boat down the Columbia River.

Two years later, four newly-wedded couples and a single man, Cornelius Rogers, followed the Whitmans and the Spaldings over the same trail. This party crossed the Continental Divide on July 15, 1838. The couples were the Reverend and Mrs. Elkanah Walker, the Reverend and Mrs. Cushing Eells, the Reverend and Mrs. Asa B. Smith, and Mr. and Mrs. William H. Gray. The four women of this party endured all of the dangers and difficulties experienced by their two sisters who preceded them. They also rode horseback on sidesaddles from the western frontier of Missouri to Fort Walla Walla. A ride of twenty-five or thirty miles a day was fairly common, and once they made a record of forty-five miles in one day!

These thirteen men and women were sent out to Oregon by the American Board of Commissioners for Foreign Missions, hereinafter referred to as the American Board or by the initial letters ABCFM. This Board, with its headquarters in Boston, is now a Congregational agency but then it enjoyed the support of both the Presbyterians and the Congregationalists. Oregon then included everything north of the present Oregon-California border and west of the Continental Divide.

All of the six women, with the possible exception of Mrs. Spalding, came out of Christian homes and were closely associated with the church from earliest infancy. Mrs. Whitman's father was ordained a Presbyterian elder on the evening of her marriage. Mrs. Spalding joined a Presbyterian church when she was nineteen years old. Mrs. Gray was a member of the Dutch Reformed Church, which was Presbyterian in its doctrine and policy. The other three women, Mrs. Walker, Mrs. Eells, and Mrs. Smith, were daughters of Congregational deacons.

The average age of the thirteen was twenty-eight for the women and twenty-nine for the men. Among the women at the time of their overland journey, Sarah Smith at twenty-five was the youngest and Myra Eells, thirty-three, the oldest. Among the men, Cornelius Rogers at twenty-three was the youngest and Dr. Whitman, thirty-four in 1836, the oldest. Spalding and Walker were each thirty-three. The other men were in their late twenties.

We have reason to be amazed at the wealth of documentary material written by these missionaries which has survived the vicissitudes of about one hundred and twenty-five years. A transcontinental journey for women in those days was, as Mrs. Whitman described it, "an unheard-of journey." The realization of this fact may explain why four of the women kept diaries of their overland travels. Mrs. Whitman and Mrs. Eells wrote their impressions in the form of travel-letters which were sent back to their families. Mrs. Spalding and Mrs. Walker seem to have written only for themselves. Mrs. Walker alone of all the members of the Oregon Mission kept an almost daily record throughout the entire period of ten years which encompassed her connection with the Board. Since she was writing for her own personal satisfaction, her diary is far more intimate and revealing than that of any of the others. This diary, consisting of about one hundred and ten thousand words, is to appear in a somewhat abbreviated form for the first time in the second volume of this work.

The diaries of Mrs. Whitman, Mrs. Spalding, and Mrs. Eells have been previously published but in little known or difficult-to-find publications. Mrs. Eells' excellent description of her journey to Oregon was published in 1889, more than seventy years ago. Moreover, the transcript of the original documents which have appeared have not always been accurate. The diary of Mrs. Gray for the years 1840-42 has not heretofore been published. Mrs. Smith is the only one of the six women who is not known to have kept a diary during the mission period. However, to complete the series of brief biographical sketches of the women of the Oregon Mission of the American Board, a brief chapter of this volume is devoted to her.

The diaries and letters of these women reflect the deep religious convictions of the New England Protestants of their generation. The religious terminology they used, which sounds somewhat sanctimonious to our modern ears, was the normal and natural language of that time. Religion was for them and their husbands the most serious concern of life. The world was divided into two parts, the saved and the unsaved. They were convinced that they had received a divine call to preach the Gospel to the heathen. Never would these six couples have ventured forth into the great unknown of the Pacific Northwest to seek wealth, adventure, or fame. The compelling motive was a missionary zeal founded on a deep religious faith. This alone accounts for, what was in that day, the unprecedented boldness on the part of the women. They quietly accepted the dictum: "God wills it!" and the corollary that that God would aid and protect his own. Here in these diaries and letters is an epic story of great devotion to an ideal and of bulldog tenacity to that ideal through ten long discouraging years.

In these two volumes is the account of how these six women happened to be sent to faraway Oregon, of how they traveled, of how they established their homes in the wilderness, of how they got along with one another, and of their success or lack of success in converting the natives. The story comes to a tremendous climax in the Whitman massacre of November 29, 1847. Nowhere else is the aftermath of this tragedy described with more poignancy than in Mrs. Walker's diary.

The introductions, annotations, and footnotes are the result of the author's researches in this field covering a period of more than twenty-seven years. The bibliography and index for both volumes will be found at the end of volume II.

THE SIX WOMEN

The two who went to Old Oregon in 1836:

Mrs Marcus Whitman (née Narcissa Prentiss), born March 14, 1808; killed by the Indians November 29, 1847. Married Dr. Marcus Whitman February 18, 1836; one child: Alice Clarissa, born March 14, 1837; drowned June 23, 1839.

Mrs. Henry Harmon Spalding (née Eliza Hart), born August 11, 1807; died January 7, 1851. Married Henry H. Spalding October 13, 1833. Four children, all born at Lapwai: Eliza, b. Nov. 15, 1837; Henry Hart, b. Nov. 24, 1839; Martha Jane, b. Mar. 20, 1845; and Amelia Lorene, b. Dec. 12, 1846.

The four who went to Old Oregon in 1838:

Mrs. Elkanah Walker (née Mary Richardson), born April 1, 1811; died December 5, 1897. Married Elkanah Walker March 5, 1838. Eight children: Cyrus Hamlin, b. Dec. 7, 1838; Abigail Boutwell, b. May 24, 1840; Marcus Whitman, b. March 16, 1842; Joseph Elkanah, b. Feb. 10, 1844; Jeremiah, b. Mar. 7, 1846; John Richardson, b. Dec. 31, 1847; Levi Chamberlain, b. Feb. 4, 1850; and Samuel Thompson, b. May 2, 1852.

Mrs. Cushing Eells (née Myra Fairbanks), born May 26, 1805; died August 9, 1878. Married Cushing Eells March 5, 1838. Two children: Edwin, b. July 27, 1841, and Myron, b. Oct. 7, 1843.

Mrs. William Henry Gray (née Mary Augusta Dix), born January 2, 1810; died December 8, 1881; married William H. Gray February 25, 1838. Nine children: John Henry Dix, b. Mar. 20, 1839; Caroline, b. Oct. 16, 1840; Mary Sophia, b. Mar. 12, 1842; Sarah Fidelia, b. Nov. 25, 1843; William Polk, b. July 26, 1845; Edwin Hall, b. Feb. 14, 1847; Truman Powers, b. Dec. 24, 1848; Albert Williams, b. June 28, 1850; and James Taylor, b. Aug. 12, 1852.

Mrs. Asa Bowen Smith (née Sarah Gilbert White), born September 14, 1813; died May 27, 1855. Married Asa B. Smith March 15, 1838. No children.

The ages of these six women at the time they arrived in Old Oregon ranged from Mrs. Smith at 25, to Mrs. Eells at 33, with an average age of 28. Their ages at the time of their deaths were Mrs. Whitman, Mrs. Smith, and Mrs. Spalding at 39, 41, and 43, respectively, and similarly, Mrs. Gray, Mrs. Eells, and Mrs. Walker at 71, 73, and 86.

Mrs. Marcus Whitman

Narcissa Prentiss Whitman

Narcissa Prentiss, the wife of Dr. Marcus Whitman and the most famous of all the Protestant missionary women who went to Old Oregon, should never have been a missionary to the Indians. This was the judgment of one of her best friends in Oregon, the Reverend H. K. W. Perkins, a member of the Methodist Mission, who was well acquainted with both Dr. and Mrs. Whitman. Attention will subsequently be given to the penetrating analysis that Perkins wrote of the Whitmans following their tragic death on November 29, 1847.[1] They were massacred by a small band of superstitious, aroused natives from the very tribe among whom the Whitmans had spent eleven years of devoted and sacrificial service.

Narcissa was the victim of circumstances. As a girl and young woman, she had grown up in a home and community where an emotional religion was the accepted form. Stimulated by the enthusiasm kindled in revival meetings, she offered herself to the American Board as a missionary. There followed a succession of events which in the course of a few months deposited Marcus and Narcissa among the Cayuses at Waiilatpu in the untamed wilderness of Oregon. The ignorance which Marcus, Narcissa, their colleagues, and the American Board, had of living conditions on the mission field and of the perplexing problems which would face them was simply colossal.

Out in her lonely home in Old Oregon, Narcissa often looked back with nostalgic longing on her happy church life before her marriage. She remembered the frequent revival meetings in which she took part as the leading soloist. She recalled the "melting times" when sinners wept openly for their sins. Writing to Mrs. H. K. W. Perkins on January 1, 1840, Narcissa confessed: "My soul longs, yea, thirst for seasons like many I have been witness of and partaker of, in my native land." [2] Out of this deeply religious background came the motivation which led Narcissa to devote her life to the foreign missionary cause. To her there was no greater task, no loftier goal, than that of carrying the Gospel to the benighted heathen. God in his mysterious providence had selected her to be one of his messengers. Glory be to God!

---

[1] The full text of the Perkins letter may be found in Drury, *Whitman*, 458-60. See also pp. 154-156 in this volume.

[2] *Transactions of the Oregon Pioneer Association*, 1893, p. 127; hereafter referred to as *T.O.P.A.*

However, in her home at Waiilatpu Narcissa quickly discovered that the actual conditions of a missionary's life among the uncivilized Indians of Oregon were far different from her idealized conception. First, there was the tremendous language barrier that took years to break down. Moreover, the natives were not as eager to accept the teachings of the missionaries as she and her husband had been led to expect. And there were other difficulties. Within two years, Narcissa was writing to her parents about the fleas that the Indians brought into the house and about their filthy habits. She wanted a bigger house where it would be possible to exclude the natives from her private rooms and where she would have "a closet to pray in." The Indians in their open lodges had no sense of privacy and, therefore, could not appreciate a white woman's views on the subject. The freedom with which the Indians walked in and out of the first Whitman home became exceedingly objectionable to Narcissa. When the second house was erected in 1840, Indians were not permitted to enter the private quarters of the Whitmans except on invitation. An Indian room was reserved for them. Thus within four years Narcissa's high idealism regarding the heavenly calling of a missionary dimmed before the inescapable facts of daily contacts with the uncivilized, flea-infested natives. This changed attitude became apparent to the Indians and they called her proud and haughty.

A combination of forces kept Marcus and Narcissa at their post in spite of recurring discouragements and later of repeated threats. So much publicity had been given to their going to Oregon that once on the field it was hard to leave. Since Whitman was the only doctor in the Mission, his presence was needed by his colleagues. Both Marcus and Narcissa had a strong sense of their religious commitment. To abandon their field was to betray a trust and to cast doubt upon the providence of God which had led them to Waiilatpu. Perkins, after reviewing the situation, wrote: "Mrs. Whitman was not adapted to savage but *civilized* life . . . It was her *misfortune*, not her *fault*."

Narcissa Prentiss was born at Prattsburg, Steuben County, in western New York, on March 14, 1808. She was the eldest daughter of Stephen and Clarissa Prentiss and the third child in a family of nine. Among her sisters and brothers to whom she frequently wrote from her home in Oregon were Jane, Harriet, and Edward. Narcissa's father was a carpenter and there still stands in Prattsburg the Presbyterian manse which he built in 1832. For a time he served as an Associate County Judge and thus earned the title of Judge. All evidence points to the Prentiss home as containing a lively, affectionate, and closely knit family.

They were loyal members of the Presbyterian Church. The first entry in the baptismal register of the Prattsburg church, founded in 1804, is for July 17, 1808, at which time two infants were baptized, one of whom was "Narcissa Prentiss, daughter of Stephen Prentiss." During the winter of 1818-19, a revival visited the community and on Sunday, June 6, 1819, fifty-nine joined the church on confession of faith. Included in the number was an auburn-haired little girl, eleven-year-old Narcissa Prentiss. When Narcissa was sixteen she had a religious experience which evidently made a deep impression upon her, for in a letter to the American Board dated February 23, 1835, eleven years later, she wrote: "I frequently desired to go to the heathen but only half-heartedly — and it was not till the first Monday of Jan. 1824 that I felt to consecrate myself without reserve to the Missionary work waiting the leading of Providence concerning me."

Gifted with a clear soprano voice of captivating quality, Narcissa was a popular member of the church choir. Years later, the Reverend Joel Wakeman, who remembered her singing, wrote: "Her voice was an important factor in the social prayer meetings and missionary concerts that were held monthly in those days." Here the word "concert" referred not to music but to a meeting for prayer. And another who remembered her singing wrote that her clear, strong voice was "as sweet and musical as a chime of bells." [3]

As a young woman, Narcissa was vivacious and popular. The Prentiss home was a center of young people's social activities. Once her mother was heard to exclaim: "I wish Narcissa would not always have so much company." Narcissa attended the public grade school in Prattsburg and in 1827 was a member of the first class of girls admitted into Franklin Academy. This academy, sponsored by the local church, was opened for boys in 1824. The instruction might be compared to that of a high school. After at least one year at Franklin Academy, Narcissa went to Troy, New York, where she was enrolled in the Female Seminary conducted by the well-known Mrs. Emma Willard. This Seminary might be likened to a normal school of today. It is not known just how long Narcissa studied there. Upon the completion of her training, she became a school teacher. For a time she taught a kindergarten in Bath, New York.

Another resident of Prattsburg who was destined to play a prominent role in the history of the Oregon Mission of the American Board was Henry Harmon Spalding. Henry had the misfortune to have been born out of wedlock. He was reared in foster homes and was denied the available educational opportunities during the early years of his youth. In 1825, when Henry was twenty-two years old, he enrolled in Franklin Academy. He was older than his fellow students, and was bashful and

---

[3] Much of the material dealing with the early life of Narcissa Whitman here given has been drawn from Drury, *Whitman*, where proper documentation may be found.

diffident. Even in those days he manifested an inferiority complex which can easily be explained by the facts of his birth, his poverty, and his limited educational opportunities.

Henry and Narcissa were members of the same church and attended the same school. Possibly they were members of the church's choir at the same time. Henry proposed marriage and was rejected. His love turned to bitter jealousy which later had unfortunate consequences in faraway Oregon. Writing on October 10, 1840, Narcissa made this fact clear to her father.

> Our trials dear father knows but little about. The missionaries' greatest trials are but little known to the churches. I have never ventured to write about them for fear it might do hurt. The man who came with us is one who never ought to have come. My dear husband has suffered more from him in consequence of his wicked jealousy, and his great pique towards me, than can be known in this world. But he suffers not alone — the whole mission suffers, which is most to be deplored. It has nearly broken up the mission.

Many years later her youngest sister, Harriet, wrote regarding Spalding: ". . . he wished to make Narcissa his wife, and her refusal of him caused the wicked feeling he cherished toward them both." [4]

The Prentiss family moved in June, 1834, to Amity (now called Belmont) about fifty miles southwest of Prattsburg. There Narcissa joined the newly organized Presbyterian Church. During the latter part of November of that year, the Rev. Samuel Parker traveled through that region telling the story of how four Indians from west of the Rocky Mountains had journeyed to St. Louis in the fall of 1831 to get Christian missionaries and the Bible. Parker, although he was then fifty-five years old, offered to go to Oregon but the Board rejected his application because of his age. On January 6, 1834, which was a day of prayer set by the Presbyterian Church, Parker spoke in the First Church of Ithaca, New York, with such enthusiasm on the subject of a mission to Oregon that the church voted to support him. Being informed of this fact, the Board gave him an appointment. Parker made an effort to go to Oregon in the summer of 1834 but arrived in St. Louis too late to join the fur company's caravan which left in the spring for the Rockies. He then returned to western New York where he visited a number of churches, appealing for money and also for some one who would go with him the next year to Oregon.

---

[4] The author, in the first edition of his *Spalding*, denied that Spalding was a rejected suitor of Narcissa Prentiss'. However, on the basis of a letter in the archives of the Oregon Historical Society from Mrs. J. W. Jackson, née Harriet Prentiss, to Mrs. Eva Emery Dye dated Jan. 11, 1893, discovered after the publication of the first edition, correction was made in the second edition of the Spalding book.

Among the churches visited was that at Wheeler, New York, a few miles south of Prattsburg, where Dr. Marcus Whitman was an elder and an active worker. After listening to Parker's stirring appeal, Whitman, who was then unmarried, offered to go. Parker soon afterwards visited the Presbyterian church at Angelica. In the audience that evening was Narcissa Prentiss. Her home in Amity was only six miles from Angelica. Following the presentation of the Oregon appeal that evening, Narcissa indicated her willingness to go if the Board could use "an unmarried female." In a letter to his family written on December 5, 1834, Parker reported his success in finding "Dr. Whitman of Wheeler" and "a daughter of Judge Prentiss of Amity." Parker wrote to the Board on December 17 asking: "Are females wanted? A Miss Narcissa Prentiss of Amity is very anxious to go to the heathen. Her education is good — piety conspicuous — her influence good. She will offer herself if is needed." Secretary David Greene of the Board replied December 24 that the Board could not then use "unmarried females."

Among those whom Parker interested in missionary work among the Indians were the Rev. O. S. Powell, pastor of the Amity church, and his wife. The Powells received an appointment from the Board on January 6, 1835, but no special field was designated. Marcus Whitman received word of his appointment to go with Parker to Oregon on January 14. He then rode to Ithaca to see Parker. The two made plans to go to St. Louis by separate routes and then to Liberty to join the American Fur Company's caravan to the Rockies. The caravan usually left the frontier about May 15.

According to a tradition in the Parker family, Samuel Parker told Marcus Whitman about Narcissa Prentiss who had also expressed an interest in going as a missionary to Old Oregon. It seems reasonable to assume that Marcus knew Narcissa, even before Parker suggested the possibility of marriage, as they had long lived in the same general area and both were active in the Presbyterian Church.

After returning from Ithaca, Whitman visited his mother and other relatives in Rushville. He then went to Wheeler where, on February 19, he received final instructions from the Board. He left the same day for St. Louis. Marcus spent the weekend of February 22 as a guest of the Powells at Amity. Sometime during this visit, Marcus proposed marriage to Narcissa and was accepted. On Monday morning, February 23, Marcus mounted his horse and continued on his way to St. Louis. That same day Narcissa wrote her first letter to the American Board which began as follows:

Dear Brethren: Permit an unworthy sister to address you. Having obtained favour of the Lord and desiring to live for the conversion of the world, I now offer myself to the American Board to be employed in their service among the heathen, if counted worthy.

After giving a short account of her life, she closed her letter with the following statement: "Feeling it more my privilege than duty to labour for the conversion of the heathen, I respectfully submit myself to your direction and subscribe, Your unworthy sister in the Lord, Narcissa Prentiss." On the reverse side of the pale green letter paper were testimonials from three Presbyterian ministers who served churches at Angelica, Cuba, and Amity, New York. All gave hearty recommendations for her appointment. O. S. Powell added a postscript to his recommendation which informed the Board of the engagement of Marcus and Narcissa. He wrote: "As it is probable that Miss Prentiss will hereafter become the companion of Doct. Marcus Whitman (should he be established missionary beyond the Rocky Mts.) it may be proper to add that he expressed a desire that she might accompany us on our mission. . ." The Powells were then thinking of going as missionaries to the Indians on the western frontier. The suggestion was made that possibly Narcissa could accompany them and thus get somewhat acquainted with the work of a missionary to the Indians. The Board acted favorably on Narcissa's application and notified her of her appointment in a letter dated March 19. However, the Powells found it impossible to go to the mission field. Narcissa spent the year teaching, waiting for Marcus to return.

A reference to the unusually short courtship of Marcus and Narcissa is found in a statement made by Narcissa in the Parker home in Ithaca in February, 1836, after their marriage and just before they left for Oregon. Narcissa was remembered as having said: "We had to make love somewhat abruptly, and must do our courtship now that we are married." [5]

The fact that the two did not have opportunity to discuss fully all aspects of an overland journey for women to Oregon is found in a letter Marcus wrote to Narcissa from Liberty, Missouri, on April 30, 1835. Evidently Marcus had just received a letter from Narcissa in which she had expressed a wish that they had been married so that she could have accompanied him that year to Oregon. Marcus replied:

> In reading your letter I was surprised exceedingly that you should have conceived it practicable for you to have crossed the mountains this spring. Had I known one half as much of the trip as I now do, when I left you, I should have been entirely willing, if not anxious, that you should have accompanied us. [6]

On the margin of this letter, the following notation in Narcissa's handwriting appears: "Mr. Parker said I could go just as well as not. N. Prentiss." If the possibility of an immediate marriage in order for Narcissa to go with Marcus on the exploring trip had been discussed,

[5] Eells, *Whitman*, 28.
[6] Mowry, *Whitman*, 56.

in all probability Marcus had abruptly dismissed the suggestion as being utterly inadvisable. No white American woman had ever ventured the hazardous journey over the Rocky Mountains. Marcus wanted to make sure that such a journey was feasible before exposing his wife to the difficulties and dangers of such an undertaking.

WHERE WAGONS COULD GO, WOMEN COULD GO

The westward thrust of the Protestant missionary movement into the Pacific Northwest was made possible by the existence of the fur trade. Three animals made this fur trade possible, the beaver, the horse (or sometimes the mule), and the buffalo. During the first decades of the nineteenth century, it was stylish for professional men to wear top hats made of beaver skins. The streams of the Rocky Mountains were alive with beaver. Enterprising fur companies, as the American Fur Company with headquarters in St. Louis, and the Hudson's Bay Company with its head office in Montreal, Canada, competed for the lucrative profits that were to be realized.

Beginning with 1825 a series of sixteen mountain fairs, called Rendezvous,[7] were held, mostly under the sponsorship of the American Fur Company, at some previously designated place in the Rockies. Here hundreds of trappers would gather and exchange their pelts for supplies brought on the backs of horses and mules from the western border of civilization in Missouri. The American Fur Company would sent out its caravan about the middle of May when the prairie grass was high enough to provide food for the animals and when the great herds of buffalo would be roaming the country through which the caravan would pass. The men of the caravan carried only enough food to permit them to reach the buffalo range. After that they lived almost exclusively on buffalo meat. Beginning with 1832, styles in men's hats began to change. The silk hat came into favor. The declining prices of beaver skins ruined the Rocky Mountain fur trade. The last Rendezvous, if indeed the small gathering of that year could be called such, was held in 1840.

In 1835 Whitman and Parker made an exploring tour for the American Board, to the Rockies. They traveled with the Fur Company's caravan. At first the rough and ungodly men of the caravan resented the presence of the missionaries. Whitman, in a letter to the Board, wrote: "Very evident tokens gave us to understand that our company was not agreeable, such as the throwing of rotten eggs at me." The caravan left Liberty, Missouri, on May 14 and moved up the Missouri River to Bellevue near the mouth of the Platte. There the dread cholera struck. Three men died and Lucian Fontanelle, the leader of the

---

[7] Contemporary references to the Rendezvous were usually without the article "the", although now it is customary to use it.

caravan, became ill. Whitman, who had had some experience in treating the disease while serving as a country doctor in western New York, ascribed the cause of the outbreak to "their intemperance, and their sunken and filthy situation." He recommended that the men move their camp to a clean site above the river and that the water used for drinking purposes come from a pure source. The health situation improved at once and soon the caravan was able to resume its march. Dr. Whitman's much appreciated services transformed the feelings of hostility into those of friendliness. Thus the way was prepared for the mission party of the following year, which included women, to cross through hostile Indian territory under the protection of the caravan. Without such an escort it would not have been possible for the small missionary band to cross to the Rockies.

As the caravan worked its way westward to the Rendezvous in the summer of 1835, Whitman made special note of the travel conditions to see if it were possible to take his wife and other women over that same trail. There were many who said that it should not be attempted. W. J. Snelling, in an article for the *New England Magazine*, February, 1832, commenting on the folly of trying to colonize Oregon, wrote: "Only parties of men could undergo the vicissitudes of the journey; none who ever made the trip would assert that a woman could have accompanied them." The well-known painter of Indians, George Catlin, who had been out on the western plains in 1832, told Spalding in the spring of 1836 that he would not take a "white female into that country for the whole continent of America." Although Whitman in 1835 was probably unaware of Catlin's views, there were undoubtedly many others who would have given him the same advice.

When Whitman arrived at the Rendezvous of 1835 on the Green River, near what is now Daniel, Wyoming, he learned that Captain Benjamin L. E. Bonneville had succeeded in taking twenty heavily loaded wagons to that place in 1832. Whitman reasoned that wherever a wagon could go, a woman could go. Custom then decreed that women should ride sidesaddle rather than astride. In contemplating the possibility of a mission party with women keeping up with the caravan, as it traveled sometimes as many as thirty miles a day, Whitman was not sure if women could endure such a gruelling experience day after day, riding on sidesaddles. However, if the mission party could take a wagon with them, then the women, when they became weary of horseback travel, could ride in the wagon. In the journal which Whitman kept on this exploring tour of 1835, and which he mailed to the Board when he returned to St. Louis in the fall of that year, he made special mention of the fact that wagons had been taken over the Rockies. And he added that what had been done once could be done again. Wherever a wagon could go, a woman could go.

The caravan of 1835 did not arrive at the Rendezvous until August

12, much later than usual, having been delayed by the outbreak of cholera. Whitman noted in his report to the Board that there were from two to three thousand Indians present in addition to several hundred trappers. Among the tribes represented were the Shoshones, the Flatheads, the Utahs, and the Nez Perces. Some of the Nez Perces showed such an enthusiastic desire for missionaries to settle among them that Whitman and Parker decided to separate. Parker would continue the exploring tour while Whitman would return for reinforcements and, incidentally, get married to Narcissa Prentiss. By this time Whitman was fully convinced that it was feasible to take his wife over the Rockies. Of course, it would be best to have at least another couple to accompany them.

Whitman with two Nez Perce boys arrived back in St. Louis on November 4 and on the seventh he wrote to Secretary David Greene of the American Board stating his desire to go out to Oregon with reinforcements the following year. Even though Whitman advanced the argument that it was possible to take women over the Rockies if one took a wagon along, Greene was not convinced. Writing from Boston on December 8, Greene asked Whitman: "Have you carefully ascertained & weighed the difficulties in the way of conducting females to those remote & desolate regions and comfortably sustaining families there?" [8] This was the crucial question.

Whitman wrote to Greene from Rushville on December 17, before he had received Greene's letter of the eighth, and repeated his statement about the wagons. "If you see fit to send [a] mission to the other side of the mountains, we can go as far as the Black Hills [i.e., Fort Laramie] with a waggon for the convenience of females, and from that to rendezvous." And in a third letter to Greene dated December 28, he reiterated his point: "We should go as far as the Black Hills with a waggon."

Actually the mission party of 1836 started out from the frontier with two wagons. The larger of the two was taken to Fort Laramie where it was abandoned. The other, a light Dearborn wagon which the Spaldings had received as a wedding present from Mrs. Spalding's parents, was taken over the Divide to the Rendezvous. After leaving the Rendezvous, the wagon was reduced to a two-wheeled cart. This was the first wheeled vehicle to be taken over the Oregon Trail as far west as Fort Boise.

WHITMAN FINDS THE SPALDINGS

A reading of the correspondence which passed between Whitman and the Board leaves us somewhat amazed at the haphazard manner in which missionaries were then appointed. No physical examinations

---

[8] Hulbert, *Whitman,* I: p. 170.

were required. Of course present day psychological tests to determine fitness for the peculiar problems inherent in a missionary's life were not dreamed of. Even educational requirements were not standardized. All that seemed to be necessary was the desire to be a missionary supplemented by some favorable letters of recommendation. It should be remembered that the whole foreign missionary program of the American Protestant churches was at that time still in its infancy and there were not many volunteers.

The Board gave Whitman the names of several possible candidates. However, as soon as Whitman wrote to them and explained the proposed overland journey to Oregon, all made excuses. Oregon then was more remote than many countries on other continents. Travelers had to obtain passports from the War Department, then in charge of Indian affairs beyond the Mississippi, to go there. Moreover, after the Whitmans arrived at their mission station at Waiilatpu, it took on the average two years to send a letter back to their homes in the East and to get a reply. No wonder candidates who might have been willing to go to Africa, China, or India hesitated to accept a call to faraway Oregon.

Whitman had taken two Nez Perce boys back with him in order that they might be placed in school to learn the English language. One he named Richard, a son of Chief Tack-en-sua-tis. The other he called John. Whitman had faithfully promised their fathers to return the boys to the Rendezvous of 1836. Also he had promised to meet Parker there at that time. With the passing of weeks and with the continued failure to find any associates, Whitman became increasingly concerned. He knew that it was not advisable to get married and go out without at least one other couple being with them.

The name of Henry H. Spalding had been suggested to Whitman shortly after his return to Rushville. The Spaldings had received an appointment in 1835 to go as missionaries under the American Board to the Osage Indians in western Missouri. Their departure had been delayed by the birth of a stillborn baby girl on October 24 at Prattsburg. When Spalding first heard that he was under consideration for the Oregon Mission, and knowing that Whitman was engaged to Narcissa Prentiss, said publicly: "I will not go into the same mission with Narcissa for I question her judgment." [9] When Whitman could not find anyone willing to go to Oregon, he overlooked the tactless remark that Spalding had made and asked him whether or not he would be willing to have his destination changed. Writing to Greene on December 17, Whitman reported: "I received a letter yesterday from H. H. Spalding saying he would be ready to accompany me across the mountains if the Board should approve it." And Spalding wrote on

---

[9] Material dealing with the life of Henry H. Spalding has been drawn from Drury, *Spalding*, where proper documentation may be found.

December 28, saying: "If the Board and Dr. Whitman wish me to go to the Rocky Mountains with him, I am willing; act your pleasure." The fact that Whitman continued to look for two months for other associates even after Spalding had expressed his willingness to go is indicative of Whitman's desire to find someone else if possible.

February, 1836, came and the time for Whitman's departure for the frontier was only three weeks or less away. On February 12 Henry and Eliza said goodby to their friends at Prattsburg and began their overland journey to Pittsburgh, from which point they were to travel by river steamer to the western frontier of Missouri. On or about the same day Whitman received a letter from Greene which gave permission for the Spaldings to go to Oregon should they be willing. He lost no time in hastening to Prattsburg to see the Spaldings. He arrived on Saturday evening, February 13, only to find that the Spaldings had started the day before. Even though Whitman shared the conviction that it was sinful to travel on the "Sabbath" day, yet the urgency of the occasion overcame his conscientious scruples. So on Sunday Whitman continued his pursuit and found the Spaldings resting in an inn in the village of Howard about twenty miles from Prattsburg. There Whitman pleaded the cause of Oregon. After consultation and prayer the Spaldings gave their consent. Plans were hastily made for the Spaldings to proceed to Cincinnati where they would await the coming of Whitman and his bride.

MARRIAGE AND DEPARTURE

The willingness of the Spaldings to change their destination from the Osage Indians to the Nez Perces solved, for the time being at least, Whitman's most pressing problem. Assured of the presence of another couple, he could now be married. There was no time for delay as he wanted to be on the frontier in April in plenty of time to join the caravan. With a light heart Whitman hastened on to Angelica to tell Narcissa of the new developments.

It so happened that Judge Stephen Prentiss and two other elders-elect of the Angelica Presbyterian Church were to be ordained to their office at a congregational meeting which had been set for Thursday evening, February 18. Narcissa quickly decided that this would be an opportune time for the wedding. Her best dress was a black bombazine, just the thing for a wedding dress. Perhaps she had gotten it ready long before. To the Puritan-minded church member of that generation, weddings were solemn occasions and black was the suitable color. Years later Matilda Sager Delaney, who was one of the orphan children received into the Whitman home in 1844, wrote that not only was Narcissa clothed in black but her whole family also.

In the sessional records of the Angelica church we may read the minute which says: "The session ordered a letter to our sister Narcissa Prentiss who is destined to the Mission beyond the Rocky Mountains." Following the ordination of the three men to the eldership on the evening of February 18, the communion was served. Judge Stephen Prentiss, as one of the newly ordained elders, assisted in serving the elements to his daughter and to his son-in-law to be, Marcus Whitman. The marriage was performed by the pastor, the Rev. Leverett Hull. Sometime during the evening, perhaps following the wedding, Hull preached a sermon. Writing back to Mr. Hull from Fort Vancouver on October 25 of that year, Narcissa said: "Brother Hull, you know not how much good that sermon I heard you preach for the last, the which you gave me, does me now in this desert land." The long evening's program closed with a congregational hymn, the first stanza of which was as follows:

> Yes, my native land! I love thee;
>   All thy scenes I love them well;
> Friends, connections, happy country,
>   Can I bid you all farewell?
> Can I leave you,
>   Far in heathen lands to dwell?

The hymn was written by the Reverend Samuel F. Smith, author of "America." The sentiment was so appropriate for the occasion that one by one members of the congregation and of the choir found lumps in their throats and tears in their eyes, and could not sing. Narcissa, with amazing self-composure, finished the hymn singing it in her clear soprano voice as a solo. The last stanza was:

> In the deserts let me labor
>   On the mountains let me tell,
> How he died — the blessed Saviour —
>   To redeem a world from hell!
> Let me hasten,
>   Far in heathen lands to dwell.

This dramatic event was long remembered in Angelica. The next day Marcus and Narcissa began their wedding journey to Oregon. We can only imagine the tearful farewells as Narcissa said goodbye to her parents and to her brothers and sisters. They were never to see each other again in this world. Although Narcissa repeatedly, especially in the closing years of the mission, begged members of her family to migrate to Oregon, no one did so during her lifetime. Years after the massacre, her younger sister, Clarissa, then Mrs. Norman Kinney, moved to San Francisco.

The Whitmans found it necessary to drive to Ithaca to get the two Indian boys, Richard and John, who were living in the Parker home.

They were in Ithaca on Sunday, February 21, where both Marcus and Narcissa spoke before audiences in the Presbyterian church. After leaving Ithaca, the Whitmans went to Rushville where they visited Marcus' mother, Mrs. Calvin Loomis, and other relatives. Sunday, February 28, was spent at Rushville. Narcissa later referred to having a pair of "gentlemen's boots" made for her in "Brother Augustus' shoe store" and also to some shirts given to her husband by the women of the church.

Finally on March 3, the Whitmans said their last farewells and with the two Indian boys began the overland drive to Pittsburgh. Since the ground was still covered with snow, the first part of the journey was made in a sleigh. Their route took them through Elmira to Williamsport, Pennsylvania, and then on to Hollidaysburg. Near the latter place they overtook Dr. and Mrs. Benedict Satterlee, who were under appointment by the American Board to the Pawnee Indians. Mrs. Satterlee was also a bride. With them was Miss Emeline Palmer who was on her way to Liberty, Missouri, where she was to be married to another missionary to the Pawnees, Mr. Samuel Allis. Thus the mission party was increased to seven. Mrs. Satterlee was in ill health and this delayed their progress somewhat. Actually she was very ill at the time, probably with tuberculosis, and died on April 30 shortly after the party arrived at Liberty. Again we are amazed that the Board would send out missionaries without first requiring a medical examination.

The Whitman party reached Pittsburgh on March 12. The next day was Sunday and they attended church. The two Nez Perce boys are reported to have created somewhat of a sensation when their identity became known. The party secured passage on the steamboat "Siam" which left Pittsburgh Tuesday morning, March 15.

Mrs. Whitman's Diary; March to July 1836

Writers dealing with the Whitman story have usually thought of Mrs. Whitman's overland diary as being only that section beginning July 18, 1836, when the Whitman-Spalding party left the Rendezvous, and continuing to October 18 when the missionaries reached Fort Vancouver. Actually, however, Narcissa's diary began with her first letter to her family, dated March 15. Before leaving her home, Narcissa's mother suggested that she keep a diary in the form of travel letters. This Narcissa gladly agreed to do for she loved to write. She also wrote several such letters to her husband's relatives. Sometimes Narcissa would copy for her husband's mother the same material sent to her own mother.

At least four of these travel letters written before the missionaries reached the Rendezvous are extant and are here given in full. They bear the dates March 15 and 31, June 3 and 27. All of these, together with that section of the diary dated July 18-October 18, appeared in the 1891 issue of the *Transactions of the Oregon Pioneer Association* except the letter of June 3. This was printed in the 1893 *Transactions*. However, these letters were not arranged in sequence to suggest their unity and the letter of June 27 was printed in an abbreviated form. At least two letters that Narcissa wrote as a part of the series are not extant. One was written to her husband's mother from the Otoe Indian Agency, about May 15, and the second was addressed to her parents from the Rendezvous, about July 7.

Myron Eells, a son of the Reverend Cushing Eells who was a member of the mission reinforcement of 1838, published his *Marcus Whitman, Pathfinder and Patriot*, in 1909. In this volume he gave in proper sequence but in an abbreviated form Narcissa's letters listed above, including the section dated July 18-October 18.

In 1936, at the time of the recognition of the centennial of the arrival of the Whitman-Spalding party in Oregon, the *Oregon Historical Quarterly*, beginning with the June issue and continuing until June of the following year, gave space in five of its numbers to the reprinting of Narcissa's letters of June 3, June 27 (again in its abbreviated form), and the section of the diary dated July 18-October 18. These appeared with splendid editorial notes by the late T. C. Elliott of Walla Walla. Again, however, the letters were not in sequence. The material was rearranged and reissued as a book by the Oregon Historical Society in 1937 under the title *Coming of the White Women.*

Now in this volume, for the first time, the complete extant overland diary of Narcissa Whitman is given in proper sequence and with the transcriptions faithfully made from the original sources.[10] Except for a few minor changes made for the sake of clarity, the following text contains the original spelling and punctuation.

LETTERS OF MARCH 15 AND 31

On Board Steamboat Siam [11]   March 15, 1836

Dear, Dear Mother: Your proposal concerning keeping a diary as I journey comes before my mind often. I have not found it practicable while traveling by land, although many events have passed which, if noted as they occurred, might have been interesting. We left Pittsburgh this morning at ten o'clock, and are sailing at the rate of thirteen miles an hour. It is delightful passing so rapidly down the waters of the beautiful river. The motion of the boat is very agreeable to me, except while writing. Our accommodations are good; we occupy a stateroom where we can be as retired as we wish. Two boats left Pittsburgh before we did, but they are now in our rear. The captain of one of them became very angry because we attempted to pass, and shot into our path before us. For a time we thought injury would be done by their coming in contact, but we passed her unhurt. The Siam was a very strong boat, and might have sunk the other without much difficulty. It is an imposing scene to see the march of these stately figures as they pass us on the waters. Some are very large, and are swarming with inhabitants. It has been quite pleasant to-day, but too cold to be on deck much of the time. We have seen no snow since we left the Allegheny mountains.

March 28.   We have just come on board the Majestic. It is rightly named, for it is one of the largest boats on the river. We are now sailing on the waters of the great Mississippi. When I commenced this sheet we had just left Pittsburgh. We arrived in Cincinnati Thursday noon. Found Brother Spalding. Said he had been waiting for us anxiously for a fortnight; spent the remainder of the week in making arrangements for our journey, and on the Sabbath had a very interest-

---

10 The location of the original Whitman correspondence, unless otherwise noted, is indicated in Appendix i of Drury, *Whitman.* Whitman items, including Mrs. Whitman's diary there listed as being in Collection u are now in Bancroft Library, Berkeley, Calif.

11 The "Siam" was the same boat that Whitman and Parker took from St. Louis to Liberty on April 8 of the preceding year. See Drury, *Whitman,* 93.

ing time with the disciples of Jesus there; felt strengthened and comforted as we left them, to pursue our journey into the wilderness.

Much good feeling was manifested in the churches — a deep interest appeared to be taken in the missions. Especially our two Indian youths attracted the gaze and admiration of a crowd on Sabbath evening. You will probably hear from us through the Rev. Mr. Norton, who promised to write Brother Hall. Miss Matthews teacher in the colored school, promises to write to Jane. We left Tuesday noon in the Junius and expected to arrive in St. Louis before the Sab. but our expectations were not realized, and Sat. night found us on the waters of the Mississipi eighty-nine miles from St. Louis. We felt it our duty not to travel on the Sab. and determined to leave the boat altho many on board tryed to persuade us to remain and have preaching on the Sab, and of the number one was a Presbyterian minister from New York who appeared quite anxious to detain us. At ten o'clock we landed at Chester, Illinois, and had a most delightful Sab. of rest with the few disciples of Jesus we found there. An aged minister who had been toiling in this part of the vineyard ever since the year 1817, we found of a kindred spirit. He preaches to several congregations. Said he had not had a brother minister to preach for him since had been there. And to have a mission family call and enjoy the privileges of the Sab. with him seemed like angels' visits. He had heard of their passing often. Mr. Spalding preached in the forenoon, and in the afternoon my Husband requested the children and youth to meet in a Sab. School and we distributed a number of books among them. Of the number we found one young man who professed to be a Roman C. but said he wanted to know our religion, had not a Protestant Bible but if he had one would read it attentively. My husband gave him a Testament for which he appeared greatful [Sic].

Since we came on board we have come on very pleasantly, our accommodations are better here than on any previous boat, excellent cooks, and enough to eat. Servants, who stand at our elbows ready to supply every want. Five o'clock, we are now fast upon a sand bar, but think we shall soon get off. It has rained all day, a dense fog covers the river so that it is impossible to shun them. We shall be obliged to lie still to night.

29. Tues morn, fog very thick this morn but now appears to be disappearing. We shall expect to see St. Louis today. Cold and damp today and am obliged to stay in my room, can scarcely resist the temptation of standing out to view the shores of this majestic river. Varied scenes present themselves as we pass up, beautiful landscapes, on the one side high and rugged bluffs, and on the other low plains. Eve. We are now in port. Husband has been to the Office expecting to find

letters from dear dear friends at home but find none.[12] Why have they not written, seeing it is the very last, last time they will have to cheer my heart with intelligence from home, home, sweet home, and the friends I love. *But I am not sad.* My health is good. My mind completely occupied with present duty and passing events. St. Louis has a commanding situation. It is so late and foggy our view of it as we came in is quite indistinct.

WEDNESDAY 30.   A boat is in port ready to take us up the Missouri and will leave to day. I intended to write several letters from here, expecting to spend some time, but as we made our purchases at Cincinnati, it is not necessary. When we were in Pittsburgh we heard that the Fur Com. Steam boat Dinnah had left St. Louis. We then expected [to] make our journey from Liberty to Bellview by land probably on horseback 300 miles which would have been the most difficult part of the journey on account of the season and high water. But providence has ordered it otherwise. Since we have arrived here we learn that the Dinnah snagged herself and sunk but in shallow water so that no lives were lost. We have the promise of overtaking her before we reach Liberty. She is now lying up for repairs and drying her freight. We had a call this morn from a gentleman who has resided in the mountains. Richard knew him very well, is going back with us. He was formerly from Cin. It seems to me now that we are on the very borders of civilization. Altho we shall pass many towns on our way to Liberty. At this moment my feelings are peculiar. I hardly know how to define them. I have not one feeling of regret at the step which I have taken but count it a privilege to go forth in the name of my Master cheerfully bearing the toil and privation that we expect to encounter. I intend to write home from Council Bluff if I am not prevented, and give some statements which I cannot now. We could not pack all contained [in] that box sent us from Angelica. What we could not, Brother Whitman took home to sell for us and send the avails to us to St. Louis.[13] How anxiously I look for a line or two from some one of the dear family in that box some where but I saw none. Jane, don't

---

[12] Narcissa, in a letter to her parents dated March 15, 1838, wrote: "More than two years have passed since I left my father's home and not a single word has been wafted hence. . .   This long, long silence makes me feel the truth of our situation, that we are far, very far removed from the land of our birth and Christian privileges." On July 11, 1838, she received two letters from her sister Jane dated Jan. and Aug., 1837. In her letter to Jane, of Sept. 18, Narcissa mentioned her "feelings of inexpressible joy" upon the receipt of the letters. It is hard to understand why her relatives did not write more often. Possibly some mail was lost in the long voyage around South America. Whitman in a letter to Levi Chamberlain dated Oct. 7, 1837 (original in the Hawaiian Mission Children's Society, Honolulu) stated: "We received no letters by land. . .   The American traders will not forward letters coming this way."

[13] Narcissa is here referring to some repacking that she and her husband did at Rushville. "Brother Whitman" refers to Augustus, a brother of Marcus.

forget to write to them for me. It is out of my power to write as much as I should like too. How often I think of the Christians in Angelica, those beloved sisters and brothers with whom we have knelt before the altar of prayer. Surely now I feel the influence of their prayers altho widely separated. Say to them we wish them to rejoice with us and thank God for his kind protection and the prosperity which has attended us since we left home. We are making arrangements for crossing the mountains and shall expect to unless prevented in the Providence of God. I think I should like to whisper in Mother's ear many things which I cannot write. If I could only see her in her room for one half hour. This much, Dear Mother, I have one of the kindest Husbands and the very best every way. Tell Father by the side of his calomile he has taken a quarter of a pound of lobelia and a large quantity of Cayenne which will answer my purpose better than some of the apothecary medicines.[14]

My Husband unites with me in sending a great deal of love to dear friends there G. and . . .[15] J.C. H. E. and N. and to Father and Mother.[16] Mr. and Mrs. Spaulding will go with us over the mountains.[17] We send our Christian regard to Broth and Sister Hull, Brother and Sister Allen, Bro. and Sister Patrick and all who inquire. I have become very much interested in the Nez Perces lads. They are very affectionate and seem to wish to please us in every way. We think they will be of great service to the Mission in various ways. We have just had a call from Dr. and Mrs. Wisner.[18] We expect the boat will leave soon —Farewell, dear dear Parents. From your unworthy children

M AND N. WHITMAN

(P.S.) Mother, I forgot to say that I heard Dr. Beecher . . . in C. while I was there.[19] . . Dr. B. appears the same in the pulpit

[14] Here is clear evidence that Judge Prentiss was a Thomsonian, which was a medical cult then popular. The founder of the cult prescribed lobelia, which acted as a powerful emetic, and "hot-drops," the principle ingredient of which was cayenne pepper. See Drury, *Whitman*, 135.

[15] The three-dot ellipsis will be used to indicate the omission of some undecipherable word or phrase, the loss of one or more words due to a torn place in the manuscript, or occasionally the elimination of irrelevant material.

[16] The initials refer to brothers and sisters of Narcissa. Galusha (sometimes J.G. was used to refer to his full name of Jonas Galusha), Jane, Clarissa, Harriet, and Edward. It is not known to whom the "N" referred. The reference to "Broth and Sister Hull" is to the Rev. and Mrs. Leverett Hull of Angelica. Mr. Hull officiated at Narcissa's wedding. The Allens and Patricks have not been identified.

[17] This statement seems to imply that there was some doubt as to whether or not the Spaldings were to go with the Whitmans to Oregon at the time of Narcissa's wedding. Perhaps final confirmation of plans reached the Spaldings at Cincinnati. Spalding spelled his name without the "u." Later Narcissa spelled it correctly.

[18] Dr. Wisner was probably the pastor of the Congregational Church in St. Louis.

[19] When the Whitmans and the Spaldings were in Cincinnati, they heard Dr. Lyman Beecher preach. Dr. Beecher was President of Lane Theological Seminary located in that city where Spalding spent two years as a student.

that he does at a distance — I mean he is a small man, quite indifferent in his appearance, I could hardly believe it was he when I saw him come.   N.W.

ON BOARD BOAT CHARITON   Thursday March 31, 1836
DEAR SISTER JANE   We did not leave last night as expected and the day being very pleasant gave me an opportunity of visiting the city. Received a call from an old acquaintance, Rev. Milton Kimball [20] and with him visited the Cathedral. It was High Mass day.[21] I wish I could describe the feelings I had in viewing their worship, if it may be so called. It appeared to me like idolatry. Their embroydered robes appeared to be of the richest material. Splendor and show characterized the place, and all their movements. But what was worse than all was to see young boys training in such a school of destruction. They appeared to be heaping all their honours upon one old man so far as I could understand their movements. Six boys dressed in white robes received each an article of dress of different discriptions at the hand of one of the priests, carried them in their arms one after the other to this old man who took them and with the assistance of one at his right hand loaded his person with them. While dressing some one stood before him with a looking-glass or a book. I could not distinkly see which, apparently very devout in all their movements. A censor completed the dress, and finally one bro't him a golden staff or rod. He took it, arose and walked to the altar, kneeled and seemed to be in the act of silent prayer, as he passed along his attendants and worshipers arose, to show their respect for the dignity of his station. His Holiness the Arch Bishop, I learned to be his title, after I left the house, from Br. Kimble. During the whole performance there was music of a character upon an organ very different from our church tunes and toward the last the Nuns sang the same strains in an unknown tongue. To us it seemed like sound without articulation. While sitting there and behold their idolatry, I thot of the "Whited Sepulcher which indeed appeared beautiful to men but within one full of dead mens bones and all uncleanness." I thot too of the many dellicate fingers that had been employed innocently perhaps, in all

---

[20] Kimball, a Presbyterian minister, was an agent of the A.B.C.F.M. for Illinois and Missouri for 1834-36.

[21] All of the first paragraph of this letter following "High Mass day" to the paragraph beginning "We left the Cathedral" was omitted in the transcription of this letter which appeared in the 1891 T.O.P.A. Both the Whitmans and the Spaldings had an anti-Roman Catholic bias. They shared a feeling common to New England Protestants of their generation. Undoubtedly, when they attended a Roman Catholic service in St. Louis, this was the first time they had ever witnessed such ceremonies. Note the comments for this day in Mrs. Spalding's diary. The Cathedral which they visited was dedicated in 1834 and is still standing in St. Louis. It is known as the Old Cathedral.

manner of needle work preparing vestments for such hypocritical characters. What cause of gratitude, have I that I am not of the number who willfully shut my eyes to the truth, deceiving and being deceived.

We left the Cathedral after staying about an hour, called and made some purchases, then returned to the boat. Found that Mr. Lovejoy had called to give us an invitation to dinner with him. Felt to regret very much that I did not see him. My husband saw him. He wished to know when we were married bcause he designed to publish it in the Observer. He still continues to edit his paper in St. Louis.[22]

We left St. Louis immediately after dinner. Passed many delightful residences in Missouri, on the banks of the Mississippi, just as we leave the city. Dwellings situated upon mounds, and many remaining ones yet to be occupyed, Natural mounds in appearance like that in Amity, only much larger. One of them is the situation of a Female Academy, now in building. My next curiosity was Uncle Sam's Tooth Pullers. Two huge looking boats lying too. They fearlessly run into danger, search out difficulties, and remove them. I should like to see them in operation, but shall not expect too now.

Twilight had nearly gone when we entered the waters of the great Missouri. But the moon shone in her brightness. It was a beautiful evening. My husband and myself went upon the top of the boat to take a commanding view of the scenery. How majestic, how grand was the scene. The meeting of two such great waters. "Surely how admirable are thy works O Lord of Hosts." I could have dwelt upon the scene still longer with pleasure but Brother Spaulding called us to prayers and we left beholding the works of God for his immediate worship.

April 1st — Nothing of much importance occured today. My eyes are satiated with the same beautiful scenery all along the coasts of this mighty river so peculiar to this western country. One year ago to day since my husband first arrived in St. Louis on his exploring route to the mountains. We are one week earlier passing up the river this spring than he was last year. While the boat stopt to take in wood, we went on shore, found some rushes, picked a branch of cedar, went to a spring for clean water (the river water is very rily at all times), rambled considerably in pursuit of new objects.

One of these circumstances I must mention, which was quite diverting to us. On the rocks near the river we found a great quantity of

---

[22] The *St. Louis Observer,* a weekly paper published in St. Louis at that time by the ardent abolitionist Elijah P. Lovejoy, carried in its April 7, 1836, issue a reference to the marriage of Marcus Whitman and Narcissa Prentiss and the note that they were "destined to the Bored Nose Indians, [i.e. Nez Perces.]" About a month after the mission party passed through St. Louis, a mob attacked Lovejoy's printing establishment because of his abolitionist sentiments. Lovejoy moved to Alton, Ill., in Oct. of that year, where other mobs attacked his press. He was murdered on Nov. 7, 1837.

prickly pears. Husband knew from an experience the effects of han-
dling them, and caution[ed] me against them, but I thot I could just
take one & I put it in my India Rubber apron pocket and carry it to
the boat. I did so, but after rambling a little, I thot to take it out and
behold my pocket was filled with needles just like catterpiller's
bristles. I became considerably anoyed with them. They covered my
hands, and I have scarcely got rid of them yet.

My Husband would have laughed at me a little were it not for his
own misfortune. He thot to discover what kind of mucilage it was by
tasting it, cut one in two, bit it, and covered his lips completely. We
then had to sympathize with each other and were glad to render
mutual assistance in a case of extermination.

[APRIL] 2. Eve. ten o'clock. We have come on well since we left
St. Louis, sailed all night last night which is a rare thing in this river
on account of the snags and sand bars. We are now at Jefferson City,
about half way to Liberty from St. L. How long we stop here, I do not
know, perhaps all night.

MON. 4TH. We passed the wreck of the Steamboat Shiana to day
about noon. It is indeed a melancholy sight. She was not quite a year
old. She ran upon a snag and sank last winter. No lives lost. We
stopped to day at Chariton about an hour. [I] We went on shore and
visited a steam saw mill. It was quite a curiosity as well as the great
engine that propells the boat upon the mighty waters. I forget and
speak in the singular number when I should [say] we.[23]

THURS. 7. Very pleasant but cold. This morning the thermometer
stood at 24 at nine o'clock. I have not seen any snow since we left the
Allegany Mountains before the 15th of March. I should like to know
about the snow in New York. Is it all gone? How did it go and the
consequences? Mary, we have had a sick one with us all the way since
we joined Doc. Satterlee. Mrs. Satterlee has had a very bad cough and
cold which has left her feeble.[24] She is now recovering and is as well
as can be expected. She is en famalle [sic]. The rest of us have been
very well except feeling the effects of drinking the river water some.
I am an exception however. My health is never better than since I
have been on the river. I was weighed last week and came up to 136
pounds.[25] I think I shall endure the journey well, perhaps better than
any of the rest of us. Mrs. Spalding does not look nor feel quite healthy

[23] Several times in this letter, Narcissa crossed out the personal pronoun "I,"
and wrote "We" over it. Such instances are indicated by using brackets around the
"I." The mission party disembarked at Liberty on a raw spring morning, April 7.
This marked the end of their travel to Oregon by water.

[24] See references in Mrs. Spalding's diary, Apr. 8-May 1, to the illness and death
of Mrs. Satterlee.

[25] Writing to her parents from Waiilatpu on Oct. 9, 1844, Narcissa said: "I
weigh one hundred and fifty-seven pounds, much higher than ever before in my
life."

enough for our enterprise. Riding affects her differently from what it does me. Everyone who sees me compliments me as being the best able to endure the journey over the mountains from my looks. Sister S. is very resolute, no shrinking with her. She possess good fortitude. I like her very much. She wears well upon acquaintance. She is a very suitable person for Mr. Spaulding, has the right temperment to match him. I think we shall get along very well together; we have so far. I have such a good place to shelter, under my husband's wings. He is so excellent. I love to confide in his judgment and act under him. He is just like Mother in telling me my failings. He does it in such a way that I like to have him, for it gives me a chance to improve. Jane if you want to be happy, get a good husband as I have got and be a missionary.

Mary, I wish you were with us. You would be happy as I am. The way looks pleasant notwithstanding we are so near encountering the difficulties of an unheard of journey for females. I think it would do your health good as well as Lyman and Brother J.G. too.

This letter is free plunder Jane. I will write to you again but on reflecting what I say to one I say to all. I should like to write to each of you separately but I wish to write so many ways that all my time is so occupied that I cannot write as much as I want to. Since have been here [I] we have made our tent. It is made of bed ticking in conical form, large enough for us all to sleep under, viz Mr. Spaulding and wife, Dr. Whitman and wife, Mr. Gray,[26] Richard Takahtoo-ah-tis, and John Aits — quite a little family, raised with a center pole and fasten down with pegs, covering a large circle. There we shall live, eat and sleep for the summer to come at least, perhaps longer. Mary, you inquired concerning my beds and beding. I will tell you. We five spread our Indian Rubber cloth on the ground, then our blankets and encamp for the night. We take plenty of Mackanaw blankets which answers for our bed and beding when we journey place them over our saddles and ride on them. I wish you could see our outfit.

I had made for me in Rushville a pair of Gentleman's boots in Brother Augustus shoe store and from there supplied ourselves with what shoes we wanted. We have each of us a life preserver so that if we fall into the water we shall not drown. They are made of India Rubber cloth, air tight and when filled with air and placed under the arms will prevent us from sinking.[27] We take each of us a plate, knife and fork and a tin cup. Mary,[28] when we are under way, I will describe the whole process to you. When I see it before my eyes & can

---

[26] William Henry Gray joined the mission party at Liberty on Apr. 19.

[27] This is the only reference discovered in the writings of the missionaries to life preservers. They were undoubtedly considered highly desirable when the women forded such rivers as the Snake on horseback.

[28] A reference probably to Mary Ann, one of Narcissa's sisters. See Drury, *Whitman*, for more information about Narcissa's family.

give a better description, for I shall have a better understanding. Husband has got me an excelent side saddle and a very easy horse.[29] He made me a present of a mule to ride the other day, so I do not know which I shall like best. I have not tried the latter. Richard says, "Thats very bad mule, can't catch Buffaloe!" That is the test with him; their speed makes them good in his eye. I shall write you from Council Bluffs and every opportunity, especially when Mr. Parker returns. We have lately received a letter from Mrs. Parker. O what a spirit it breathes. When we were there, she said if we could not get a minister to go with us, we might keep Mr. Parker untill one came, if we would only go on and even now she has given permission for him to stay a year longer and visit another tribe to the south. I wish I could show you her letter.

You say Brother J.G. has been to Ithaca and wife. Why did he not go when I was there. . . He sent me the Missionary's Farewell by Dr. Satterlee, music by himself. Alas! my Husband dont come to night, the wind has blown so hard that I expect he has not been able to cross the river.[30] Brother Gray is with him. I shall not feel so anxious about him on that account, so adieu for tonight. It is most ten o'clock and the families have all gone to rest.

I should like to tell you how the western people talk if I had room. Their language is so singular that I could scarcely understand them, yet very amusing. In speaking of quantity they say "heap of money, heap of water, she is heap sick, &c" "How does your wife do to day?" "O she is smartly better, I reckon, but she is powerful weak. She has been mighty bad. What's the matter with your eye?" [31]

THE MISSION PARTY ALMOST LEFT BEHIND

Since we have no extant travel letters of Mrs. Whitman's for the latter part of April and for May, a brief summary of events that took place during this time is necessary to understand her later letters. Mrs. Spalding in her diary comments only briefly on these events.

Liberty, Missouri, where the missionaries disembarked on April 7, was about the halfway point between their eastern homes and their final destination in Old Oregon. Here they began to assemble their equipment for the overland journey. A heavy farm wagon was pur-

---

[29] The sidesaddle used by Mrs. Elkanah Walker to cross the country to Oregon in 1838 is now in the Oregon Historical Society, Portland. See vol. II illustration.

[30] Narcissa probably wrote this section of her letter about the middle of April when her husband was temporarily absent.

[31] This letter of Narcissa's bears no signature. Since the cost of postage was determined either by the number of sheets or weight, Narcissa economized by writing on the margins and on that part of the outside page not needed for the address. About one-half of the letter, or all that followed after "Thurs. 7." was written in fine script on the margins. There was no envelope.

chased together with twelve head of horses, six mules, and seventeen cattle including four milch cows. While the men were busy with their purchases, Mrs. Whitman and Mrs. Spalding made a conical shaped tent out of bedticking.

On April 19 a single man, William Henry Gray, unexpectedly arrived with an appointment from the American Board to join the Whitman-Spalding party as a mechanic. The missionaries hired a young man by the name of Dulin to assist them. A Nez Perce lad, Samuel Temoni, also joined the party. Shortly after the mission company got started, a red haired, nineteen-year-old youth from New Haven, Connecticut, attached himself to the company. He was Miles Goodyear who later became the first white settler in what is now Utah. Thus the mission party was increased to ten — five missionaries, three Nez Perces, and two hired men.

Whitman made arrangements for himself and the women to go up the Missouri River on one of the Company's boats to Bellevue, where they would join the caravan. Spalding, in the meantime, would go overland with the wagons, the camping equipment and supplies, and the livestock. He was to cross the Missouri River at Leavenworth and then strike out in a northeasterly direction to the Platte. Spalding, the Nez Perces, and the hired men with their outfit, left Liberty on April 27.

Mrs. Satterlee died on April 30. The next day when the funeral service was about to begin, the Fur Company's boat appeared, but, to the dismay of the small mission band, the Captain refused to stop. This put Whitman and the women in a serious predicament. Since it was unsafe for the small mission party to cross the prairies apart from the caravan, they either had to catch up with Spalding and then with the caravan by making forced marches overland or give up any attempt to go to Oregon that year.

Whitman hired a man with a team and wagon. He and the women left Liberty about May 3. Dr. Satterlee and Samuel Allis accompanied them. Whitman hoped to find Spalding at Leavenworth, but when the party arrived there Whitman discovered that Spalding had not tarried but had continued his journey. Since the tent and camping equipment had been taken by Spalding, the men and women of Whitman's party had to sleep in the open without any other protection than that afforded by their blankets. Thus Mrs. Whitman and Mrs. Spalding had a rather rough initiation into the rigors of prairie travel.

In spite of the need for haste, Whitman and his associates spent Sunday, May 8, at the Methodist Kick-a-poo mission. The observance of the Sabbath was a most important consideration in their religious life. While at St. Louis, Whitman had received a letter from Secretary Greene dated March 4, in which Greene had stressed the importance of Sabbath observance. "Keep it strictly," Greene wrote, "and let the

Indians & all others see that you do so. Make the distinction between that and other days as broad and obvious as you can, always using the day for public or private religious purposes." [32]

By Saturday, May 14, the Whitman party was within eighteen miles of the Otoe Agency near Bellevue. By that time they had caught up with Spalding. Again they rested on Sunday. On that day the Fur Company's caravan under command of Thomas Fitzpatrick left Bellevue for the Rendezvous. Whitman rode on ahead to plead with Fitzpatrick to wait. Fitzpatrick, who had been with the 1835 caravan and knew Dr. Whitman, had no objections to the missionaries joining the caravan, but felt that he could not wait. The mission party would have to catch up by forced marches or be left behind. To overtake the caravan, the need for haste was so great that the missionaries travelled on Sunday, May 22. They crossed the Elkhorn River, on the north side of the Platte, on Monday, May 23. The next day they made a hard drive of sixty miles and reached the Loup Fork of the Platte at eleven o'clock that night. To their joy they saw the caravan on the other side of the river. They were none too soon as the next day the caravan with the mission party in the rear passed some large Indian villages.

LETTERS OF JUNE 3 AND 27

PLATTE RIVER, JUST ABOVE THE FORKS.
June 3d, 1836   Friday eve, six o'clock.

DEAR SISTER HARRIET AND BROTHER EDWARD. We have just encamped for the night near the bluffs over against the river. The bottoms are a soft, wet plain, and we were obliged to leave the river yesterday morning for the bluffs. The face of the country yesterday afternoon and to day has been rolling sand bluffs, mostly barren quite unlike what our eyes have been satiated with for weeks past. No timber nearer than the Platte, and the water to night is very bad, got from a small ravine. We have usually had good water previous to this.

Our fuel for cooking since we left timber (no timber except on rivers) has been dried buffalo dung. We now find plenty of it and it answers a very good purpose, similar to the kind of coal used in Pennsylvania. (I suppose Harriet will make up a face at this, but if she was here she would be glad to have her supper cooked at any

---

[32] Hulbert, Whitman, I, p. 195.

[33] On the treeless prairies, travelers found that dried buffalo dung made excellent fuel. It was called prairie coal. An Oregon emigrant of 1852 wrote in his diary for June 12: "Buffalo chips scarce and in good demand. Many of the ladies can be seen running over the prairie with sacks in hand, searching for a few buffalo chips to cook their evening meal. Some of the ladies are seen wearing gloves, but most of them have discarded their gloves and are gathering the buffalo chips with their bare hands." T.O.P.A., 1905, p. 441. Evidently by the time Narcissa wrote this letter, she had no squeamishness on this subject.

rate, in this scarce timber country.) [33] The present time in our journey
is a very important one. The hunter brought us buffalo meat yesterday,
for the first that has been seen to day to have been taken. We have
some for supper to night. Husband is cooking it, no one of our company
professes the art but himself. I expect it will be very good.

Stop — I have so much to say to your children, that I do not know in
what part of my story to begin. I have very little time to write. I will
first tell you what our company consists of. We are ten in number, five
missionaries, three Indian boys and two young men employed to assist
in packing animals.

SAT. 4. Good morn H. & E. I wrote last night till supper, after that
it was so dark I could not see. I told you how many bipeds there was
in our company last night, now for the quadrupeds, — 14 horses and
six mules and fifteen head of cattle. We milk four cows.[34] We started
with seventeeen but we have killed one calf and the Fur Company
being out of provisions have taken one of our cows for beaf. It is
usually pinching times with the company before they reach the buffalo.
We have had a plenty because we made ample provision at Liberty.
We purchased a barrel of flour and baked enough to last us with killing a calf or two untill we reached the buffalo.

The Fur Com. is large this year. We are really a moving village —
nearly four hundred animals with ours, mostly mules and seventy men.
The Fur Com. has seven wagons and one cart, drawn by six mules
each, heavily loaded; the cart drawn by two mules carries a lame man,
one of the proprieters of the Com.[35] We have two waggons in our
com[pany.] Mr. & Mrs. S. and Husband and myself ride in one, Mr.
Gray and the baggage in the other. Our Indian boys drive the cows
and Dulin the horses. Young Miles leads our forward horses, four in
each team. Now E. if you wish to see the camp in motion, look away
ahead and see first the pilot and the Captain Fitzpatrick, just before
him — next the pack animals, all mules loaded with great packs — soon
after you will see the waggons and in the rear our company. We all
cover quite a space. The pack mules always string along one after the
other just like Indians. There are several gentlemen in the Com. who
are going over the Mountains for pleasure. Capt. Stewart, Mr. Lee
speaks of him in his journal — he went over when he [Mr. Lee] did
and returned. He is an Englishman, — Mr. Chelam. We had a few of

[34] So far as is known, this was the first herd of cattle to be driven across the
prairies and over the Rockies to Oregon. The availability of fresh milk daily undoubtedly made it possible for Mrs. Spalding to survive the journey.

[35] The reference is to Milton Sublette, long time friend and partner of Thomas
Fitzpatrick. Sublette suffered an amputation of one of his legs in February 1835.
Even though thus handicapped, he tried to carry on his activities as a fur trader.
However, the hardships of travel forced him to turn back to Fort Laramie where
he died on Apr. 5, 1837.

them to tea with us last Monday eve — Capts. Fitzpatrick, Stuart, Maj. Harris and Chelam.[36]

I wish I could discribe to you how we live so that you can realize it. Our manner of living is far preferable to any in the States. I never was so contented and happy before. Neither have I enjoyed such health for years. In the morn as soon as the day breaks the first that we hear is the word — arise, arise. Then the mules set up such noise as you never heard which puts the whole camp in motion. We encamp in a large ring baggage and men, tents and waggons on the outside and all the animals, except the cows [which] are fastened to pickets, within the circle. This arrangement is to accommodate the guard who stand regularly every night and day, also when we are in motion, to protect our animals from the approach of Indians who would steal them. As I said the mule's noise brings every man on his feet to loose them and turn them out to feed.

Now H. & E. you must think it very hard to have to get up so early after sleeping on the soft ground. When you find it hard work to open your eyes at seven o'clock, just think of me, every morn at the word "Arise," we all spring. While the horses are feeding, we get our breakfast in a hurry and eat it. By this time the word "Catch up, catch up," rings throu the camp for moving. We are ready to start usually at six — travell till eleven, encamp, rest and feed, start again about two — travel until six or before if we come to a good tavern — then encamp for the night.[37]

Since we have been in the prairie, we have done all our cooking. When we left Liberty we expected to take bread to last us part of the way but could not get enough to carry us any distance. We found it awkward work to bake at first out of doors, but we have become so accustomed to [it] now we do it very easy.

Tell Mother I am a very good housekeeper in the prairie. I wish she could just take a peep at us while we are sitting at our meals. Our table is the ground, our table-cloth is an Indian rubber cloth used when

---

[36] Here Mrs. Whitman refers to the Rev. Jason Lee, a Methodist missionary who crossed the Rockies with his nephew, the Rev. Daniel Lee, and three assistants, in 1834. They were the first Protestant missionaries to cross the Rockies. All were men. Captain William Drummond Stewart (or Stuart) was a wealthy Scottish nobleman who made several trips to the Rockies with the fur company's caravan. Moses Harris, often called Black Harris or Major Harris, was one of trappers of the pioneer company that entered the Rockies under Gen. Wm. H. Ashley in 1823. When Whitman made his famous ride East in the latter part of 1842, Moses Harris is reported to have been his guide for a part of the way through the mountains. Drury, *Whitman*, 295. Nothing further is known about Chelam.

[37] It was customary for the caravan to make two camps a day, a short one in mid-day for food and rest and then the over-night camp. In the writings of the traders and of the missionaries the word "camp" was sometimes used as a synonym for "march." They spoke of a "long camp" or a "short camp" to indicate the length of marches between camps.

it rains as a cloak; our dishes are made of tin — basins for tea cups, iron spoons and plates, each of us, and several pans for milk and to put our meat in when we wish to set it upon the table — each one carries his own knife in his scabboard and it is always ready for use. When the table things [are] spread, after making our forks of sticks and helping ourselves to chairs, we gather around the table. Husband always provides my seat and in a way that you would laugh to see us. It is the fashion of all this country to imitate the Turks.

Mr. Dunbar and Allis have supped with us and they do the same.[38] We take a blanket and lay down by the table and those whose joints will let them follow the fashion. Others take out some of the baggage (I suppose you know that there is no [stone] in this country. Not a stone have I seen of any size on the prairie.) For my part I fix myself as comfortably as I can, sometimes on a blanket, sometimes on a box, just as it is convenient. Let me assure you of this, we relish our food none the less for sitting on the ground while eating. We have tea and a plenty of milk which is a luxury in this country. Our milk has assisted us very much in making our bread since we have been journeying. While the fur company has felt the want of food, our milk has been of great service to us, but was considerable work to supply ten persons with bread three times a day. We are done using it now. What little flour we have left we we shall preserve for thickening our broth, which is excellent. I never saw anything like buffalo meat to satisfy hunger. We do not want any thing else with it. I have eaten three meals of it and it relishes well. Supper and breakfast we eat in our tent. We do not pitch it at noon. Have worship immediately after sup & breakfast.

NOON   The face of the country to day has been like that of yesterday. We are now about 30 miles above the forks and leaving the bluffs for the river. We have seen wonders this forenoon. Herds of buffalo have hove in sight. One, a bull, crossed our trail and ran upon the bluffs near the rear of the camp. We took the trouble to chase him so as to have a near view. Sister Spaulding and myself got out of the waggon and ran upon the bluff to see him.[39] Husband was quite willing to gratify our curiosity since it was the first. Several have been killed this forenoon. The Company keep a man out all the time to hunt for the camp.

---

[38] The Rev. John Dunbar and Samuel Allis were appointed missionaries to the Pawnees in 1834. They went to their field at the time Samuel Parker made his abortive attempt to go to Oregon. In a letter to the Board dated July 14, 1836, Allis expressed his doubts as to the wisdom of sending women over the Rockies. He wrote: ".   .   .   I think it a hasty step to taking Females across the mountains at present but if it is the Lords will and he has a work for them to do, he will protect them." *Kansas Historical Collections*, vol. xiv, p. 709.

[39] This is one of the few references, found in the writings of either Mrs. Whitman or Mrs. Spalding, to their riding in the wagon. This they seemed to have done during the first part of their journey.

Edward, if I write much more in this way, I do not know as you can read it without great difficulty.[40] I could tell you much more but we are all ready to move again. So farewell for the present. I wish you were all here with us going to the dear Indians. I have become very much attached to Richard Takaktooahtis. It is the one you saw at our wedding. He calls me Mother. I love to teach him, to take care of him and hear them talk. There are five Nez Perces in the company and when they are together they chatter freely. Samuel Temoni, he would be the oldest one, has just come in to the camp with the skin and some of the meat of a buffalo which he has killed himself. He started this forenoon of his own accord. It is what they like dearly, to hunt buffalo. So long as we have him with us we shall be supplied with meat.

I am writing backwards. Monday morn[ing.] I began to say something here that I could not finish. Now the man from the mountains has come who will take this to the [post] office. I have commenced one to Sister Hull which should like to send this time if I could finish it. We have just met him and we have stopped our waggons to write a little. Give my love to all. I have not told you half I want to. We are all in health this morn and making rappid progress in our journey. By the fourth of July our Capt. intends to be at the place where Mr. Parker and husband parted last fall. We are a month earlier passing here than they were last spring. Husband has begun a letter to pa and ma and since he has cut his finger so that it troubles him to write to the rest.[41] As this is done in a hurry, I dont know as you can read it. Tell mother if I had looked the world over I could not have found one more careful and better qualified to transport a female such a distance.

Farewell all.   NARCISSA PRENTISS.[42]
Husband says "Stop."

The caravan with the mission party arrived at Fort William (named after William Sublette) on Monday, June 13, where it remained until Tuesday, June 21. There the women had a chance to wash their clothes. Narcissa noted in her diary that they had only three such opportunities en route; once at Fort William, or Fort Laramie as it was also called, again at the Rendezvous, and the third time at Fort Boise. The fol-

---

[40] In order to make the fullest possible use of the letter page, Narcissa would sometimes reverse the page and write between the former lines. Such a page is indeed read with difficulty.

[41] The letter that Marcus wrote to his wife's parents is now in the Oregon Historical Society's collection and was printed in *T.O.P.A.*, 1893, p. 109. Marcus wrote that they were most favored in their weather. "We have not been once wet even to this time, and we are now beyond where the rains fall much in summer." However, in all probability rain did fall during some of the nights on this part of their journey.

[42] Narcissa signed her maiden name.

*lowing letter of Narcissa's, addressed to Augustus Whitman and his
wife Julia, is in a damaged condition. The words within the brackets
have been supplied to complete the sense of what Narcissa probably
wrote.*

PLATTE RIVER, SOUTH SIDE,   Six days above the Fort Larimys Fork,
            near the foot of the Rocky Mountains.   June 27, 1836
DEAR BROTHER AND SISTER WHITMAN   Husband told you in one of his
letters that I was a little selfish in not writing to our friends in Rushville. If I could prevail on him to write one letter, even, to Angelica, I
should have more time to write to his relatives. As it is this will make
the third while he has written only one hasty letter to Father and
Mother.[43] I have no disposition to complain however for he has been
pressed above measure with care, labours, and anxieties, all the way.

We were in perplexity when we left Liberty but it has been over-
ruled for good. I wrote Mother Loomis from the Otoe Agency. We
were in a still greater perplexity there. While crossing our baggage,
husband became so completely exhausted with swimming the river on
Thurs. May 19th that it was with difficulty he made the shore the last
time swiming it. Mr. S. was sick; our two hired men were good for
nothing. We could obtain not much assistance from the Otoes for they
had gone away from the village — had but one canoe and that partly
eaten up by the dogs the night before. Got them all over by Friday
night.

We did not get ready to start untill Sat afternoon [May 21]. By this
time the Com had 4½ days the advance of us. It seemed scarcely
possible for us to overtake them, we having two more difficult streams
to pass, before they would pass the Pawnee villages. Beyond there we
dare not venture more than one day. We were at a stand. But with the
advice of Brethren Merrill [44] and Dunbar after a concert of prayer on
the subject, we concluded to start and go as far as it would be prov-
ident for us. Brother Dunbar kindly consented to become our pilot
untill we could get another one. He started with us and came as far as
the Elk Horn river — there the man Maj. Dougherty [45] sent for, for us,
came up and Mr. Dunbar returned. We had passed the river Monday
Morn and taken down the rope when our pilot and his Indian came
up. It was with difficulty we crossed him and returned Bro Dunbar.
While on the opposite shore, just ready to leave us, he called to us to
receive his parting advice with a word of caution which will never be
forgotten. Our visit with him and Br Merrill's family was indeed re-
freshing to our thirsty spirits — kindred spirits rejoicing in self denials
and labours of a missionary life.

---

[43] The two previous letters Narcissa wrote to her husband's family are not known
to be extant.
[44] The Rev. Moses Merrill was a Baptist missionary stationed with the Otoes.
[45] Major Dougherty was Indian agent at the Otoe Agency on the Platte.

Sat in the morn we met a large party of the Pawnees going to the fort to receive their annuities. Some of the principle men in each tribe. We stopped, shook hands with some of them, told them who we were and where we were going etc. They seemed very much surprised and pleased to see white females, many of them had never seen any before. They are a noble Indian — large, athletic frames, dignified countenances bespeaking an immortale exhistance [sic] within. They did not detain us long. When we had said what we wished, we took our leave of them and hurryed on and arrived at the Elk Horn in time to cross all our effects. Here I must tell you how much good Richard, John, and Samuel did us. They did the work of driving the cattle and loose horses principally. Occasionally Husband and myself would ride with them for company and encouragement. They came up to the river before us, and seeing a skin canoe on the opposite side, they striped themselves, wound their shirts round their heads and swam over and back again with the canoe by the time we came up — did not have much difficulty in crossing — stretched a rope across the river and pulled the goods over in the canoe.

Monday and Tuesday we made hard drives, Tuesday especially. We attempted to reach the Loup Fork that night and did succeed. Part of us, those in the waggons, drove there by eleven o'clock but it was too much for the cattle. There was no water nor fuel short of that. We rode with Richard and John untill nine o'clock — we were all very much fatigued. Rich proposed to us to go on and he and John would stay in the prairie with the cattle and drive them in in the morn. We did not like to leave them and so we concluded to stay. Husb. had a cup tied to his saddle in which he milked what we wished to drink — this was our supper. Our blankets upon our saddles with our Indian rubber cloaks was all we wished for a bed, having spread them upon the ground and offering up our thanksgiving for the blessings of the day and seeking protection for the night, we committed ourselves to rest.

We awoke in the morn much refreshed and rode into camp before breakfast, five miles. The Fur Com was on the opposite side of the river. We forded it, and without unloading our waggon much, and were ready to move again about noon. We wished to be with the Com when they passed the Pawnee villages. This obliged us to make a day's drive of the camp in a half-day. This was too hard for our horses after crossing the river twice. We did not reach them untill one o'clock at night. The next day we passed all their villages. We especially were visited by them both at noon and night. We ladies were such a curiosity to them, they would come and stand around our tent — peep in and grin in their astonishment to see such looking objects.

Since we came up with the Com. I have rode in the waggons the most of the way to the Black Hills. It is astonishing how [well we] get along with our waggons where there are no roads. I think I may say [it is] easier traveling here than on any turnpike in the [States] . . . have no spring seats simply sit upon some . . . baggage and are as well suited as if in the s . . . [On the] way to the Buffalo country we had to bake br . . . a day for ten persons, it was difficulty at f[irst as] we did not understand working out of doors we [became accustomed to it,] so that [it] became quite easy. We passed the [forks of the] Platte on the second of June. It has not been [necessary] to kill but one of our calves for our own use . . . Com quite out of provisions, they wished . . . to repay us again at the fort. June found [us ready to receive our first] taste of Buffalo, since that time I ha[ve had but little] to do with cooking, not one in our num[ber relishes] Buffalo meat as well as my husband and [I be]lieve Mother Loomis would give up to [him if] she was here, he has a different way for every different piece of meat. We have had no bread since. We have meat and tea in the morn and tea and meat at noon. All our variety consists in the different ways of cooking. I relish it well and it agrees with me, my health is excellent, so long as I have buffalo meat I do not wish any thing else. Sister S. is affected by it considerably, has been quite sick.[46]

We feel that the Lord has prospered us in our journey beyond our most sanguine expectations. We wish our friends at home to unite with us in thanksgiving and praise for his great mercies to us. We are a month earlier this year than husband was last and the Com wish to be at rendezvous by the fourth of July. We have just crossed the river and shall leave here tomorow morning.

[Back page] Now Sister Julia, between you and me, I just want to tell you how much trouble I have had with Marcus two or three weeks past.[47] He was under the impression that we had too much baggage and could not think of anything so easy to be dispensed with as his own wearing apparel, those shirts the Ladies made him just before we left home, his black suit and overcoat, these were the condemned articles, sell them he must as soon as he got to the fort. At first I could not believe him in earnest. All the reasons I could bring were of no avail, he still said he would get rid of them. I told him to sell all of mine too, I could do without them better than he could — indeed I did not wish to dress unless he could. I had already mended and repaired the coat he wears untill it seemed it would not stay on him untill we

---

[46] Whitman, writing to Secretary Greene from the Rendezvous on July 16, said: "Mrs. Spalding has suffered considerably from change of diet but in the end I am confident her health will be greatly improved by the journey."

[47] Here is one of the rare instances in the writings of Mrs. Whitman when she referred to her husband by his Christian name. Usually she called him "Husband" or "the Doctor." The same reticence to use Christian names is found also in the writings of all of the members of this Mission. It was never "Henry" or "Eliza" Spalding but "Mr. Spalding" and "Mrs. Spalding."

could get to our journey's end. I finally said to him that I would write and get Sister Julia to plead for me for I knew you would not like to have him sell them better than I should. This was enough; he knew it would not do to act against or contrary to her wishes — he said no more about it.

JULY 16th.   When I wrote this letter I expected an opportunity to send it immediately but we did not meet the party we expected and have had no opportunity since. We are now west of the Rocky Mountains at the encampment of Messrs. McLeod and McCay [McKay] expecting to leave here Monday morn for Walla Walla. It seems a special favour of Providence that that Company has come to Rendezvous . . .   this season for we [otherwise would have had] to have gone with the Indians, a difficult rou[te, and so] slow that we should have been late at Walla Walla and [not had] the time we wanted for making preparations for winter. Hus[band has] written the particulars concerning our arrival, meeting [the] Indians, etc. to Brother Henry. One particular I will mention which he did not. As soon as I alighted from my horse, I was met by a company of native women, one after the other, shaking hands and salluting me with a most hearty kiss. This was unexpected and affected me very much. They gave Sister Spaulding the same salutation. After we had been seated awhile in the midst of the gazing throng, one of the Chiefs whom we had seen before came with his wife and very politely introduced her to us. They say they all like us and that we have come to live with them. It was truly pleasing to see the meeting of Richard and John with their friends.[48] Richard was affected to tears, his father is not here but several of his

---

[48] After the arrival of the missionaries in Oregon, John went to live with the Spaldings and Richard stayed with the Whitmans. For a short time the youths were helpful as interpreters. John died a year or so later. In a letter to Parker dated Feb. 21, 1837, Spalding reported: "The Dr's boy ran away last fall, taking considerable property; which with the clothing and books given him in the States, he has gambled away. He is a profane, gambling youth." See Drury, *Whitman*, 172. Following the death of Ellis, head chief of the Nez Perces, in 1848, Indian Agent H. A. G. Lee selected Richard to be head chief. However, lacking leadership qualities, Richard resigned within a year in favor of Lawyer. Evidently Richard had been selected because he knew some English and had been to a white man's school.

E. W. Conyers, who was an Oregon emigrant in 1852, relates the following experience he had when his wagon train entered Grand Round Valley in Aug. 1852: "While standing a few feet from our wagons, viewing the arrival and departure of different squads of Indians, I noticed a small-sized Indian riding towards our camp on a full gallop. Just then I heard some one just back of me exclaim: 'I wonder where that d——d Indian came from.' On looking around I saw that it was a full-blooded Indian that had made this remark. I said to him: 'You seem to talk the white man's language quite well. Where did you learn it?' He answered that he had lived with Mr. Whitman a long time, and he had taught him to speak and read the white man's language. He told me that his name was 'Dick' and that Mr. Whitman was a good man." *T.O.P.A.* 1905, p. 493.

band and Brothers. When they met each took off his hat and shook hands as respectful as in civilized life. Richard does not give up the idea of seeing again Rushville.

I must close for want of room. Please give my love to Deborah and Harriet and all other friends. I hope you will all write us now as Husband has given directions how to send. Remember me affectionaly to Sister Alice [49] — tell her to write us immediately. We want to hear from you all.

Your affectionate sister, NARCISSA WHITMAN

[49] Alice was a sister of Marcus.

The Oregon Trail as Followed by
the Missionaries

The old Oregon Trail, followed by the missionaries on their way to the Pacific Northwest in 1836, was nothing more than overlapping segments of old Indian trails used long before the white man came. When the explorers and fur traders pushed their way into the Rocky Mountain country, they used the trails that followed the streams. Here they found water for themselves and their animals. Usually along the water courses, even in desert areas, were patches of grass which provided food for the animals. The clumps of trees that often lined the streams gave wood for the camp fires.

The route of the Oregon Trail from the western frontier of Missouri or Iowa followed the wide but shallow Platte River to the forks, then up the North Platte past such landmarks in what is now western Nebraska as Chimney Rock and Scotts Bluff. Sometimes travelers took the north side of the Platte, at other times the south bank. This depended largely upon their point of departure. There was no single road as such, but rather a broad band of roads. When the great emigrant wagon trains began rolling toward Oregon, beginning with that of 1843, the wagons spread out to avoid the heavy dust stirred up by the plodding feet of the animals and the iron tires of the heavy wagons.

The mission party of 1836 crossed the Platte River a few miles above its mouth in order to travel with the Fur Company's caravan already on the north bank. The caravan stayed on the north side of the Platte and of its north fork until shortly before their arrival at Fort Laramie when a crossing was made to the south side of the North Platte. After leaving Fort Laramie, the Oregon Trail, following the south bank of the North Platte, turned in a northwesterly direction to what is now Casper, Wyoming. There the river swung to the southwest. Near the mouth of the Sweetwater, a tributary of the North Platte, the road crossed the river again to follow the Sweetwater to the Rockies' summit.

The ascent to the Continental Divide along the Sweetwater was comparatively easy.[1] There were no long steep grades or mountain

---

[1] Paul C. Henderson, *Landmarks on the Oregon Trail*, (published by Peter Decker for the Westerners, New York, 1953) gives an excellent discussion of the Oregon Trail from Fort Laramie through South Pass with a detailed map.

defiles to impede travel. Along the stream were such famous landmarks as Independence Rock, the great register of the desert where through the years, when the Oregon Trail was the main highway to the Pacific Coast, hundreds of westward bound travelers paused to carve their names. A little farther west was Devil's Gate where the Sweetwater boiled through a narrow defile of high perpendicular rocks. Just before reaching the summit of the Rockies, the stream curved to the north to its source on the eastern slope of the southern end of the Wind River Mountains.

After leaving the Sweetwater the Oregon-bound travelers had to go about twenty miles over a high plateau through South Pass before coming to water again at Pacific Springs on the west side of the Continental Divide. South Pass is a saddle of land from fifteen to twenty miles wide, with the southern tip of the Wind River Mountains to the north and the Oregon Buttes to the south. The ascent within the Pass is so gradual that the exact summit, with an elevation of 7,550 feet, can not easily be determined.

The first documented account of the discovery of this Pass is to be found in the records of the small party of Astorians under the command of Robert Stuart who returned this way from the mouth of the Columbia River in the latter part of 1812. Then for a number of years the location of this important gateway to the Pacific Coast was lost. The Pass was rediscovered by a party of trappers under the command of Jedediah Smith early in 1824, as they were looking for the Colorado River.

Today Wyoming state highway No. 28 goes through the Pass from Lander to Farson. The recently built highway passes a few miles to the north of the Oregon Trail. Interested travelers can easily see the exact place where the Trail crossed the Divide by following a dirt road which branches off the highway to the east of the summit. This road zigzags for three or four miles through the sage brush to where the ruts dug by the wheels of the heavily loaded emigrant wagons may still be seen. Along this original Oregon Trail at the summit stand two monuments. The larger bears the inscription: OLD OREGON TRAIL 1843-57. The smaller has the following: NARCISSA PRENTISS WHITMAN. ELIZA HART SPALDING. FIRST WHITE WOMEN TO CROSS THIS PASS. JULY 4, 1836.[2]

These two missionary women were in the vanguard of a great procession of men, women, and children, who were to travel that same way during the three decades immediately following. Narcissa and Eliza proved that it was possible for women to cross the Rockies. As

---

[2] Jim Harrower of Pinedale, Wyoming, in a letter to the author dated Sept. 21, 1960, wrote that Capt. Herman G. Nickerson of Lander, Wyoming, erected the monument to the women at his own expense "many years ago." See frontispiece of this vol.

will be noted later in this work, another party of missionaries including four women was sent out by the American Board to Oregon in 1838. In 1839 and 1840 five missionary couples, independent of any established board or agency, went this same way.[3] Thus, altogether, eleven missionary women had crossed the Rockies before the first trickle of Oregon-bound immigrants ventured to attempt the overland journey.

The route of the Oregon Trail can be traced with comparative ease until it emerges from the west end of South Pass. After that it spread out like the strands of a frayed rope. Since the 1836 Rendezvous was held on Green River at the junction of Horse Creek, we know that the trail followed by the mission party turned in a northwesterly direction along the west side of the Wind River Range for about forty-five miles to what is now Daniel, Wyoming.

THE RENDEZVOUS OF 1836

About one mile south of Daniel, Wyoming, is a roadside sign erected by the Sublette County Historical Society, which marks the place where the local people have presented an historical pageant on the first Sunday of July for the years 1934-58 inclusive. The site has now been changed to nearby Pinedale and the time from the first to the second Sunday of July. The sign reads as follows:

1824   GREEN RIVER RENDEZVOUS   1840

A market place of the fur trade from the Mississippi to the Pacific, from Canada to Mexico, where trappers traders and indians came to barter for the first great resource of the west. Six rendezvous were held here gathering not only furs but information of geographical importance to weld the final link in exploration of the new world. It is a tribute to the brave men, both red and white, who blazed the trails for culture and progress and to the lowly beaver who gave it impetus.

The annual Rendezvous in the Rockies, where the fur company's caravan with supplies from civilization met several hundred trappers and sometimes thousands of Indians, was a unique feature of the Rocky Mountain fur trade. In 1824 General William H. Ashley, one of the American pioneers in the development of the beaver trade, made arrangements for his company of about one hundred trappers to meet him and a caravan on the Green River in the summer of 1825. About one hundred and fifty whites were gathered at the mouth of Henry's Fork of the Green River together with about eight hundred Indians

---

[3] They were the Rev. and Mrs. John S. Griffin and Mr. and Mrs. Asahel Munger, in 1839; and the Rev. and Mrs. Harvey Clark, Mr. and Mrs. Philo B. Littlejohn, and Mr. and Mrs. Alvin T. Smith, in 1840.

when Ashley arrived and began trading about July 1. This was the first of sixteen annual Rendezvous, the last being held in 1840.

The companies sponsoring the caravans changed during the years. The American Fur Company, with its headquarters in St. Louis, was one of the most important of these concerns. The location of the Rendezvous also varied from year to year. Three — 1829, 1830, and 1838 — were held on the Popo Agie or Sweetwater Rivers east of the Rockies. Twelve were held west of the Continental Divide. Of this number the Rendezvous for the following years were held on the Green River — 1833, 1835, 1836, 1837, 1839, and 1840. The Rendezvous for 1831 began on the Green River but moved to a site on the Powder River east of the Big Horns. The Rendezvous of 1834 was on Hams Fork of the Green near the present Kemmerer, Wyoming. The other gatherings were held in various places in Utah or Idaho. As far as the relationship of the Rendezvous with the Whitman-Spalding story is concerned, the site at Green River near the present towns of Daniel and Pinedale, Wyoming, was the important place.

At the heyday of the fur trade, as many as five thousand Indians were reported to have been at the Rendezvous. These came from the Shoshone and its related tribe, the Bannocks; the Nez Perces, the Flatheads, and the Utahs. These tribes were usually at peace with each other. The feared Blackfeet to the north were not known to have taken part in any of these gatherings. Perhaps at the peak of the fur trade, as many as four hundred trappers would be present, including the independent men. For a number of years the Hudson's Bay Company sent a small party from one of its forts in Old Oregon to take part in the trading.

The large assemblage of whites and Indians meant that sometimes as many as ten thousand horses and mules would be present. They had to have forage grounds and water. The Rendezvous site on the Green River provided the ideal location. Here was a great flat prairie well watered by the sprawling Green River and its several tributaries. About one hundred and twenty-five square miles were available in a valley that measured on the average about ten miles wide and twelve miles long. To the east was the imposing Wind River mountain range with Fremont Peak rising to a height of thirteen thousand seven hundred feet. This range, with a spectacular series of high peaks, many of which are covered with snow most of the year, extends for some ninety miles.

Thus, in a place of surpassing beauty the fur traders, the mountain men, and the Indians met in a great mountain fair which was usually held in July but was sometimes delayed until August. It usually lasted for about two weeks. This was the great social event of the year in the life of the trappers who were often obliged to spend the remainder of the year in lonely isolation. Hence there was a tendency for the moun-

SITE OF THE GREEN RIVER RENDEZVOUS OF 1836, NEAR DANIEL, WYOMING
Green River appears at left center, and Horse Creek in lower left and right center.
The junction of the two streams may be seen. The site of Fort Bonneville is to the
left of the upper left of picture. The mission party of 1836 camped in that area.

tain men to "let themselves go" in complete abandonment at the Rendezvous. The caravan would bring out casks of liquor. There would be drinking, carousing, gambling, and the Indians provided the women.

It was the custom of the caravan to send a messenger to the Rendezvous several days in advance of its arrival. In 1836 the messenger naturally passed on the exciting news to the trappers and Indians that missionaries with white women were with the caravan. As a result a party of Nez Perces including Tack-en-sua-tis (or Rotten Belly),[1] Ish-hol-hol-hoats-hoats (later better known as Lawyer), their wives, and some others rode out to meet the missionaries. The Indians met them on the evening of July 4 when the caravan was camped at what Mrs. Spalding described as "the head waters of the Colorado." Among the Nez Perces was Kentuc, who had been Parker's assistant and guide during much of his travels the preceding year. Kentuc carried a letter from Parker to Whitman, dated May 16, which conveyed the disheartening news that Parker was not planning to return to the States by the overland route, rather he intended to go home by sea.

Parker's failure to meet Whitman at the 1836 Rendezvous as he had promised, and also his failure to pass on any advice growing out of his explorations, was a great disappointment to the mission party. In a letter to Greene dated May 10, 1839, Whitman was outspoken in his criticism:

> We cannot say how much good Mr. Parker's tour will do others. It has done us none, for instead of meeting us at the Rendezvous as he agreed, he neglected even to write a single letter containing any information concerning the country, company, Indians, prospects, or advice whatever.

The caravan and the missionary party arrived at the Rendezvous on July 6. There the Fur Company took over the rude Fort Bonneville, which Gray described as being nothing more than "a square log pen 18 x 18 . . . covered with poles, brush on top of the poles." This trading post had been erected by Captain Bonneville in 1832. It afforded the best available protection for the precious freight brought from civilization and as a temporary storage place for the furs which would be taken in exchange. Gray gives the following description of the assembly:

> West of the fur company's camp or store were most of the camps of the hunters and trappers; east of it, close to the river,

---

[1] Tack-en-sua-tis received the opprobious nickname from a festering wound suffered in his abdomen. He was very friendly at first to the missionaries, going with them to Fort Walla Walla. Later he became cool and indifferent. Years later, in his old age, Spalding returned to his Nez Perces and led in a great revival. On November 12, 1871, he baptized Rotten Belly giving him the name of Samuel. Chief Lawyer was baptized at the same time.

was the missionary camp, while to the south, from one to three miles distant along Horse Creek, from its junction with Green River, where the Snake and Bannock Indians were camped, to six miles up the stream, were the camps of the Flatheads and Nez Perces. . . The whole city was a military camp; every little camp had its own guards to protect its occupants and property from being stolen by its neighbor.[2]

The arrival of the missionary women created a sensation not only among the one hundred and fifty or so trappers, some of whom had not seen a white woman for years, but also among the natives, most of whom were seeing a white woman for the first time. Whitman in his report to Greene, dated from the Rendezvous on July 16, wrote of the Indians: "They were greatly interested with our females cattle & waggon."[3] The Indians called the wagon a "land canoe." The mission party remained at the Rendezvous from Wednesday, July 6, to Monday, the eighteenth. The presence of the women attracted many of the mountain men to the daily prayers which the missionaries conducted. From fifteen to twenty came either for the morning or evening devotions. In a letter to her husband's family, dated July 15, Narcissa wrote:

> If we had packed one or two animals with bibles & testaments we should have had abundant opportunity of disposing of them to the traders & trappers of the mountain who would have received them gratefully. Many have come to us for tracts & bibles which we could not supply. We have given away all we have to spare.[4]

Among the few mountain men who later wrote their memoirs was Osborne Russell, whose *Journal of a Trapper; or, Nine years in the Rocky Mountains, 1834-1843* first appeared about 1914 and has been twice republished. In this *Journal* Russell describes the reception the missionary women received at the Rendezvous. "The two ladies were gazed upon with wonder and astonishment by the rude Savages," he wrote, "they being the first white women ever seen by these Indians, the first that had ever penetrated into these wild and rocky regions."[5] The Reverend George H. Atkinson, a prominent Congregational missionary to the white settlers in Oregon who arrived in 1848, wrote: "Orville (sic) Russell, Esq., a trapper from a Baptist family in Maine, who had been converted while reading his Bible in his lonely hunter's

[2] Gray, *History of Oregon*, 121-22.

[3] Hulbert, *Whitman*, I: p. 206.

[4] Elliott, *Coming of the White Women*, 19.

[5] Russell, *Journal of a Trapper*, 1955, p. 41. For reference to his Bible, see *idem.*, p. 109.

cabin in the Rocky Mountains." [6] Russell may have been one of the trappers to whom the missionaries gave a Bible. In his *Journal*, Russell refers to the fact that he had a Bible. He migrated to the Willamette Valley in 1843 where he became a charter member of the First Presbyterian Church of Oregon City, organized on May 25, 1844.[7]

In recognition of the kindly spiritual influence exercised by the missionary women at the Rendezvous, a monument has been erected to them at the site near Daniel, Wyoming, where the annual pageant has been presented. The monument consists of a bronze plaque attached to a great boulder with the following inscription:

To

NARCISSA PRENTISS WHITMAN

AND

ELIZA HART SPALDING

MISSIONARIES

FIRST WHITE WOMEN IN WYOMING

AND

FIRST WOMEN OVER OREGON TRAIL

1836

July 6 to July 18 was spent at "Green River Rendezvous"

These pilgrim women took an active part in
religious services held here.

Since the Rendezvous was the terminus of the caravan, the missionaries knew that some arrangements had to be made for a guide or an escort for the remainder of their journey to the Columbia River. In a letter to Greene dated July 8, Spalding estimated that they had traveled about thirteen hundred miles from Westport and that the distance from the Rendezvous to Fort Walla Walla was about six hundred miles.[8] The Nez Perces, delighted to know that finally missionaries were on their way to their people and fearful that something might happen to divert them, urged the mission party to travel with them.

There were at least two routes the Nez Perces could follow from the Rendezvous into the Bitterroot Valley through which they intended to

---

[6] Atkinson, *Biography of Rev. G. H. Atkinson,* 177.

[7] There were only three charter members, one of whom was a staunch Presbyterian by the name of Robert Moore, hence the name. Shortly after its organization, Moore moved to another locality. Upon his departure the name of the church was changed to the First Congregational Church of Oregon City.

[8] Estimates of the distances traveled by the missionaries from Westport to the Rendezvous vary. For a detailed report on distances, see records kept by Asa B. Smith and Mrs. Cushing Eells, vol. II of this work.

pass on their way back to their homes in the Clearwater Valley of what is now northern Idaho. The first trail led northward through the Jackson Hole country, then through Pierre's Hole in what is now northeastern Idaho (now called Teton Basin), and on over the mountains into the Bitterroot Valley. This is the route the Indians had taken the previous year when Parker traveled with them. A second way was by a circuitous route to Fort Hall and then over the mountains into the Bitterroot Valley. The first suggested route would have taken the missionaries through some very mountainous terrain. Moreover, the Nez Perces were planning to travel in a leisurely fashion, killing such buffalo as might be found en route. Whitman and Spalding estimated that if they went with the Indians, it would take them at least two months longer to reach their destination.

A second possibility for the mission party was to hire a guide and travel independently of the Indians by going first to Fort Hall, then following the Snake River across what is now southern Idaho. In his letter of July 8, Spalding indicated that they were considering the latter plan.

However, to the great relief of the missionaries, a small party of Hudson's Bay men under the command of John L. McLeod and Thomas McKay arrived at the Rendezvous on July 12. McLeod and McKay invited the missionaries to return with them to Fort Walla Walla. In a postscript to his letter to Greene, Spalding added: "It seems the most marked Providence in our favour, of any we have yet experienced. . ."

The Hudson's Bay party and the missionaries left the Rendezvous on July 18. The Nez Perces decided to accompany them as far as Fort Hall. On this part of their route, McLeod, McKay, and the missionaries adapted their manner of travel to that of the Indians who were accustomed to make but one camp a day of about fifteen miles. The mixed company of traders, Indians, and missionaries followed a trail that led in a southwesterly direction for about sixty miles to Smith's Creek in the vicinity of what is now Cokeville, Wyoming. This was reached on July 25. Thus they were able to skirt the high mountains, some peaks of which rose to eleven thousand feet or more, on the west side of Green River. On the twenty-seventh they reached Bear River, which flowed into the Great Salt Lake, near what is now Montpelier, Idaho. They arrived at Soda Springs on July 30 and on the third of August they reached Fort Hall. Some of the Indians left the main party before arriving at the Fort.

Mrs. Whitman's Diary, July to December 1836

After the mission party started on July 18 on the last segment of their overland journey, Narcissa had no opportunity to mail letters until she reached Fort Vancouver. Thus this part of her diary covers a period of three months. Before mailing her diary to her mother, Marcus persuaded her to make a copy for his mother. Both of these documents are still extant. For the sake of designation, the first will be known as Diary A, now on deposit in Whitman College, Walla Walla, Washington, and the second as Diary B.[1]

Diary A, together with a collection of Narcissa's letters, passed into the possession of a sister of Narcissa's, Mrs. Harriet P. Jackson, who in 1893 was living in Oberlin, Ohio. Mrs. Jackson, retaining the diary, presented the letters to the Oregon Historical Society which published them in the 1891 and 1893 *Transactions of the Oregon Pioneer Association*. Unfortunately, however, there were many omissions and errors in the printed copies.[2] In 1932 some of Mrs. Jackson's descendants presented Diary A to Whitman College. Judging from a statement in Narcissa's letter of September 18, 1838, to her sister Jane, she was much annoyed to learn that this diary had been published in a local newspaper. She wrote: "I regret you should have it printed, or any of it, for it never was designed for public eye." So far as is known, this is the only time Diary A was ever printed until Elliott used this copy in his *Coming of the White Women, 1836*.

Diary B appeared in the 1891 *Transactions* with the following introduction by George H. Himes, Secretary of the Association:

> The following was secured through Rev. Myron Eells, of Union City, Washington, a member of the Association, who writes as follows to your Secretary under date of August 31, 1891: "I have fortunately been able to obtain a copy of this journal, which has lain in manuscript among some relations of Dr. Whitman's in New York [State] for the past fifty-two years, and is now for the first time given to the public, with some important omissions.[3]

[1] Now in Bancroft Library, Berkeley.

[2] *T.O.P.A.*, 1891, p. 79; 1893, p. 53. Some of these transcriptions of Mrs. Whitman's letters were reprinted in Hulbert, *Whitman*, vol. I., without being compared with the original documents and corrected.

[3] *Op. cit.*, p. 40.

We do not know whether Myron Eells himself made the transcription of Diary B or whether this was made by another.

When Mrs. Whitman copied her diary for her husband's mother, she took a sheet of paper which measured about eight inches wide and twelve and a half inches long — approximately the size of an ordinary sheet of typewriter paper. This was divided at the center and each half folded. Each page then measured four inches wide by six and a quarter inches long. The two folded pages were referred to by Narcissa as "leaves." Each leaf would have four pages of finely written material. In order to make the best use of the paper and thus save postage, Narcissa wrote to the very edges of the paper leaving no margins. Diary B originally contained twenty-three of these leaves of which one-half of the first page and all of the fourth leaf are now missing. An examination of the copy that appeared in the 1891 *Transactions* shows that the fourth leaf was then lost. The diary as published in 1891 contained about twelve thousand words.

Diary B begins with a short letter to Mrs. Loomis, the mother of Marcus Whitman. This letter is here published for the first time.

VANCOUVER,   Oct. 13th. 1836

MRS. ALICE LOOMIS,

DEAR MOTHER   At the request of my husband I send you a copy of the journal I have kept from Rendezvous here, originally dedicated to my own Mother. If the perusal of it will afford you any satisfaction, I shall be amply rewarded for copying it.

Your affectionate daughter,   NARCISSA WHITMAN

Narcissa must have taken about a week to make the transcription for Diary A begins with the following short letter to her parents:

VANCOUVER,   Oct. 20th, 1836

DEAREST PARENTS,   I have been able to write something of a journal from Rendezvous here, did not expect to be able to copy it, but as I have been situated for a few weeks past, have taken time to copy it & as it requires several sheets, have put it in this form as being the most compact for sending.[4] It must answer for all in the room of letters, for I have not time to say more.

Your affectionate Daughter   NARCISSA WHITMAN

The following copy of Narcissa's diary for that part of her overland journey extending from the Rendezvous ot Fort Vancouver is taken from Elliott's Coming of the White Women, 1836. *A careful comparison of Diaries A and B shows a few variant readings. Material in Diary A*

---

[4] According to this statement, Narcissa copied both of the diaries from some original notes which she evidently afterwards destroyed.

*not included in B will be in (parentheses), and material in Diary B
and not in A will be marked {thus}. It must be assumed that the
missing manuscript pages of Diary B contained the same information
as found in the same section in Diary A.*

THE RENDEZVOUS TO FORT HALL

WEST OF THE ROCKY MOUNTAINS

DEAREST MOTHER We commenced our journey to Walla Walla July
18th 1836, under the protection of Mr. McLeod & his company. Came
ten miles, in a southwesterly direction. The Flat Head & Nez Perce
Indians & some lodges of the Snake tribe, accompany us to Fort Hall.
While they are with us, we shall make but one camp in a day. On the
19th we did not move at all. 20th Came twelve miles in the same
direction as on the 18th over many steep & high mountains. On the
21st our course was south east in the morning. Traveled fifteen miles.
Yesterday the 22nd was a tedious day to us, we started about nine
o'clock A.M. rode untill half past four, P.M. Came twenty one miles.
Had two short showers in the afternoon which cooled the air considerably. Before this the heat was oppressive. I thought of Mother's
bread & butter many times as any hungry child would, but did not
find it on the way. I fancy pork & potatoes would relish extremely well.
Have been living on fresh meat for two months exclusively. Am cloyed
with it. I do not know how I shall endure this part of the journey.
Find it much harder to make one camp in a day than we did to make
two while with Fitzpatric, for our dinner and two hours rest in the
heat of the day prepared us for a lengthy ride in the afternoon. Our
ride today has not been so fatiguing or lengthy as yesterday. Rode
from nine o'clock A.M. untill 1 o'clock P.M. in the same direction, south
west as yesterday. Felt a calm and peaceful state of mind all day. Had
sweet communion with him who delights to dwell with the humble &
contrite in heart. Especial in the morning. I had a freedom in prayer
for my beloved Parents. Earnestly desired that God would bless them
in their declining years, & smooth their passage to the tomb; that in
the absence of their earthly comforts, he would fill their souls with
his more immediate presence, so that they may never have cause to
regret the sacrifice they have made for his Name Sake. Father, accept
the sacrifice & may they prove a blessing to the world.

24th Sab Eve. Our route today has been a very mountainous one.
Came about eight miles. Painful as it is for me to journey on the Holy
Sabbath, I have enjoyed notwithstanding a melting sense of the presence of that Being who has promised to be "with his desciples always."
Found it good to rest my soul on this today. Although I can truly say
"my soul thirsts yea even faints for the courts of God," the word of his
saints below; the privation has been made good to me by a rich supply

from the fountain head God, the Father, Son & Holy Ghost. O blessed blessed privaledge, that such a sinner as I may have access to a mercy seat through such a Saviour as Jesus Christ. It is good to feel that he is all I want, & all my righteousness, & if I had ten thousand lives I would give them all to him. I long to be more like him, to possess more of his meek Spirit.

25th.   Came fifteen miles today. Very mountainous. Encamped on Smith's creek, a small branch of Bear River. Bear River emties into Salt Lake, called on maps, Timpanogos.[5] That Lake has not outlet & is said to be a great curiosity by those who have visited it. Large quantities of Salt may be obtained from the Shore and that of the finest quality. We do not expect to pass it, said to be a tedious route, no water or buffalo in going from it. Endured the ride today very well notwithstanding its difficulties. Very mountainous. Paths winding on the sides of steep mountains. In some place the path is so narrow as scarcely to afford room for the animal to place his foot. One after another, we pass along with cautious steps. Passed a creek on which were a fine bunch of Gooseberries, nearly ripe, relished them very much. They were not as sweet when ripe as those in the states nor prickly.

Husband has had a tedious time with the waggon today. Got set in the creek this morning while crossing, was obliged to wade considerably in getting it out. After that in going between two mountains, on the side of one so steep that it was difficult for horses to pass, the waggon was upset twice. Did not wonder at this at all. It was a greater wonder that it was not turning a somerset continually. It is not very greatful to my feelings to see him wear out with such excessive fatigue as I am obliged to.[6] He is not as fleshy as he was last winter. All the most difficult part of the way he has walked in his laborious attempt to take the waggon over. (Ma knows what my feelings are.)

26th.   Did not move camp today. McKay has been preparing to send out trappers from this place. Husband has been sick today and so lame with the rheumatism as to be scarcely able to move. It is a great privalege that we can lie still today on his account, for he needs rest. Heat oppressive. About noon some of the Indians set the willows on fire near the camp, which came near burning us out. It was stopped before any injury was done to us save it caused some to move their lodges and we our tent.

27th   Had quite a level route today. Came down Bear River and encamped on Tommow's [Thomas] Fork, a small branch. Mr. McKay sent off about 30 of his men today as trappers. Several lodges of In-

---

[5] A map showing this name for the Great Salt Lake has not been located.

[6] Gray, *Oregon*, 130. "Soon after we reached camp, along comes Dr. Whitman with his wagon, notwithstanding all parties and persons, except the Indians, advised him to leave it. He was literally alone in his determination to get his old wagon through on to the waters of the Columbia."

dians left us also, to go in another direction, & we expect more will leave us tomorrow. They wish to go a different route from Mr. McLeod, ʃand desire us to go with them. It would be more difficult and lengthy than Mr. McLeod's.ʔ We are still in a dangerous country but our company is large enough for safety. Our cattle endure the journey remarkably well.[7] They are a source of great comfort to us in this land of scarcity, they supply us with sufficient milk for our tea & coffee which is indeed a luxury. We are obliged to shoe some of them on account of sore feet. Have seen no buffalo since we left Rendezvous. Had no game of any kind except a few messes of Antelope which John's Father gave us. We have plenty of dry Buffalo meat which we purchased of the Indians & dry it is for me. I can scarcely eat it, it appears so filthy, but it will keep us alive, and we ought to be thankful for it.[8]

We have had a few meals of fresh fish also, which relished well. Have the prospect of obtaining plenty in one or two weeks more. Found no berries. Neither have I found any of Ma's bread. (Girls do not waste the bread, if you know how well I should relish even the dryest morsal you would save every piece carefully.) Do not think I regret coming. No, far from it. I would not go back for a world. I am contented and happy notwithstanding I sometimes get very hungry and weary.

Have six weeks steady journeying before us. Will the Lord give me patience to endure it. Feel sometime as if it was a long time to be traveling. Long for rest, but must not murmur. We are told we shall find the heat greater as we go on than we have found it previously to this. Feel to pity the poor Indian women who are continually traveling in this manner during their lives & know no other comfort. They do all the work, such as getting the wood, preparing food, piching their lodges, packing & driving their animals, the complete slaves of their husbands. I am making some little progress in their language — long to be able to converse with them about the Saviour. They all appear anxious to converse with us & to be understood by us.

28th   Very mountainous all the way today, came over another ridge. Rode from eight A.M. till two P.M. We thought yesterday the Indians were all going to leave us except two or three but not one has. They fear to on account of the Black Feet tribe, who are their enemies, and would destroy them all if they could. The Flat Head tribe are nearly extinguished by them.

[7] The missionaries were able to drive only eight head through to Fort Walla Walla of the seventeen with which they started. Two were killed for their meat; two calves were lost; and five were left at Fort Boise because of exhaustion.

[8] Spalding in a letter to Greene, Sept. 20, 1836, commented as follows about the dried buffalo meat: ". . . the poorest kind of buffalo bull meat, sour, mouldy, & full of all manner of filth, such as I once would not have fed to a dog."

One of the axle trees of the waggon broke today. Was a little re-joiced, for we were in hopes they would leave it and have no more trouble with it. Our rejoycing was in vain however for they are making a cart of the hind wheels this afternoon & lashing the forward wheels to it, intending to take it through in some shape or other. They are so resolute & untiring in their efforts, they will probably succeed. Had a little fresh fish for breakfast & some Antelope for supper sent us by Mr. McLeod, and other friends in camp. Thus the Lord provides and smooths all our way for us, giving us strength.

July 29th   Had a tedious ride today. Started the usual time, but did not come into camp untill nearly four o'clock P.M. Mr. Gray was quite sick this morning & inclined to fall behind camp. Husband & myself thought it would not be prudent to leave him alone & rode with him about two hours & half when he became very feeble & inclined to lie down. By this time we were so far behind the camp that Husband thought it not prudent for me to remain with them any longer & sent me on to overtake them. Soon after Mr. Gray gave out entirely & Husband left him to come for the cart & return for him. I had over-taken an Indian & told him how sick he was, who went back met Husband & both returned to Mr. Gray.[9] The Indian helped him on his horse, got on behind him, supported him in his arms & in this manner rode slowly into camp. This was a welcomed relief. All rejoyced to see them come in for some of us had been riding seven hours, others eight, without any nourishment. It is good to stop a while under such cir-cumstances, I think.

July 30th   Went today ten miles off our route with Husband Mr. McLeod & a few others, to visit Soda Springs.[10] Was much delighted with the view of the wonders of Nature we saw there. The first object of curiosity we came to were several white mounds on the top of which were small springs of soda. These mounds were covered with a crustation made from the evaporation of the water which is con-tinually running in small quantities from these springs. The next object we saw was a little singular. It consisted of an opening like a crater about three feet in diameter, by the side of a small stream. On some rocks a little below in the opening were dead flies & birds in abundance which had approached so near the crater, as to be choked with the gas which it constantly emits. On putting the face down, the breath is stoped instantly, & a low rumbling noise like the roaring of fire is

---

[9] Gray became so ill one day that he could not ride. He was left lying on the bank of a stream as the caravan moved on six miles to camp. Gray in his *Oregon*, p. 130, tells how Lawyer got him on a horse and brought him into camp. Gray, who later developed an anti-Hudson's Bay Company bias, wrote: "My impression of this transaction has always been that McLeod wished to get rid of this young American, who was then in the service of the mission party."

[10] Narcissa gives a good description of this well known phenomenon on the Oregon Trail.

heard beneath. Having satisfied our curiosity here we passed through a grove of juniper & pitch pine trees, & a small distance from them came to a large spring of soda water. Clear as crystal, effervescing continually. It appeared of great depth. At a considerable distance below the surface, there were two white substances, in appearance like lumps of Soda in a concrete state. We took with us some soda & Acid to try the effect of a mixture & found that it effervesed with both, but the effervescence was greater with the Acid, than with the Soda. Drunk freely of the water, found it very pleasant. There were five or six other springs near Bear River which we did not visit, in consequence of loosing sight of part of our company & being obliged to hasten back. The ground in every direction was covered with lava. Gathered several fine specimens. We desired more time to visit other curiosities there but was unable to, for camp was moving from us continually. Rode in all thirty miles, & found them encamped under a bluff covered with black basalt.

31st. Our ride was not lengthy today which I felt to be a great favour. Am nearly sick in consequence of excessive fatigue yesterday. Heat oppressive in the middle of the day.

August 1st (Monday) Monthly Concert day. How sweet & sacred the influence of this day upon the weary & solitary Missionary.

2nd Had an unusual long ride today. Heat excessive. Truly I thought "the Heavens over us were brass, & the earth iron under our feet." [11] Our route for two or three days past has been quite level. But the same scenery prevails, rocks & sandy plains covered with a species of wormwood called sage of a pale green, offensive both to the sight & smell. We meet with frequent fertile spots however, often enough to furnish us & our animals with a comfortable Inn for the night. Had a feast of service berries today, the first ripe ones we have seen.[12] They are a small black berry, very sweet, something like the Pear in its flavour. Stoped & gathered some which rested me much, & answered the place of a dinner very well.

3d Came to Fort Hall this morning distance eight miles. A cool breeze made our ride very pleasant. Husband & myself were alone entirely behind the dust of camp & enjoyed a sweet repast in conversing about home & dear friends. Particularly Mother Loomis in her new situation. Thought a sight of her in her dairy would be particularly pleasant. Was much cheered with a view of the Fort at a considerable distance. Any thing that looks like a house makes us glad. Called and

[11] Narcissa's quotation from Deut. 28:23, so appropriate in describing the excessive heat of the day, reveals her thorough knowledge of the Bible. The verse in the King James version reads: "And thy heaven that is over thy head shall be brass, and the earth that is under thee shall be iron."

[12] The serviceberry is common to Idaho. The fruit is a juicy, full-flavored berry. The Indians used to dry the berry for winter use.

were hospitably entertained by Capt Thing who keeps the Fort. It was built by Capt Wyeth a gentleman from Boston, whom we saw at Rendezvous, on his way to the east. Our dinner consisted of dry buffalo meat, turnips & fried bread, which was a luxury. Mountain bread is simply coarse flour & water mixed & roasted or fried in buffalo grease. To one who has had nothing but meat for a long time this relishes (very) well. For tea we had the same with the addition of some stewed service berries.

FORT HALL TO FORT WALLA WALLA

Fort Hall was located on the south bank of the Snake River, about twelve miles north of the present city of Pocatello, Idaho. The Fort was established as a trading post in July 1834 by Nathaniel Wyeth as an independent venture in the fur trade. In 1837 Wyeth sold Fort Hall to the Hudson's Bay Company. Gray, in his History of Oregon, *gives the following description of the Fort as he remembered seeing it in 1836:*

Fort Hall, in 1836, was a stockade, made of cotton-wood logs, about twelve feet long, set some two feet in the ground, with a piece of timber pinned near the top, running entirely around the stockade, which was about sixty feet square. The stores and quarters for the men were built inside. . .[13]

Captain Joseph Thing, one of Wyeth's men, was in charge of Fort Hall when the mission party of 1836 arrived. He was a cultured southern gentlemen whose gracious hospitality was long remembered by the missionaries. He drew upon the produce of his little garden to supplement the heavy diet of meat on which they had been living. And especially appreciated was the bread he gave them. Both Mrs. Whitman and Mrs. Spalding commented on this in their respective diaries. At Fort Fall the young Iowa lad, Miles Goodyear, severed company with the missionaries. Gray states that this was because Dr. Whitman insisted on taking the wagon and Miles refused to struggle with it any longer.[14]

According to the mileage figures compiled by the Rev. A. B. Smith,

---

[13] Gray, *op. cit.,* p. 131.

[14] Gray, *op. cit.,* p. 133. For a life of Miles Goodyear see Charles Kelly and Maurice L. Howe, *Miles Goodyear, First Citizen of Utah,* 1937. Dulin had left the mission party at the Rendezvous. However, a colored man by the name of Hinds joined the party at the Rendezvous "on account of his health and for the purpose of taking medicine." See Narcissa's letter of Oct. 24, 1836, to "Oren and Nancy." Hinds was unable to render much service as an assistant. He died at Waiilatpu sometime between Nov. 18 and Dec. 8, 1836, and was the first to be buried in the little cemetery at the base of the hill near the Whitman home.

*who went out to Oregon with the 1838 party of reinforcements, Fort
Hall was twelve hundred and twenty-one miles from Westport. This
estimate compares favorably with figures taken from present day auto-
mobile maps which give eleven hundred sixty-five for a somewhat
parallel route.[15] Since the last of the mission party of 1836 left the
frontier on May 1, this means that some ninety-five days had elapsed
before their arrival at Fort Hall on August 3. Thus they averaged
about thirteen miles a day including the time spent at Fort Laramie
and at the Rendezvous. They still had about five hundred miles to go
before reaching Fort Walla Walla — and this was across the deserts of
what is now southern Idaho in the blazing heat of August.*

4th   Enjoyed the cool retreat of an upper room this morning while
writing. The buildings of the Fort are made of hewed logs, roof
covered with mud bricks, chimney & fireplaces also of the same.[16] No
windows, except a square hole in the roof & in the bastion a few port
holes large enough for guns only. The buildings are all enclosed in a
strong log wall. This affords them a place of safety when attacked by
hostile Indians, as they frequently are, the Fort being in the Black Feet
country.

We were invited to breakfast & dinner, dined with them only. Since
dinner visited the garden & corn field. The turnips in the garden
appear thrifty, the tops very large & tall but the roots were small. The
peas looked well, but had most of them been gathered by the mice.
Saw a few onions that were going to seed, these looked quite natural.
This was all the garden contained. He told us his corn did extremely
well untill the eighth of June when the frost of one night completely
prostrated it. It has since come up again but does not look as well as
before. This is their first attempt at cultivation. The buildings at Fort
William on Larimy's Fork of Platte, Black Hills, are made in the same
way, but larger & more finished than here. Here we had stools to sit
on, there we had very comfortable chairs, bottomed with buffalo skins.
Thus you see we have a house of entertainment almost or quite as
often as Christian of Pilgrim's Progress did. We expect one more before
we get to Walla Walla. That is Snake Fort belonging to Mr. McKay
who is journeying with us. If prospered we expect to be there in fifteen
days. From this on our company will be small. The Indians (will)
{all} leave us today except one or two who go with us to assist in

[15] For the detailed estimate of distances between principal points on the Oregon
Trail, see A. B. Smith's figures in Drury, *Diaries of Spalding and Smith*. It should
be remembered that the Rendezvous of 1838, which Smith attended, was on the
Wind River east of the Rockies.

[16] The reference to the "mud bricks" is to the adobes which the missionaries
noticed being used both at Fort Laramie and at Fort Hall. This was a type of
construction new to both Whitman and Spalding.

driving the cattle. Kentuck [17] who went with Mr. Parker last year & Chief Rotten Belly. The whole tribe are exceedingly anxious to have us go with them, use every argument they can invent to prevail on us to do so, & not only arguments, but stratagem. We all think it not best. We are very much fatigued & wish to get through as soon as possible. To go with them would take us two months or more, when now we expect to go to Walla Walla in twenty-five days, or be there by the first of September. When we get there rest will be sweet to us. So it will be to the Christian when he gets to heaven. Ah! will Mother & Father get there before I do? if so then they will be ready to greet me upon its threshold. Here we have raised our Ebenezer, saying, "Hitherto the Lord hath helped us." Now we leave it & pass on. Farewell dear Parents for the present. Our animals are nearly ready. It is now half past two, expect to go but a short distance & encamp.

5th   FRIDAY MORN.   Came all of ten miles last eve, did not arrive here untill after dark.[18] Mr McLeod & his company started earlier than we did intending to come but a little way from the Fort just to make a commencement. We could not get ready to start with him & the man who piloted us, led us wrong, much out of the way. Those on whom we depended to drive our cattle, disappointed us. Husband & myself fell in behind to assist John Aits, who was alone with them. This made us later into camp than the rest of our com. We came through several swamps & all the last part of the way we were so swarmed with musquetoes as to be scarcely able to see, especially while crossing the Pourtniff [19] which we did just before we came into camp. It is the widest river I have forded on horseback. It seemed as if the cows would run mad for the Musquetoes.[20] We could scarcely get them along. Mr. McLeod met us and invited us to tea, which was a great favour. Thus blessings gather thick arround us.

---

[17] In a letter to Parker dated Sept. 18, 1836, Whitman stated: "We employed Kentuc (your favorite Indian) but he did not do well." Kentuc left the mission party. Hulbert, *Whitman*, I, p. 232.

[18] After leaving Fort Hall, the Hudson's Bay men and the missionaries could travel more leisurely. The missionary women were especially thankful for the opportunity to rest during the mid-day. After leaving Fort Hall, the trail followed the south bank of the Snake River all the way to Glenn's Ferry where the Snake was crossed on Aug. 13.

[19] The Portneuf River, a tributary of the Snake.

[20] The mosquitoes and flies are still bad in many of these places visited by the missionaries. The author of this work visited the site of the 1836 Rendezvous on Green River in July 1960 and found the mosquitoes and flies most annoying. Horses especially were plagued with the horse fly, the deer fly, and the botfly. There was also a small black fly which bit both man and beast. Some of the flies tried to deposit their eggs in the nostrils of the horses while others stung the animals in the tender spot back of the ankle just above the hoof. Perhaps some of these same insect pests were making life miserable for the cattle here mentioned by Narcissa.

Fort Hall is situated on a flue of Snake River, called on maps Lewis, about ten miles above the junction of the Pourtniff in its valley. We have been in the mountains so long find the scenery of this valley very greatful to the eye, with a large river on my right and one on my left hand skirted with timber. This is our first sight of Snake River at Fort Hall. We shall follow the course of it on the south side, for many days. We have passed many places where the soil is good and would be fertile if there were frequent rains. Usually the country is barren & would be a sandy desert were it not for the sage, which is its only production, in some places it grows in bunches to the height of a mans head, & it is so stif and hard as to be much in the way of our animals & waggon. Its common height is just above the ancles.

Eve. We passed the American falls in Snake river just after dinner. The roar of the water is heard at a considerable distance. Our ride has not been very tedious today for us for we stoped during the greatest heat for rest & dinner. Now the Indians are not with us, we shall expect to make two camps. I feel this to be a great mercy to us weak females for it was more than we could well endure to travel during the heat of the day without any refreshment.

6th Route very bad & difficult today, especially in the forenoon. We crossed a small stream, full of falls a short distance above where it emties into the Snake River. The only pass where we could cross was just on the edge of rocks above one of the falls. While the pack animals both ours & the Company's were crossing there was such a rush as to crowd two of our horses over the falls, both packed with dry meat. It was with great difficulty they were got out, one of them was in nearly an hour, much to his injury. Had a fine breeze during most of the day. Heat very great when otherwise. No game taken today. We have a little rice to eat with our dry meat given us by Mr. McLeod, which makes it relish quite well.

7th Sab. Came fifteen miles without seeing water, over a dry parch{ed} earth, covered with its native sage as parched as the earth itself. Heat excessive, but mitigated with a gentle breeze. We have encamped on a fine place, plenty of good grass for our weary animals. Thus are blessings so mingled, that it seems as if there was nothing else but mercy and blessings all the way. Was there ever a journey like this, performed where the sustaining hand of God has been so manifest every moment. Surely the children of Israel could not have been more sensible of the "pillar of cloud by day & of the pillar of fire by night," than we have been of that Hand that has led us thus safely on. God has heard our prayer in our behalf, & even now while I am writing on this Holy day is the sweet incence of prayer ascending before the throne of Heavenly Grace. Nor are we forgotten by our beloved churches at home in the prayers of the Sanctuary. We are too sensible of its blessed effects to believe otherwise & O how comforting is this thought to the heart of the Missionary. We love to think & talk of home with such feelings as (that) {these}. It warms our hearts, strengthens & encourages us in the work of our beloved Master & makes our journeyings easy.

8th. Mon. Eve. Snake River. Have an excellent camp of ground tonight, plenty of excellent fead for our horses & cattle. Quite a change in the temperatures of the atmosphere since yesterday noon. It was so cool last night & we have such a wind today, that we and our animals have traveled more comfortably for it. We think it remarkable that our cattle should endure the journey as well as they do. We have two sucking calves that appear to be in very good spirits, they suffer some from sore feet, otherwise they have come on very well {& will go through}.

Have come eighteen miles today & have taken it so deliberately that it has been easy for us. The hunters came in last night well loaded. They had been in the mountains two days after game. Killed three Elks & two Antelopes. This is the first Elk meat we have had & the last opportunity we expect to have of taking any more game. We are told many have traveled the whole distance from Rendezvous to Walla Walla without any fresh, living entirely upon the dry. We think ours will last us untill we reach the Salmon fishery at Snake Falls. Thus we are well provided for all the way, contrary to expectations. Mr. McLeod has excelent hunters, this is a reason why we live so well. There is but {little} game & that little is found at a great distance from the route.

11th   Tuesday & Wednesday have been very tedious days, both for man and beast. Lengthy marches without water. Not so tedious today for length, but the route has been rocky & sandy. Had a present tonight of a fresh Salmon, also a plate of fried cakes from Mc McLeod (Girls if you wish to know how they taste, you can have the pleasure of taking a little flour & water & make some dough roll it thin, cut it into square blocks, then take some beaf fat & fry them. You need not put either salt or pearl ash in your dough.) Believe me I relish these as well as I ever did any made at home.

12th   Frid.   Raised camp this morn at Sunrise. Came two hours ride to the Salmon fishery. Found a few lodges of Diggers of the Snake tribe (so called because they live on roots during winter) who have just commenced fishing. Obtained some and boiled for our breakfast, find it good eating. Had we been a few days earlier we should not have been able to obtain any fish, for they had but just come up. They never go higher than these falls, but come here every season.

Friday eve.   Dear Harriet, the little trunk you gave me has come with me so far & now I must leave it here alone. Poor little trunk, I am sorry to leave thee. Thou must abide here alone & no more by this presance remind me of my Dear Harriet. Twenty miles below the Falls on Snake River. This shall be thy place of rest. Farewell little Trunk.

The Crossing of the Snake River

Believed to be the place, showing two islands near Glenn's Ferry, Idaho, where the mission party of 1836 crossed the Snake River. See text page 85.

Descending the Blue Mountains

An unknown artist made this drawing of the Whitman-Spalding party descending the west side of the mountains. The description of the scene may have been furnished by Joe Meek who knew the missionaries and who supplied much information for Victor's *River of the West* in which this drawing appeared. The first couple probably represent the Whitmans; the third figure is Spalding in clerical dress; and Mrs. Spalding is in the rear. One of the two men must be Gray. The women are shown riding side-saddle. Actually the Whitmans were in advance of the Spaldings at the time they descended the Blue Mountains. See text page 91.

FORT WALLA WALLA

This site is now covered by the waters of the Columbia River which have been backed up by the McNary Dam. No post of the Hudson's Bay Company figured more in the story of the Oregon Mission of the American Board than did this. From Stevens, *Pacific Railroad Report.* See text pages 93-95.

I thank thee for thy faithful services & that I have been cheered by thy presance so long. Thus we scatter as we go along.

The hills are so steep ∫and⟩ rocky that Husband thought it best to lighten the waggon as much as possible & take nothing but the wheels, leaving the box with my trunk. I regret leaving anything that came from home especially that trunk, but it is best. It would have been better for us not to have attempted to bring any baggage whatever, only what ∫was⟩ necessary to use on the way. It costs so much labor, besides the expense of animals. If I were to make this journey again, I would make quite different preparations. To pack & unpack so many times & cross so many streams, where the packs frequently get wet, requires no small amount of labour, besides the injury done to the articles. Our books what few we have, have been wet several times. In going from Elmira to Williamsport, this trunk fell into the creek and wet all my books & Richard's too, very much. The sleigh box came off, and all of us came near a wetting likewise. The custom of the country is to possess nothing & then you will loose nothing while traveling. Farewell for the present.

13th Sat. (Dear H.) Mr McKay has asked the privaledge of taking the little trunk along, so that my soliloquy about it last night was for nought, however it will do me no good, it may him. We have come at least fifteen miles & have had the worst route in all the journey for the cart, we might have had a better one, but for being misled by some of the company who started out before their leaders. It was two o'clock before we came into camp. They are preparing to cross the Snake River.

The river is divided by two islands into three branches & is fordable. The packs are placed upon the top of the highest horses & in this way crossed without wetting. Two of the tallest horses were selected to carry Mrs. S & myself over. Mr McLeod gave me his & rode mine. The last branch we rode as much as a half mile in crossing & against the current too which made it hard for the horses the water being up to their sides.[21] Husband had considerable difficulty in crossing the cart. (Both the cart & the mules were capsized in the water and the mules entangled in the harness.) ∫Both the cart and mules turned upside

---

[21] The missionaries forded the Snake River at Island Ford about three miles below present-day Glenn's Ferry, Idaho. Miles Cannon in his *Waiilatpu*, p. 24, wrote: "The writer has examined this ford and finds the conditions today unchanged. There are two islands in the river at this point and the distance between the second and the north bank of the river is computed to be 2600 feet. The current passes over a bar and is quite rapid. The main channel at low water is from five to seven feet deep. Mrs. Whitman and Mrs. Spalding forded the river on horseback. It is a safe presumption that few men could be found today who would undertake this ford under any conditions short of life itself." If the missionaries still had their Indian rubber life preservers, they no doubt used them at this time. After crossing the Snake, the mission party remained on the north bank to Snake Fort or Fort Boise. See illustration at page 83.

down in the river, entangled in the harness.⎰ (They) ⎱The mules⎰ would have drowned, but for a desperate struggle to get them ashore. Then after putting two of the strongest horses before the cart & two men swimming behind to steady it, they succeeded in getting it over. I once thought that crossing streams would be the most dreadful part of the journey. I can now cross the most difficult stream without the least fear. There is one manner of crossing which Husband has tried, but I have not, neither do I wish to. Take an Elk Skin and streach it over you spreading yourself out as much as possible. Then let the Indian women carefully put you on the water, & with a cord in the mouth they will swim & drag you over. (Edward how do you think you would like to ride this way.)

15th   Yesterday Mr McLeod with most of his men left us, wishing to hasten his arrival at Snake Fort, leaving us a pilot & his weakest animals to come in with us at leisure. This (is) ⎰was⎱ a relief to us for it is difficult to bring our cattle up to the speed they wish to travel. We have had such a cool wind today & it has been so comfortable traveling that we have made better progress than usual. Considerable stony however. We passed the hot Springs just before noon which are quite a curiosity. Boiled a bit of dry Salmon in one of them in five minutes.

16th   This evening found a plenty of berries called hawthorn on the stream where we have encamped. They are as large as a cherry & taste much like a mealy sweet apple. Our route on this side of the river is less hilly & difficult than on the south side & said to be two days shorter.

19th   Arrived at Snake Fort about noon.[22] It is situated on Big Wood River, so called because the timber is larger than any to be seen this side of the mountains. It consists chiefly of cotton wood, and is small compared with timber in the States. Snake Fort is owned & built by Mr McKay, one of our company whom we expect to leave here. He with Mr McLeod gave us a hearty welcome. Dined with them. Mr. McLeod was ready to leave on the morrow, but said he would stay a day longer to give us the opportunity of doing some necessary work, for which we were thankful.

20th   SAT.   Last night I put my cloths in water & this morning finished washing before breakfast. I find it not very agreeable to do such work in the middle of the day when I have no shelter to protect me from the sun's schorching rays. This is the third time I have washed

---

[22] Fort Boise had several locations. In 1836 it was on the Boise — or the Big Wood River, as Narcissa called it — about six miles up from its mouth. The trail followed by the missionaries crossed a dry tableland from Glenn's Ferry to Emigrant Point overlooking the Boise River a few miles east of the present city of Boise. A crossing to the north side of the Boise River was made near the present city of Caldwell, Idaho.

since I left the states, or home either. Once at Fort William & at Rendezvous. Mr. McLeod call this eve to see if we were ready to leave. Observed that we had been so engaged in labor as to have no time for rest & proposed for our sakes (the Ladies) to remain over the Sabbath. This I can assure you was a favour for which we can never be too thankful for as our souls need the rest of the Sab as well as our bodies.

21st SABBATH. Rich with heavenly blessings has this day of rest been to my soul. Mr S was invited to preach in the Fort at eleven o'clock. The theme was the character of the blessed Saviour & how pleasing to dwell upon its beauties, his love to us, as exhibited in his life & actions. All listened with good attention to the subject.

22d Left the Fort for Walla Walla. (We) came a short distance to the crossing on Snake river, crossed & encamped for the night. The river had three branches, divided by islands as it was where we crossed before. The first & second of these were very deep but we ʃhadʅ no difficulty in crossing on horseback. The third was deeper still. We dare not venture on horseback. This being a fishing post of the Indians, we easily found a canoe made of rushes & willows on which we placed ourselves & our saddles (Sister S. & myself) when two Indians on horseback with each a rope attached to the canoe, towed us over. (0 if Father Mother & the girls could have seen us now in our snug little bark floating on the water) we are favourites of the company, no one else was privaledged with a ride on it. I wish I could give you a correct idea of the little bark. It is simply bunches of rushes tied together & attached to a frame, made of a few sticks of small willows. It was just large enough to hold us & our saddles. Our baggage was transported on the top of the tallest horses without wetting.

As for the waggon it is left at the fort, & I have nothing to say about crossing it this time. Five of our cattle we left also to be exchanged for others at Walla ʃWalla, three of themʅ only exchanged. Perhaps you will wonder why we have left the waggon having taken it so near through.[23] Our animals were failing & the route in crossing the Blue Mountains is said to be impassable for it. We have the prospect of obtaining one in exchange at Vancouver. If we do not, we shall send for it when convenient & pack it over. We regret now to loose the use of it when we have been at so much labour in getting thus far. It is a useful article in this country.

Now for Edward's amusement & that he may know how to do when he comes over the Rocky Mountains, I will tell how we get the cattle over the rivers. Our two boys, Richard and John, have had the chief management (of) ʃin drivingʅ them all the way, & are commendable for the patience they have manifested. They have had some one or two

---

[23] The Joseph Meek party took wagons over the Blue Mountains in 1840. Narcissa, in a letter to Marcus dated Oct. 4, 1842, mentions the presence of a cart at Waiilatpu.

to help them usually but none so steady drivers as themselves. When a stream is to be forded, where it is necessary for the ʃanimalsʅ to swim, Richard comes to my husband and asks if he may go over with his horse & clothes then & come back after the cows. Having obtained consent he rides over accompanied by his fellow drivers, all strip themselves to the shirt, then return with their horses, if the stream is wide & difficult, if not they leave their horses, tie their shirts on their heads, swim back, collect the cows & drive them through, all swiming after them. If the stream is very wide & they return with their horses, they drive them (over), swiming on their horses after them. This saves them from the too great fatigue of swiming the river twice.

They love to swim as they love to eat & by doing it have saved me many an anxious feeling, for the relief it has given my Husband many times. In the commencement of the journey, we were not able to ford all the streams. In this case all the horses & mules were to be driven across likewise. Usually the best Indian swimmer was selected & mounted the horse that was good for leading, to go before the animals as a guide, while many others swim after them to drive them over. When once under way, such a snorting & hallowing you never heard, at the same time you can see nothing save so many heads floating upon the water. Soon they gain the opposite shore, triumphantly ascend its banks, & retire to their accustomed employment.

Mrs. Whitman made no entries in her diary for August 23, 24, and 25. However, in a letter written by W. H. Gray dated September 9, 1836, we learn that the mission party travelled twenty-six miles on Tuesday, the 23rd. The missionaries were then in eastern Oregon. They crossed the Malheur River, opposite the present site of Payette, Idaho, on the noon of that day. By the evening of the twenty-fourth, they had reached the Burnt River. That day they covered twenty-two miles over some exceedingly difficult mountain terrain. Nowhere along their entire journey did they find such mountainous country as in eastern Oregon. Gray, using his own inimitable system of phonetic spelling, wrote: ". . . our trail beeing along the sides of the Mountain and only wide enough for a single animal to pass winding around and along steep presipisses and among the rocks which scarcely permits the foot of man or beast to secure a firm foot hold, while passing along." [24] Gray does not indicate how far the party travelled on the 25th but judging from Mrs. Whitman's diary, they reached the Powder River Valley that day. After crossing the Wallowa Mountains, the trail took them through beautiful Grande Ronde Valley, then over the Blue Mountains into the Columbia River Valley.

26th FRIDAY. On account of our worn out cattle & horses, it was

[24] Original in Coll. A.

thought best to separate from Mr McLeod's party at least some of us and travel more deliberately. Two mules & a horse have almost entirely given out, having been very much hurt in packing. It is also necessary that some of our party go to Vancouver immediately for supplies & see Mr. Parker before he leaves. It was thot best for my Husband & Mr Gray to go. As Mr McLeod intended to make but a day stop at Walla W we came on with him leaving Mr & Mrs S, the hired men, with the most of our baggage, & the Nez Perces Chief Rottenbelly to pilot them in. We parted from them about three O'clock P M & came on as far as the Lone Tree.[25] The place called Lone Tree is a beautiful valley in the region of Powder river, in the centre of which is a solitary tree quite large, by the side of which travelers usually stop & refresh themselves. We left our tent for Mrs S expecting to be out only a few nights, while she might be many. Mr McLeod kindly offered his for my use & when I arrived in camp found it piched and in readiness for me. This was a great favour, for the wind blew quite hard & the prospect was for a cool night. Took tea with Mr McLeod.

27th   Came in sight of the hill that leads into Grand Round & should have come quite to it, had it not been for a circumstance that occured during the day. This morning Mr McLeod remained behind in persuit of game, & did not come into camp untill we had made a long nooning. Began to feel a little concerned & it was proposed to send back in persuit of him when, at about three o'clock P M he came into camp loaded with wild ducks, having taken twenty two. Now Mother he did just as he always did, during the whole journey, sent me nine of them.[26] Here also Richard caught a fresh Salmon which made us another good meal & if we had been out of provisions we might have made a dinner upon fresh water clams for the river was full of them where we nooned.

We left at four o'clock P.M. and rode untill seven o'clock. Felt exceeding languid & worn out with fatigue in the morn, but took a long sleep at noon while waiting which refreshed me very much. Girls, how do you think we managed to rest ourselves every noon having no houses to shelter us from the schorching heat of the noon day sun, or sofas on which to recline. Perhaps you think we always encamp in the shade of some thick wood. Such a sight I have not seen lo these many weeks. If we can find a few small willows or a single low tree, we think ourselves amply provided for. But often our camping places are in some open plain, & frequently a sand plain, even here is comfort & rest. My Husband who is one of the best the world ever knew is always ready

---

[25] At the point where the Oregon Trail reached the Powder River, there was a lone pine tree which remained as a land mark until some needy emigrant cut it down in 1843. When Fremont passed that way that year, he looked for it and found it freshly fallen.

[26] Here is evidence of special favors which McLeod extended to Mrs. Whitman.

to provide a comfortable shade with one of our saddle blankets spread upon some willows or sticks placed in the ground. Then our Saddles & pishmores,[27] with the other ⟨blanket⟩ placed upon the ground, constitute our sofa. Here we recline & rest untill dinner is ready. How do you think you would like this? Would you not think a seat by Mother in some cool room preferable? Sometimes my wicked heart has been disposed to murmur, thinking I should have no rest for the heat when I stoped. But have always been reproved for it by the comfort and rest I received under these circumstances. I never have wished to go back. Such a thought finds no place in my heart. "The Lord is better to us than our fears." I always find it so.

28th   This morn lingered with Husband on the top of the hill that over looks Grand Round for berries, untill we were some distance behind camp. Have no distressing apprehensions now the moment we are out of sight of camp for we have entirely passed the dangerous country. Always enjoy riding alone with him, especially when we talk about home friends. It is then the tedious hours are sweetly decoyed away. We decend a very steep hill in coming into Grand Round at the foot of which is a beautiful cluster of pine trees, pitch and spruce ⟨pines⟩, but no white pines like that I have been accustomed to see at home. Grand Round is indeed a beautiful place. It is a circular plain, surrounded with lofty mountains & has a beautiful stream coursing through it, *skirted with timber quite large timber. The scenery while passing through it* in some places is delightful & the soil rich, in other places we find the white sand & sage as usual, so peculiar to this country. We nooned upon the Grand Round River.

The Cammas [28] grow here in abundance & it is the principal resort of the Cayouses & many other tribes to obtain of it, of which they are very fond. It resembles an onion in shape & colour, when cooked is very sweet, taste like a fig. Their manner of baking them is very curious. They dig a hole in the ground, throw in a heap of stones, heat them to a red heat, cover them with green grass, upon which they put the Cammas & cover the whole with earth, when taken out it is black. This is the chief food of many tribes during winter. After dinner we left the plains & ascended the Blue Mountains. There a new & pleasing scene presented itself, mountains covered with timber through which we rode all the afternoon, a very agreeable change. The scenery reminded me of the hills in my native county Steuben.

29th   Had a continuation of the same scenery as yesterday afternoon. Rode over many logs, an obstruction that we had not found in our way since we left the states. Here I frequently met old acquaint-

---

[27] Usually spelled "apishamores" — the Indian name for a saddleblanket made from buffalo calf skins.

[28] The camas root was an edible tuber somewhat like an onion. This was one of the main items of food for the Nez Perces and other Indians of that area.

ances, in the trees & flowers & was not a little delighted. Indeed I do not know as I was ever so much affected with any scenery in my life. The singing of the birds, the echo of the voices of my fellow travelers, as they were scattered through the woods, all had a strong resemblance to bygone days.

But this scene was of short duration. Only one day. Before noon we began to descend one of the most terrible mountains for steepness & length I have yet seen. It was like winding stairs in its decent & in some places almost perpendicular. We were a long time descending it. The horses appeared to dread the hill as much as we did. They would turn & wind in a zigzag manner all the way down. The men usually walked but I could not get permission to, neither did I desire it much. We had no sooner gained the foot of the mountain when another more steep & dreadful was before us. We did not mount this untill we had taken some refreshment & rest. ∫Mount Pleasant in Prattsburg would not compare with these Mount Terribles.⌡ Our ride this afternoon exceeded everything we have had yet & what rendered it the more aggravating the path all the way was very stony resembling a newly McAdamized road. Our horses feet were very tender, all unshod, so that we could not make that progress we wished. [Illustration p. 83.]

The mountains in many places was covered with this black broken basalt. We were late in making camp tonight. After ascending the mountain immediately after dinner, we kept upon the main divide untill sunset, looking in vain for water and a camping place. While upon this elevation, we had a view of the valley of the Columbia river. It was beautiful. Just as we gained the highest elevation & began to decend, the sun was dipping his disk behind the western horizon.[29] Beyond the valley we could see two distant Mountains, Mount Hood & Mount St Helens. These lofty peaks were of a conical form & separate from each other by a considerable distance. Behind the former the Sun was hiding part of his rays which gave us a more distinct view of this gigantic cone. The beauty of this extensive valley contrasted well with the rolling mountains behind us & at this hour of twilight was enchanting & quite diverted my mind from the fatigue under which I was labouring. We had yet to decend a hill as long but not as steep or stony as the others. By this (time) our horses were in haste to see camp as well as ourselves & mine made such lengthy strides in descending that it shook my sides surprisingly. It was dark when we got into camp but the tent was ready for me & tea also, for

[29] On clear days from several vantage points along the roads that led down into the Columbia River Valley from the Blue Mountains, at an elevation of about 5,000 feet, one can see over 200 miles across eastern Oregon to the snowy peaks of the Coast Range. Marcus and Narcissa were most fortunate to have such an unforgettable view break upon their sight when they made their first descent of the Blue Mountains. To be there just when the sun was setting behind Mt. Hood made it even more impressive.

Mr McLeod invited us to sup with him. We are now on the west side of the Blue Mountains, crossed them in a day and half.

This marks the half-way point in Narcissa's account of her journey from the Rendezvous to and including her stay at Fort Vancouver. Her entries for September, so rich in detail, constitute one of the most fascinating sections of the entire diary. She made no entries from October first through eighteenth.

DEAREST MOTHER.   Let me tell you how I am sustained of the Lord in all this journey. Yesterday & for two or three days past, I have felt weak, restless and scarcely able to sit on my horse. Yesterday in particular. But see! how I have been diverted with the scenery and carried out of myself in conversation, about home & friends. Mother will recollect what my feelings were and had been for a year previous to my leaving home. The last revivals I enjoyed, my visit on Onondaga & the scenes there. This I call my last impressions of home, and it is of such a character, that when we converse about home these same feelings are revived & I forget that I am weary & want rest. This morn my feelings were a little peculiar. Felt remarkably well and strong, so much as to mention it, but could not see any reason why I should feel any more rested than on the morning previous. Then when I began to see what a day's ride was before me, I understood it. If I had had no better health today than yesterday, I should have fainted under it. Then the promise appeared in full view "as thy day is so shall thy strength be" and my soul rejoyced in God and testifys to the truth of another evidently manifest "Lo I am with you alway."

30th   In consequence of the lengthy camp yesterday & failure of animals two of the company's men left four of their behind with packs also. This occasioned some anxiety lest the wolves would destroy their beaver. Today they send back for them & we remain here untill they return or make but a short move to find more grass. In following the course of the stream on which we encamped last night, found cherries in abundance, had time to stop to gather as many as we wished. Indeed we rambled untill noon before we went into camp.[30] The cherries are very fine equal to any we find in the States.[31]

When we arrived Mr Gray had the dinner ready, waiting for us. Our employment this afternoon is various. Some are washing their shirts & some are cutting their (hair) others shaving, preparing to seeing Walla Walla, and some are asleep. For my part I endeavoured to divert myself the best way I could, doing a little mending for

[30] A detailed discussion of the route followed by the Whitmans over the Blue Mountains may be found in Elliott, *Coming of the White Women,* 1836.

[31] Probably a reference to the chokecherry which most people do not like to eat raw.

Husband, & trying to write while he & Mr Gray are streatched upon the ground enjoying the refreshment of a sound sleep. The men who went for the animals returned late. We all regreted this hindrance, for Mr McLeod intended to see Walla W today & return again with a mushmellon for Mrs Whitman (so he said). He will go in tomorrow, It is the custom of the country to send heralds ahead to anounce the arrival of a party and prepare for their reception.

31st Came to Walla Walla river within eight miles of the Fort. Both Husband & myself were very much exhausted with the fatigue of this day's lengthy ride. Sandy most of the way, and no water for many miles. When we left Mr Spalding, Husband rode an Indian horse, one that he had never mounted before, found him a hard rider upon every gate except a gallop and slow in all his movements, especially on a walk. He could not pace as mine did, so as to make up the deficiency in that easy way, so for the last six days when the ground would admit we galloped most of the way.

According to Elliott, in his Coming of the White Women, *1836, the Whitmans moved down Pine Creek on August 30 and camped near the present Weston, Oregon. On the thirty-first they rode about thirty miles over dry hills devoid of trees but covered with a carpet of long dry grass. Their camp that night was on Walla Walla River near what is now Nine-mile Bridge, on the highway between Wallula and Walla Walla. Narcissa's diary pulsates with the excitement she felt as she drew near her journey's end. At this time the Whitmans did not know that they would find it advisable to go to Fort Vancouver for supplies. For the time being Fort Walla Walla on the Columbia River, strategically located near the place where they intended to settle, was the terminus of their travels. Six and a half long months of tedious and sometimes hazardous travel had come to an end.*

The site of old Fort Walla Walla is now covered by the waters of the Columbia River which have been backed up by the recently built McNary dam. It was located on a sandy elevation on the south bank of the Columbia near the mouth of the Walla Walla River. It was sometimes called Fort Nez Perce. At the time of the arrival of the mission party, Pierre C. Pambrun was the Hudson's Bay official in charge. He retained this responsibility until his death on May 15, 1841. Too much praise can not be given to the Hudson's Bay Company and to its various servants who did so much to assist the missionaries in establishing their stations and in supplying them with their necessities at reasonable prices. The cordial reception Pambrun extended the Whitmans is indicative of the continuing spirit of goodwill.

SEPTEMBER 1st, 1836. You can better imagine our feelings this morning than I can describe them. I could not realize that the end of our long journey was so near. We arose as soon as it was light, took a cup of coffee and eat of the duck we had given us last night, then dressed for Walla W. We started while it was yet early, for all were in haste to reach the desired haven. If you could have seen us now you would have been surprised for both man & beast appeared alike propeled by the same force. The whole company galloped almost all the way to the Fort. The first appearance of civilization we saw was the garden, two miles this side of the Fort. The fatigues of the long journey seemed to be forgotten in the excitement of being so near the close. Soon the Fort appeared in sight & when it was announced that we were near, Mr. McLeod, Mr. Pambran, the gentleman of the house, & Mr. Townsend,[32] sallied forth to meet us. After the usual introductions & salutations, we entered the Fort & were comfortably seated in cushioned armed chairs.

They were just eating breakfast as we rode up, soon we were at the table & were treated to fresh salmon, potatoes, tea, bread & butter. What a variety, thought I. You cannot imagine what an appetite these rides in the mountains give a person. I wish some of the feble ones in the States could have a ride over the mountains, they would say like me, victuals even the plainest kind never relished so well before.

After breakfast we were shown the novelties of the place, they are so to us. While at breakfast, however, a young cock placed himself upon the cell [33] of the door and crowed. Now whether it was the sight of the first white females or out of compliment to the company I know not, this much for him. I was pleased with his appearance. You may think me simple for speaking of such a small circumstance as this. No one knows the feelings occasioned by seeing objects once familiar after a long {de{privation, especially {when{ it is heightened by the expectation of not meeting with them. The dooryard was filled with hens turkeys pigeons & in another place we saw cows hogs & goats in abundance, & I think the largest & fattest cattle & swine I ever saw. We were soon shown a room, which Mr Pambran said he had prepared for us by making two bedsteads {or{ (of) bunks, on hearing of our approach. It was the west bastion of the fort, full of port holes in the sides but no windows, & filled with fire arms. A large cannon always loaded stood behind the door by one of the holes. These things did not {disturb{ (move) me. I am so well pleased with the possession of a room to shelter us from the scorching sun, that I scarcely notice them. Having arranged our things, we were soon called to a feast of mellons, the finest I think I ever saw or tasted. The mushmelon was

---

[32] John K. Townsend, a travelling naturalist, happened to be at the Fort at the time of the arrival of the Whitmans. He published several books on his travel experiences in Old Oregon.

[33] Mrs. Whitman was referring to a "sill." Even the crowing of a rooster was a thrilling sound to those who had been so long removed from civilization.

the largest measuring eighteen inches in length, fifteen arround the small end and nineteen arround the large end. You may be assured we were not any of us satisfied or willing to leave the table untill we had filled our plates with chips.

At four o'clock we were called to dine. It consisted of pork, potatoes, beets, cabbage, turnips, tea, bread & butter, my favorite dinner, and much like the last dinner I eat with Mother Loomis. I am thus particular in my description of eatibles so that you may be assured we find something to eat beyond the Rocky mountains as well as home. We find plenty of salt but very many here prefer to do almost & some entirely without it on their meat & other eatibles.

SEPT 2d. Have busied myself today in unpacking my trunk & arranging my things, for a visit to Vancouver. Mother will wonder at this, & think me a strange child, for wishing to add three hundred miles to this journey not from necessity but because my Husband is going, and I may go as well as to stay here alone. If we were obliged to go on horseback, I think I should not wish to undertake it, but we are going in a boat, & it will not take us more time than six days to go there. A very agreeable change & I think I shall enjoy it as well as to stay here (alone). I feel remarkably well and rested, do not need to lounge at all, & so it is with us all. I can scarcely believe it possible of myself but it is true. I feel as vigourous & as well able to engage in any domestic employment as I ever did in my life. Covered a stock yesterday for my first work here for Husband.[34]

I have not yet introduced you to the Lady of the House. She is a native. From a tribe east of the mountains. She appears well, does not speak English but her native language & French. The cooking and house work is done by men chiefly. Mr. Pambran is from Canada. Is very agreeable & much the gentleman in his appearance.

FORT WALLA WALLA TO FORT VANCOUVER

SEP 3d. Mr. McLeod & Townsend left for Vancouver today. Since our arrival new arrangements have been made about our going. Mr. Pambran is going in a boat by himself & offers us a passage with him. Mr. McLeod is so loaded as not to be able to give us a comfortable passage. (We) expect to leave next week. About noon Mr & Mrs. S[palding] arrived with their company, having made better progress than was anticipated. The animals all came in except one horse that has been injured in packing & entirely gave out & is left. Here we all are at W Walla through the mercy of a kind Providence, in health and all our lives preserved. What cause for gratitude & praise to God. Surely my heart is ready to leap for joy, at the thought of being so near

---

[34] The word "stock" probably referred to some sort of neckpiece or cravat to be worn by her husband.

the long desired work of teaching the benighted ones a knowledge of a Saviour & having completed this hazardous journey under such favourable circumstances. Mr Pambran said to us the day we arrived, there never had been a company previous to ours that came into the Fort so well fed as we had been for the last days of the journey. All our friends of the East Company, who knew anything about the country dreaded this part for us very much.[35] But the Lord has been with & provided for us all the way, & blessed be his Holy Name. Another cause of gratitude is the ∫preservation⟩ of our animals in this difficult dangerous & lengthy route, while many parties previous to this have had every animal taken from them & left on foot in a dangerous land exposed to death. Two horses have given out with fatigue & left, two have been stolen or lost. Most that we have now have come all the distance from the Settlements & appear well. two calves only have been lost, the remainder came on well except those we left at Snake Fort.

SAB 4th.   This has been a day of mutual thanksgiving with us all. Assembled in the Fort at twelve o'clock for worship. Our feelings are better imagined than described. This first Sab(bath) in September, a sabbath of rest, first after completing a long journey, first in the vicinity of our future labours. All of us here before God. It is not enough for us alone to be thankful. Will not my beloved friends ∫at home⟩, the disciples of Jesus, unite with us in gratitude & praise to God for his great Mercy. It is in answer to your prayers that we are here and are permitted to see this day under such circumstances. Feel to dedicate my∫self⟩ renewedly & unreservedly to his service, among the heathen & may the Lords hand be as evidently manifest in blessing our labours among them as it has been in bringing us here, & that too in answer to your prayers, beloved christian friends.

5th.   Mr & Mrs Spalding have concluded to go with us to Vancouver, as nothing can be done by either of the party about location, untill the Indians return from their Summer hunt. Expect to leave tomorrow. Have had exceeding high winds for two days & nights past, to which this place is subject. Our room shakes and the wind makes such a noise, that we can scarcely hear each other converse.

SEPT 7th   We set sail from W[alla] W yesterday 2 o'clock P.M. Our boat is an open one, maned with six oars & the steersman. I enjoy it much, it is a very pleasant change in our manner of traveling. The Columbia is a beautiful ∫river⟩. Its waters are clear as crystal & smooth as a sea of glass, exceeding in beauty the Ohio of the east. But the scenery on each side of it is very different. No timber to be seen. High perpendicular banks of rocks in some places, rugged bluffs and plains of sand is all that greets the eye, as we pass down the waters of this Majestic river. We sailed untill near sun set, landed, pitched our tents,

---

35 Undoubtedly a reference to the fur companies east of the Rockies.

supped on tea, bread & butter, boiled ham & potatoes, commited ourselves to the care of a kind Providence, then retired to rest. This morn arose before sunrise, embarked & have sailed untill nine o'clock & are now landed for breakfast. Mr. Pambran's cook is preparing it while Husband & myself are seated by a little shrub in the sand writing. We are this moment called. Farewell.

8th.   Came last night to the Chutes, a fall in the river not navagable where we slept & this morning before breakfast made the portage.[36] All were obliged to land, unload, carry our baggage & even the boat for a half mile. I had frequently seen the picture representing the Indians carrying their canoes, but now I saw the reality. We found plenty of Indians here to assist in making the portage. After loading several with our baggage & sending them on, the boat was capsized & placed upon the heads of twenty Indians, who marched off with it with perfect ease.

Below the main fall of water are rocks, deep narrow channels, many frightful precipices, all this distance. We walked deliberately among the rocks viewing the scene with astonishment, for this once beautiful river seems to be cut up and destroyed by these hugh masses of rocks. Indeed it is difficult to find where the main body of water passes. In high water we are told these rocks are all covered, the river rising to such an astonishing height. After paying the Indians for their assistance, (which was a twist of tobacco, each about the length of a finger), reloaded went on board, sailed about two miles, then stopped for breakfast. This was done to get away from a throng of Indians. Many followed us however, to assist in making another bad portage three miles below this.

SEPT 9th   We came to the Dalls yesterday just before noon. Here our way was stopped by two rocks of immense size & height, all the waters of the river passing between them, in a very narrow channel, & with great rapidity. Here we were obliged to land, make a portage of two & half miles carrying the boat also. The Dalls is the great resort of Indians of many tribes for taking fish, we did not see many however for they had just left.

Now Mother if I was with you by the fireside, I would relate a scene that would amuse you, & at the same time call forth your sympathies. It may {not} appear well on paper, or worth mentioning, but for my own gratification I will write it let the consequences be

---

[36] The Chutes were later called Celilo Falls. The Pambrun party with the missionaries camped on the north bank near what is now Wishram, a few miles above The Dalles. Between Celilo Falls and The Dalles were a number of rapids and falls, some of which could be navigated during low water. Portages had to be made around the others. Narcissa in her diary is not specific as to how many portages had to be made. The construction of dams along the Columbia has completely changed the topography. After passing The Dalles, there was clear sailing the remainder of the way down the Columbia to its mouth.

what they may. After we landed curiosity would lead us to the top of the rock to see the course of the river through its narrow channel. But as I expected to walk this portage, Husband thought it would be giving me to much fatigue to do both. I went with him to its base to remain there untill his return. Took with me a handful of hazel nuts that I would divert myself with cracking & eating them. had just seated myself in the shade of the rock ready to commence work when feeling something unusual on my neck, put my hand under my cape & took from thence two insects, which I soon discovered to be fleas. Immediately I cast my eyes upon my dress before me and to my astonishment found it was black with these creatures making all possible speed to lay siege to my neck & ears. This sight made me almost frantic. What to do I knew not. Husband was away. Sister S had gone past hearing. To stand still I could not. I climbed up the rock in pursuit of my Husband, who soon saw & came to me. I could not tell him but showed him the cause of my distress. On opening the gathers in my dress around my waist, every plait was lined with them. Thus they had already laid themselves in ambush against a fresh attack. We brushed & shook & brushed for an hour, not stopping to kill for that would have been impossible. By this time they were reduced considerably & I was prepared to go to the boat.

I was relieved from walking by the offer of a horse to ride from a young Chief. This was a kindness for the way was through sand mostly & would have been a fatigueing walk. Found the confinement of the boat distressing on account of my miserable companions who would ⟨not⟩ let me rest for a moment in any one position. But I was not the only sufferer, every one in the boat was alike troubled, both crew and passengers. As soon as I was able to make a change in my apparel I found relief. We made fine progress this morning untill nine o'clock when we were met with a head wind & obliged to make shore. The wind that works against us will assist others that are going up stream. We met Mr. Cowee last night with the Montreal express.[37] This express goes from & returns to Vancouver twice a year.

EVE.   Have lain still all day for the wind. This is a detention. Intended to have been at Vancouver by to morrow eve. A party of Indians came to our camp this eve. Every head was flattened.[38] These

---

[37] This was the fall express of the Hudson's Bay Company which carried mail and sometimes passengers from Fort Vancouver to Montreal. The express ascended the Columbia River to Athabaska Pass in what is now British Columbia where a portage was made over the Continental Divide to navigable waters on the eastern side.

[38] The Indians of the lower Columbia River often deformed the head of a newly born child to make it wedge-shaped. Narcissa gives a good description of how it was done. One of the four Indians who went to St. Louis in the fall of 1831 as a member of the Nez Perce "delegation" had such a flattened head. Before this Indian died during the winter of 1831-32, William Walker made a sketch of the

are the first I have seen so near as to be able to examine them. Their eyes have a dull & heavy expression.

10th   High winds & not able to move today.

11th   Came to the Cascades to breakfast. Another important fall in the river where we are obliged to make a portage of a mile. The boat was towed along by the rocks over the falls with a rope. This is another great place for Salmon fishery. A boat load was just ready for Vancouver ʃas weʔ arrived. I saw an infant here whose head was in the pressing machine.[39] This was a pitiful sight. Its mother took great satisfaction in unbinding & showing its naked head to us. The child lay upon a board between which and its head was a sqiurrel skin. On its forehead laid a small square cushion, over which was a bandage drawn tight around pressing its head against the board. In this position it is kept three or four months, or longer, untill the head becomes a fashionable shape. There is a variety of shapes among them. Some are sharper than others. I saw a child about a year old whose head had been recently released from its pressure as I suppose from its looks. All the back part of it was of a purple colour as if it had been sadly bruised. We are told this custom is wearing away very fast, there is only a few tribes on this River who practice it.

SEP 12th   Breakfasted at the sawmill five miles from Vancouver & made preparations for entering it. You may be surprised to hear of a Saw Mill here when I said there was no timber on the Columbia. Since we passed the Cascades the scene is changed & we are told there is timber all the way to the Coast, above the Cascades we saw none.

AT FORT VANCOUVER

During the heyday of the Hudson's Bay Company's activities in Old Oregon, it was customary for the fur traders when going down the Columbia River by boat to stop at the sawmill a few miles from Fort Vancouver to permit the men to shave and dress up for their arrival. At this time a messenger would be sent on ahead informing those at the fort of the approach of the boats. On this particular occasion in September 1836, the messenger passed on the most interesting news to Dr. John McLoughlin, Chief Factor at Fort Vancouver, that two American ladies were in the party.

deformed head which was published in the March 1, 1833, issue of the New York *Christian Advocate and Journal and Zion's Herald*. It was the publication of this drawing together with the account of the "Macedonian Appeal" of the Nez Perces which inspired the Methodist Church and the American Board to send missionaries to the Oregon Indians in 1834 and 1836.

[39] Narcissa in a letter to Mrs. Parker written from Fort Vancouver Oct. 24, included this same description of how a child's head was deformed. In this letter, however, she stated that the child she saw was only three weeks old. See Hulbert, *Whitman*, I, p. 236 ff.

There were at that time at the fort two English ladies, Mrs. Capen-
dale, wife of the manager of the dairy farm, and Mrs. Jane Beaver,
wife of the Anglican chaplain, the Reverend Herbert Beaver. The
Beavers arrived at Fort Vancouver on September 6, 1836, shortly before
the coming of the missionaries. A clash of personalities developed
between Dr. McLoughlin and his chaplain, which resulted in the
Beavers returning to England in 1838.[40]

Also at Fort Vancouver, and mentioned by Mrs. Whitman in her
diary, were the wives of several of the Hudson's Bay officials who had
part Indian blood. Mrs. McLoughlin, formerly Margaret Waden, was
the daughter of Jean Etienne Wadin, a Swiss merchant in Canada, and
a Cree Indian woman. She is described as being a woman of unusual
ability. She was the widow of Alexander McKay and the mother of
Thomas McKay, who with John L. McLeod had escorted the mission
party from the Rendezvous. Chief Factor James Douglas, for sixteen
years an associate of Dr. McLoughlin and in 1845 his successor in
charge of Fort Vancouver, also had a half-breed woman for his wife.
Also present at the fort and later mentioned by Mrs. Whitman was
Dr. William F. Tolmie, a Scottish trained physician who had arrived
in 1833.

When the messenger from the sawmill informed Dr. McLoughlin of
the approach of the party with the two American ladies, he hastily
ordered that preparations be made to give all, and especially the
women, a suitable welcome. Servants were directed to prepare rooms
for the women. At that time two ships happened to be lying at anchor
before the fort — the English man-of-war, the "Neriade," and the
"Columbia." McLoughlin requested that each ship be dressed out in
all her flags.

As the boats bearing the missionaries moved around the bend in the
river, the missionaries saw the ships "dressed in complete regalia from
stem to stern." Gray described the scene as follows:

> In a short time, as the boats neared the shore, two tall, well-
> formed, neatly- dressed gentlemen waved a welcome, and in a
> moment all were on shore. Rev. Mr. Spalding and lady were
> introduced, followed by Dr. Whitman and lady, to the two gentle-
> men. One, whose hair was then nearly white, stepped forward
> and gave his arm to Mrs. Whitman. The other, a tall- black-
> haired, black-eyed man, with rather slim body . . . gave his
> arm to Mrs. Spalding.[41]

If the missionaries were not fully aware of the significance of their

---

[40] An excellent study of Herbert Beaver was published in 1959 by Dr. Thomas E.
Jessett. In spite of the appropriateness of his name, Herbert Beaver was not tem-
peramentally suited to be a chaplain for the Hudson's Bay Company.

[41] Gray, *Oregon*, 149.

accomplishment in bringing white women across the continent, there can be no doubt but that Dr. McLoughlin and James Douglas were greatly impressed. Gustavus Hines in his Wild Life in Oregon, commenting on the arrival of the missionary women at Fort Vancouver, said that this marked "an epoch in the history of Oregon." [42]

EVE. We are now in Vancouver. The New York of the Pacific Ocean. Our first sight as we approached the Fort were two Ships, lying in the harbour, one of which, the Neriade, Capt. Royal, had just arrived from London. The Columbia, Capt. Darby, came last May & has since been to the Sandwich Islands & returned. On landing we first met Mr. Townsend whom we saw at Walla W but did not then say who he was. He is from Philidelphia, has been in the mountains two years. He is sent here by a Society to collect the different species of bipeds & quadrupeds peculiar to this country. We brought a parcel of letters to him the first he has received since he left home. Mr. Townsend led us into the Fort. But before we reached the house of the Chief Factor Doct McLaughlin, ʃweʔ were met by several gentlemen, who came to give us a welcome. Mr. Douglas, ʃthenʔ Doct Tolmie & Doct McLaughlin of the Hudson Bay Company who invited us in and seated us on the sofa. Soon after we were introduced to Mrs. McLaughlin & Mrs. Douglas, both natives of the country (half-breed.) After chatting a little we were invited to a walk in the garden. And what a delightful place this. What a contrast this to the rough barren sand plains through which we had so recently passed. Here we find fruit of every description. Apples peaches grapes. Pear plum & Fig trees in abundance. Cucumbers melons beans peas beats cabbage taumatoes and every kind of vegitable to numerous to be mentioned. Every part is very neat & tastefully arranged ʃwithʔ fine walks each side lined with strawberry vines. On the opposite end of the garden is a good Summer house covered with grape vines. Here I must mention the origin of these grapes & apples. A gentleman twelve years ago, while at a party in London put the seeds of the grapes & apples he eat in his vest pocket & soon after took a voyage to this country and left them here. Now they are greatly multiplied.

After promonading as much as we wished and returning were met by Mrs. Capendel, a Lady from England who arrived in the Ship Columbia last May, and Mrs. [Miss] Mariah, daughter of Doct McLaughlin, quite an interesting young Lady. After dinner we were introduced to Rev. Mr Beaver & Lady, Clergiman of the Church of England who arrived last week in the Ship Neriade. I mentioned in a former letter that they were expected by the way of Montreal. But they have come (by sea around) ʃby the way ofʔ Cape Horn. This is more than we expected when we left home that we should be priv-

---

[42] *Op cit.,* p. 17.

aleged with the acquaintance & society of two English Ladies. Indeed we seem to be nearly allied to old England itself, for most of the Gentlemen of the Company are from thence & Scotland.

We have not found Mr. Parker here to our great disappointment. He went to Oahu in the Ship Columbia a few weeks before we arrived. We have mourned about it considerably for we thought it would be so acceptible to our dear Parents & friends at home, to hear him say that he had seen us alive, here, after completing this long unheard of journey [43] & besides I wish to send home many things which I can not now. More than all this his counsels & advice would have been such a relief to us at this important time concerning location character of the Indians &c. But it is wisely ordered & we submit. He appears to have been a favourite here & to have done much good. The Messrs Lees [i.e. Jason and Daniel] left Vancouver on Sat∫urday⟩ last for their Station on the Wallamut. Mr Daniel Lee has been out of health & for the year past has been at Oahu, returned in the Neriade, benefited by his visit.

13th   This morning visited the School to hear the children sing. It consisted of about 50 Scholars, children who have French fathers and Indian mothers. All the labourers here are Canadian French with Indian wives. Indeed some of the gentlemen of the Company have native wives & have adopted the custom of the country not to allow their wives to eat with them. French is the prevailing language here.[44] English is spoken only by a few. Just before dinner we went on board the Ship. The first I ever saw. (She) ∫The Neriade⟩ is a man of war & goes to the North west Coast soon. The Com∫pany⟩ have lost three ships on this Coast. The Columbia returns to London this fall.

14th   Were invited to a ride to see the farm, have rode fifteen miles this afternoon. Vancouver is finely situated on the Columbia, 130 miles from the ocean. Just above the mouth of the Wallmuth, called on maps Multnomah. We visited the barns, stock &c. They estimate their wheat crops at 4,000 bushels this year, peas the same. Oats & barley between 15 & 1700 bushels each. The potatoes & turnips fields are large and fine. Their cattle are numerous, estimated at 1,000 head in all their settlements, also sheep & goats, but the sheep are of an inferior kind. We find also Hens, Turkeys, Pigeons, but no geese. You will ask what kind of beds are used here. I can tell you what kind ∫of bed⟩ they made for us after we arrived, & I have since found it a fashionable bed for this country. The bedstead is in the form of a bunk with rough board bottoms, upon which were laid about one dozen of the Indian blankets. These with a pair of pillows covered with calico cases constitute our bed ∫sheets⟩ and covering. There are several feather beds

---

[43] Narcissa here repeats her April 7 reference to the "unheard of journey for females."

[44] It is not known that any of the missionary party was able to speak French.

in the place, but they are made of the feathers of wild game, such as
ducks, cranes, wild geese, &c. I intend to make me one of these
materials as soon as I can obtain them, not this winter however There
is nothing here suitable for ticking, the best and only material is brown
linen sheeting. The Indian Ladies make theirs of deer skin. Could we
obtain a pair of geese from any quarter, I should think much of them.

16th   Every day we have something new to see. Went to the stores
& found them filled with the cargos of the two ships both above &
below, all in unbroken bails. They are chiefly Indian goods & will be
sent away this fall to the several different posts of the Com∫pany⟩ in
the Ship, Neriade. Find here also every article for comfort & dura-
bility we need ,but many articles for convenience & all Fancy articles
are not here. Visited the Dairy also, here we find butter & cheese in
abundance. Saw an improvement in the manner of raising cream.
Their pans are of an oblong square, quite large, but shallow, flareing
a little, made of wood & lined with tin. In the center is a hole with a
long plug. When the cream has all arisen to the surface, place the pan
over a tub or pail, remove the plug & the milk will all run off leaving
the cream in the pan only. I think these in a large dairy must be very
convenient. They milk between fifty & sixty cows (here). On visiting
the mill did not find it in a high state of improvement. It goes by
horse power, has a wire bolt. This seemed a hard way of getting bread,
but better so than no bread, or to grind by hand. The Com∫pany⟩
have one at Colvile that goes by water (& two on the Wallamut.
Colvile is) five days ride above Walla W from whence we expect to
obtain our supplies of flour, also potatoes & pork. They have three
hundred hogs (there). Doct McLaughlin promises to loan us enough
to make a beginning, & all the returns he asks is that we supply other
settlers in the same way.[45] He appears desireous to afford us every
facility for living in his power. No person could have received a more
hearty welcome or be treated with greater kindness than we have been
since our arrival.

17th   A subject is now before the minds of a certain number of
individuals, in which I feel a great interest, especially in its termina-
tion. It is that we Ladies spend the winter at Vancouver, while our
husbands go seek their locations & build. Doct McLaughlin our host is
certain that it will be best for us, & I believe is determined to have us
stay. The thots of it is not very pleasing to either of us for several reasons. I had rather go to Walla Walla where if we failed of making our
location or of building this fall, we could stay very comfortably & have
enough to eat, but not as comfortable nor have as great variety to eat
as here, & besides the difficulty of ascending the river in high water,
not to say anything of a six months separation when it seems the least
desirable. But all will be ordered for the best.

---

[45] Both the Whitmans and the Spaldings got some hogs from the Hudson's Bay
Company in 1837.

18 SAB.   Mr. Beaver held two services ſin a roomʆ in Doct Mc-
Laughlin house today. His form of worship, or that of the Church of
England, differs in no respect from the forms of the Episcopal's in the
States. Enjoyed the privaledge much. The most of the gentlemen of
the Fort are Scotch Presbyterians & but very few that are Episcopa-
lians. The great mass of labourers are Roman Catholics who have
three services during the Sab[bath], one of which is attended at this
house in which Doct McLaughlin officiates in French, translates a
sermon or a tract & reads a chapter in the Bible & a prayer. The singing in Mr Beavers church was done by the children. Some of their
tunes were taught them by Mr Parker. Others by Mr Shepherd of the
Methodist Mission.

19th   The question is decided at last that we stay here perhaps four
or five weeks. There is so much baggage to be taken up now that the
boat will be sufficiently loaded for safety without us. Have the cheering promise that they will come for us in a short time if prospered.
One thing comforts us they are as unwilling to leave us as we are to
stay & would not if it was possible for us to go now. From this we
(infer that) ſare sureʆ they will make every possible effort to return
for us soon. We are told the rainy season will commence soon & continue through the winter & late in the Spring, while at Walla W there
is none. Vancouver is subject to Ague and Fever. These are quite good
reasons for prefering W.W. even if we have to live in a lodge. Have
been making some necessary purchases for our two boys Richard &
John, which we are glad to do, partly as a reward for their faithful
care of the cattle during the journey. We left them at W.W. They
regretted our leaving them & now to stay away from them all winter,
I cannot feel willing too. Their anxiety to study continues the same,
especially Richard's. We love them both & feel deeply interested in
their welfare & shall treat them as our own so long as they deserve it.

20th   Doct McLaughlin gave my Husband a pair of Lether pantaloons today. All the gentlemen here wear them for economy. Riding
horseback & carrying a gun is very destructive to cloth pantaloons.[46]
Our Husbands have been making every preparation to leave us today,
but have found so much to do as not to get ready to leave much
before night. Have concluded to start the boat a short distance and
camp, while they with Mr Pambran & Mr Gray remain in the fort to
leave early in the morning.

21st   Our friends left us this morning early. One thing I should
have mentioned as decided before they left, was the propriety of
making two stations. After consideration it was concluded best to for
several reasons.[47] The Cayouses as well as the Nez Perces are very

---

[46] Here is evidence of the fact that Whitman carried a gun on his overland
travels, as Spalding probably did also.

[47] One reason for the establishment of two stations which Mrs. Whitman does
not mention may have been the memory of an old love affair. After the reinforce-

anxious to have teachers among them. They are a numerous tribe and speak the same language as the Nez Perces. There are many other fields open ready for the harvest. O! that there were many other labourers here ready to occupy them immediately. Several places have been recommended which they will visit before (fixing) ∫they fix∤ upon any place. You will recollect that we had Grand Round in view when we left home, as a location. Our reasons for not fixing upon that place are insurmountable. The pass in the Blue Mountains is so difficult & the distance so great, that it would be next to impossible to think of obtaining supplies sufficient for our support. We could not depend upon game for it is very scarce & uncertain. Mr. Parker recommended a place on the Koos Koos ke river six days ride above Walla W. [48] I hope to give you our exact location before I send this.

22d Doct McLaughlin has put his Daughter in my care & wishes me to hear her recitations. Thus I shall have enough to do for diversion while I stay. I could employ all my time in writing & work for myself if it were not for his wishes. (I sing with the children every evening also which is considered a favour.) [49]

---

ment of 1838 arrived, Elkanah Walker is reported to have asked Spalding why he went so far away from Waiilatpu to establish a second station. Gray in a letter to Greene, dated October 14, 1840, reported that Spalding replied: "Do you suppose I would have come off here all alone a hundred & twenty miles if I could have lived with him or Mrs. Whitman?" Drury, *Diaries of Spalding and Smith*, 231.

[48] This statement, contrary to Whitman's complaint to Greene of May 10, 1839, seems to indicate that Parker had made some recommendations regarding the location of a mission station. The reference to the Koos-koos-ke is to the Clearwater River. Parker was impressed with the site now occupied by the city of Lewiston, Idaho, where the Clearwater joins the Snake, as a good place for a mission station.

[49] Although Narcissa makes no mention of it in either her diary or her letters, other evidence shows that Narcissa's singing with the children became a point of friction between Chaplain Beaver and Dr. McLoughlin. Narcissa, in her diary for Sept. 13, refers to her visit in the school to hear the children sing. Undoubtedly Dr. McLoughlin soon learned of Narcissa's singing ability and of her experience as a school teacher. According to this reference of Sept. 22, Narcissa was asked to be a private tutor to Eloisa Maria, a daughter of Dr. McLoughlin, who was married about sixteen months later to William Glen Rae of the Hudson's Bay Company. Chaplain Beaver considered all such activity by Mrs. Whitman as a personal affront.

Jessett in his *Herbert Beaver*, pp. 7 ff., published a series of letters that passed between Beaver and McLoughlin on this subject. Beaver objected to children in the school being "distracted by the various systems of instruction." He considered himself to have sole charge of the school. Dr. McLoughlin, on Sept. 30, firmly informed Beaver that: "I beg therefore explicitly to state that the school is under my direction. . ." Even after receiving such a letter, Beaver on Oct. 1 wrote to "Mesdames Whitman and Spalding" reminding them that ". . . it is unusual in England for any person to take part, without his permission and request, in the parochial duties of the minister. . ." When this letter came to the attention of Dr. McLoughlin, he demanded an immediate explanation and apology from his chaplain. In a note to Beaver, dated Oct. 3, McLoughlin wrote: "Mr. McL. must view it in the light of a deliberate Insult to the Honble. Company and would feel

23d   I have not given you a description of our eatables here. There
is such a variety I know not where to begin. For breakfast we have
coffee or coaco. Salt Salmon & roast duck, wild & potatoes. When we
have eaten our supply of them, our plates are changed & we make a
finish on bread & butter. For dinner we have a greater variety.[50] First
we are always treated to a dish of soup, which is very good. Every
kind of Vegetable in use is taken & choped fine & put into water with a
little rice & boiled to a soup. The tommatoes are a promanant article.
Usually some fowl meat, duck or any kind, is cut fine & added, if it has
been roasted once it is just as good (so the cook says) then spiced to
the taste. After our soup dishes are removed, then comes a variety of
meats to prove our tastes. After selecting & tasting, change plates &
try another if we choose, & so at every new dish have a clean plate.
Roast duck is an every day dish, boiled pork, tripe & sometimes
trotters, fresh Salmon or Sturgeon, yea to numerous to ʃbeʔ mentioned. When these are set aside a rice pudding or an apple pie is next
introduced. After this (melons) ʃa water & mushmelonʔ next make
their appearance, (some times grapes) & last of all cheese, bread or
biscuit & butter is produced to complete the whole. But there is one
article on the table I have not mentioned & of which I never partake,
that is wine. The gentlemen frequently drink toasts to each other but
never give us the opportunity of refusing for they know we belong to
the tetotal Society. They have a Temperance Society here & at Wallamut formed by Mr. Lee. Our tea is very plain, bread & butter, good
tea plenty of milk & sugar.

(30th) ʃ31stʔ   We are invited to a ride as often as once a week

---

much flattered by the removal of the impression, being most anxious to avoid
every cause of collision. . ." Beaver replied in a note to Dr. McLoughlin the
same day saying that ". . . not the slightest insult was intended."

On Nov. 15, 1836, Beaver wrote to Benjamin Harrison, one of the influential
members of the Hudson's Bay Company in London and reported: "When the
missionaries went from the Fort the other day, I was shocked, not as being present,
but at hearing that the scholars, by command, had been paraded on the River
Beach, and sung there an hymn. Sacred music should only be used on solemn
occasions, but it is made here a common entertainment of an evening, without the
slightest religious feeling or purpose." *Op. cit.*, p. 22. Used by permission.

Narcissa, writing to the Rev. and Mrs. Leverett Hull from Fort Vancouver on
Oct. 25, mentioned the preaching of Beaver. "But to contrast it with the preaching
at home," she wrote, "I find a great want of plainness and heart. He is a great way
behind the times. The standard of piety is low with him and other professed Christians here. He seldom draws the line of distinction between the righteous and the
wicked, and when he does it is so faintly that it is scarcely perceptible."

[50] In Mrs. Whitman's letter to Mrs. Parker of Oct. 24, 1836, she stated: "Since
we have been here, they have set a table for us in Dr. McLaughlins sitting room,
and we have had the company of Mrs. Douglas, Miss Maria (McLaughlin) and
two of the Gentlemen." The dining room furniture, china, and some of the silver
used by Dr. McLoughlin at Fort Vancouver are now on display in the McLoughlin
House, Oregon City, Ore.

for exercise & generally ride all the afternoon. Today Mrs. McLaughlin rode with us. She keeps her old habit of riding gentleman fashion. This is the universal custom of Indian women generally, they have saddles with high backs & fronts. We have been recommended to use these saddles as being a more easy way of riding but have never seen the necessity of changing our fashion. I sing about an hour every evening with the children, teaching them new tunes at the request of Doct McLaughlin. Thus I am wholly occupied & can scarcely find as much time as I want for writing.

Oct 18th (This afternoon) the Montreal express arrived ∫this afternoon⟩ and a general time of rejoycing it is to every one. News from distant friends both sad & pleasing. Mr. Spalding has come with it & brought a letter from my Husband filled with pleasing information. The Lord has been with them since they left us & has prospered them beyond all expectation. They have selected each a location & ∫my⟩ Husband remains there to build while Mr S∫palding⟩ comes after us.[51] Cheering thot this to be able to make a beginning in our pleasing work so soon.

This concludes the extant copy of Diary B. Whereas it is possible that Narcissa did not complete her transcription of the diary she wrote for her Mother, the probability is that the remaining part of Diary B has been lost. The break comes at the end of the twenty-third leaf. Since the transcript of Diary B as given in the Transactions of the Oregon Pioneer Association *for 1891 also breaks off at this point, it may be assumed that the manuscript by that date existed in its present abbreviated form.*

A close comparison of the text of the two diaries shows that Mrs. Whitman made some corrections in spelling and in grammar when copying the diary for her husband's mother. Such corrections have been accepted in this transcription. Diary A continues with the entry for October 18 and contains also entries for October 22, 25, and November 1. The closing section of Narcissa's diary details her experience at Fort Vancouver. The following passage begins with a continuation of the entry for October 18. Mrs. Whitman is writing of her husband:

He writes me that our location is on the Walla Walla River an eastern branch of the Columbia about 25 miles east of the Fort & about

---

[51] The three men of the mission party left Fort Vancouver on September 21 to select locations for their mission stations. On Oct. 5 Whitman chose a site in the bend of Walla Walla River called Waiilatpu, "the place of rye grass." Spalding, on the 12th, selected a location on Lapwai Creek, a branch of the Clearwater, about twelve miles from what is now Lewiston, Idaho. Lapwai in the Indian tongue meant "Butterfly Valley." While Whitman and Gray began building at Waiilatpu, Spalding returned to Vancouver for the women.

the same distance South east of the mouth of Snake or Lewis River. He is pleased with the situation thinks the soil very favourable & will be able to cultivate next year quite extensively. The spot selected can be enclosed with 80 rods of fence & brushing up the rest along two streams, by which it is most surrounded & by which may be watered. It is thought to contain 300 acres. There is no want of good land for cultivation & herding. This is the country of the Cayouses, who speak the same language as the Nez Perces. Mr. Spalding has fixed upon a place 110 miles east of us on the North side of Snake river near the mouth of CoosCoos river a small branch. The land is very good but not very extensive but sufficient for the establishment, & most of the Indians. Enough may be found near on other streams for the remainder. Plenty of good timber, stone clay & water that is, fine spring, more timber on this location than on ours. We have enough for present use however such as it is, no pine all cottonwood shall be obliged to go to the mountains fifteen miles for pine. The Nez Perces are exceedingly anxious for the location. Make many promises to work & listen to instruction. They do not like to have us stop with the Cayouses. Say they do not have difficulty with the white men as the Cayouses do & that we shall find it so.

The Walla Walla river has many branches and much good land on all of them. The Fort is on Columbia river just above Walla W river. We shall be near neighbors to them. They intend to build both houses this fall & winter and be prepared for crops next spring. Say they shall put in their crops next spring & if they cannot fence, employ Indians to guard during the day, and yard the animals at night. When they left here did not expect to make but one location this fall, feel that they are greatly prospered in making both. We expect to leave here on the first of Nov, would be glad to go if we could get our things made on account of the rain; have had none yet which is quite remarkable. Have the promise of having a room ready for me as soon as I get there. Mrs. S. goes immediately to her location without waiting for a house to be built.[52]

Oct 22d. It has rained today considerably the first I have seen since 22d July. In all the journey have not suffered any inconvenience from rain, while last year in the early part of it their was rain almost continually.

25   I thot I would tell what kind of a dish we had set before us this morning. It is called black pudding.[53] It is not a favourite dish with us Americans. It goes from the table untouched. It is made of blood & the fat of hogs well spiced & filled into a gut. The grapes are just ripe & I

---

[52] The Spaldings planned to live in an Indian lodge until their log cabin was erected. This they did.

[53] Also known as "haggis," once a popular English dish but now considered specially Scottish.

am feasting on them finely. There is abundance now on the table before me   they are very fine. I save all the seeds of those I eat for
planting & of apples also.[54] This is a rule of Vancouver. I have got
collected before me an assortment of garden seeds which I take up
with me, also I intend taking some young sprouts of apple peach &
grapes & some strawberry vines &c from the nursery here. Thus we
have every thing we could wish for supplied us here. We brought an
assortment of seed from Cincinnati with us over the mountains. I think
every time I look into the glass if Mother could see me now she
would not think my cheek bones were very promenant. We have every
comfort we can ask for here, enough to eat & drink & are as well provided for as we should be in many boarding houses in the States.

*On October 24, a few days after she had completed copying the
diary for her husband's mother, Narcissa wrote to Oren, a younger
half-brother of Marcus', and his wife Nancy.[55] Sections of this letter
are omitted in the following transcription because Narcissa had copied
parts of her diary given above. It is significant that she repeated the
prophetic warning given by the Nez Perces regarding the treacherous
nature of the Cayuses.*

VANCOUVER, Oct. 24th, 1836

DEAR BROTHER OREN AND SISTER NANCY   You will be pleased to hear
of our safe arrival & prosperous journey. We are all well & enjoying
excellent health. . .   What fortune we shall have in going up the
river I do not know. It is a dangerous river to navigate, especially in
high water. The Chutes, Dalls & Cascades are a serious impediment
in our progress Were it not for these the river would be navigable for
ships much higher than this place and it would be easier transporting
our baggage than it now is. . .

Husband has sent for the seeds of the large Locust, Chestnut &
Walnut trees. I should like to have the butternut included for experi-
ment. Timber of every description is very scarce about Walla Walla.
But above that on the Columbia near the mountains there is plenty
and that is very large. When Brother Weld [56] comes please remember
to fill his pockets with peaches, plums & pear seeds, some of the best
kind, & some good apple seed, what they have here is not of the best
kind nor a great variety. Another very important article for us house-
wives, some broom corn seed. We brought a little but we are afraid it

---

[54] The last of the old apple trees of the original orchard is still standing at Fort
Vancouver.

[55] A copy of this letter appeared in the *Chronicle Express of* Penn Yan, N.Y.,
on Jan. 8, 1931.

[56] Before leaving the western frontier for Oregon, Whitman learned that a
friend, David Weld of Cohocton, Steuben Co., N.Y., had volunteered to go to
Oregon as a missionary. For some reason, he was never appointed.

will not do well. They have nothing of the kind here, but use hemlock boughs for broom, hemlock I say, there is no such tree known here. It is balsam.

If we had a wheel or two we might spin our stocking yarn for we find wool here. We should first want cards to put it into a state to spin. All Indian goods comes principally ready made. The wives here are not first rate housekeepers. Indeed it is not very fashionable for women to do any kind of work, especially house work. This is done by men & servants. In speaking of white men's wives, all of them have Indian wives. Some are half-breeds and are so white than you can scarcely tell the difference. All kinds of work is done at the greatest disadvantage having no conveniences or any one who knows how to make things as they should be. Husband has employed two Sandwich Islanders to assist in building, etc.[57] And we keep one of the men who came from the Rendezvous with us, a black man [Hinds] who came with us on account of his health & for the purpose of taking medicine.

The Nez Perces are exceedingly anxious to have a location among them. . . so Husband writes. Say they do not have difficulty with the whites as the Cayouses do & we will find it so. This reminds me of a quarrel among the women while we were at Rendezvous. The Nez Perce women said we were going to live with them & the Cayouses said No, we are going to live with them. The contradiction was so sharp they nearly came to blows. . .

Richard often speaks of you both. . . I am anxious to return to him that he may pursue his studies as he did in Rushville. Have taken up supplies of butter, sugar, flour, pork, as we want, so you see we have not come here to starve. Find enough to eat wherever we go. . .

Your sister,   NARCISSA WHITMAN

The last entry in Diary A is dated November 1. On the same day Narcissa wrote another letter to her family. This was published in the September 1936 issue of the Oregon Historical Quarterly *and subsequently in Elliott's* Coming of the White Women, 1836. *Both of Narcissa's diaries and the several letters written by members of the mission were left at Fort Vancouver for mailing on the first ship destined for the States. When Jane, Narcissa's sister, replied in her*

---

[57] The two Hawaiians are not identified. In June, 1838, the Whitmans hired Joseph and Maria Maki, members of the mission church in Honolulu. They became charter members of the First Presbyterian Church of Oregon organized at Waiilatpu on Aug. 18, 1836. Joseph died on Aug. 8, 1840. His wife was then sent back to the Islands. The use of Hawaiians for laborers in Oregon goes back to 1813, when Astor brought some from the Islands. The Hudson's Bay Company likewise found them useful. Members of the Oregon Mission at various times had a number of Hawaiians in their employ, all of whom were secured from the Hudson's Bay Company.

letter of August, 1837, she made some mention of how much postage
they had to pay on the diary. Narcissa in reply to Jane of September
18, 1838, commented: "I am sorry my journal cost you so much."

Spalding had returned to Fort Vancouver on October 18 for supplies
and to escort the two women to the upper Columbia country. Narcissa's
entry of November 1 in her diary together with her letter to her family
of the same date brings the account of her overland travels to a close.

Nov. 1st. I have seen a sight today which makes me shudder. A
poor Indian woman sailing in a boat with her husband just below here
yesterday who was shot dead by the chief of the tribe. The ball that
killed him went through her arm & just grazed her breast but did not
kill her. She came into the Fort today a pitiful object. Mr. S. has told
us of a case which occured just after they arrived at Walla W. from
here a woman sickened & died leaving a little child. She was buried.
Her husband obtained a woman to nurse the child for him. A few days
after in the absence of the Father of the Child, the Father of the
Childs mother came & took the child away from the woman & carried
it to the grave of the Mother, dug it open and placed the child in &
buried it alive with its mother. When the Father returned & heard
what had become of the child was very much greved, & wished to have
the man shot. But no measures were then taken to redress the wrong.
These things with others make me feel that I am on heathen ground.

Eve. My school of singers are assembling, & invite my attendance.
They have improved much in their singing & learned very many tunes
for the short time I have been here. Doct thinks it is a great assistance
to them in learning to speak the English language. All regret my
leaving   Doct says if I was not situated so far off he would send them
all to me. 18 of them are orphans which the Doct has pick'd up & saved
alive. Mrs. McLaughlin has a fine ear for music & is greatly delighted.
She is one of the kindest women in the world. Speaks a little French,
mostly Cree, her native tongue. She wishes to go & live with me, her
Daughter & Mrs Douglas also. The Lord reward them for their love &
kindness to us.

9 o'clock. The Doct urges me to stay all winter, he is a very sympa-
thetic man is afraid we shall suffer, presents many obstacles in the way
of our going which appear so to him but not to us. I have just learned
that we cannot leave tomorrow. The new boat is not ready quite. No
work done for us today because it is the Roman Catholic All Saints
day, a Holladay. You will see the Seal of my host upon the enclosure
of this journal. They are over nice in following the rules of etiquette
here in some particulars. It is considered impolite to seal a letter with
a wafer for the reason that it is wet with spittle. Very impolite to send
spittle to a friend. You will laugh at this I know, but so it is. We are
both of us without a Seal & if I use wax I shall have to make a stamp
of my thimble.

How does Frances do C & J.G. I want to hear from them, also Mary ann. But when shall I? You will write me every one, I hope. I want to hear every one speak H & Livinia Clarissa & J.A.H. & Edward all all write.[58] Husband is so filled with business that I must write for him untill he is less hurried in his business (he is far away now poor husband three hundred miles. If I had wings I would fly) adieu.

I intended to have written this so plain that Father & Mother could read it without difficulty. Perhaps I have failed in doing so.

VANCOUVER   Nov 1st 1836

DEAR PARENTS BROTHERS & SISTERS   This is the last opportunity I shall have of writing you untill next Spring. We shall intend writing by the Montreal express, which leaves here in March. Possibly you may hear from us by that route, before you get this. We send these in the Ship Columbia, to Oahu, to the care of Rev. Hiram Bingham,[59] to be forward by the first opportunity. I expect to leave here tomorrow, for my future home among the Cayouses. Doct McLaughlin sends two boats to carry our baggage up the river. The water is very low at present in the river & we have had no rain yet of any consequence. . . Usually the rain commences before this season & continues all winter, so we are told. We are greatly blessed in finding conveniences for building, housekeeping &c far, very far from our expectations when we left our home. The Company let us have goods as cheap as can be afforded, & cheaper probably than we can get them from the States. They only charge us a hundred per cent more than the prime cost, or England prices. All their goods are of the best quality & will be durable. Husband has obtained a good stove of Mr. Pambran of W.W. & we take up enough sheet iron for the pipe. My Tin ware has all been made within a week past of the first rate block tin. I have six large milk pans Coffee & Tea pots, Candle sticks & moles. Covered pails & a baker, very good, the first of the fashon seen here, &c, &c.[60]

And besides this the blacksmiths have all been employed in making our farming utensils &c and are nearly or quite finished, so that we shall be able to have our accounts closed up & goods boxed ready to leave tomorrow. There are a few deficiencies in the cloth line. No provision is made for beding except blankets & these are dear. No

---

58 The references here are to the brothers and sisters of Narcissa, except Frances and Livinia who remain unidentified.

59 Bingham was the head of the American Board's Mission in the Hawaiian Islands.

60 Mrs. Whitman was most fortunate in getting the use of a heating stove. Perhaps the fact that she was pregnant at the time prompted the offer. Her baby was born on March 15 of the following spring. A comparison of the inventories of the Waiilatpu and the Lapwai stations made after the massacre of November, 1847, shows that the Whitman home was much more comfortably furnished than the Spalding.

sheets, nothing for shirting except striped or calico. I have found a piece of bleach linen which I take for sheets, the only one in the store price 75 cents per yard. I miss the cotton batting for quilts & comfortables very much, but can make the blankets do me very well, only it will be heavy washing for they are all white.

We are supplied with good butter & cheese, which I know you will not expect us to find so soon. Indeed every thing we could wish for to make us comfortable contented & happy is at hand. I could not have received more attention at home than I have here. I feel that I have come to a fathers house indeed, even in a strange land has the Lord raised up friends & praise be to his holy Name. Beloved friends, all comfort your hearts concerning us. The Lord *has provided* & *"the Lord will provide" for us,* even to the *end of our pilgrimage here.* I expect we shall be two weeks in going to W W where we have another excelent & kind Friend in Mr Pambran & wife, they will be our near neighbors, only twenty five miles apart, Mr S 110. We find that we shall be under the necessity of teaching the English language considerably, indeed we can not escape it. We are in want of books, elementary books in every branch & we shall look home for supplies of that kind, for they are not to be obtained here. We should like all the best help, to teach the English language, cards, prints &c if they could be sent us.

We expect Brother Weld here from Cohocton *just as soon as he can come* & we could hope many others. Husband & Mr S has written to Robert L Porter [61] & given him an invitation to come, we hope he will except. Another request I would make, if our friends wish to do us good, they will send us religeous books, papers, etc. We were obliged to leave nearly all we purchased at Cincinati with Brother Merrill at the Otoe Village & those we attempted to bring are nearly destroyed. If any one wishes to come by land (& by the by it is the best for the health & the cheapest) let them send all their outfit to Oahu by ship & take only the suit they wish to wear & a few changes of under garments, packing their provisions only & they will make an easy pleasant trip & less expensive than we made. Our expenses over were 3295.58 which Dr. McLaughlin says is cheaper than we could have come by sea. I mean the whole expense from home for us all, seven in number, & *we might have come* much cheaper if we had not undertaken to brought so many things with us. *We see now* that it was not necessary to bring anything *because we find all here.* But I see I shall exceed the limits I have marked for myself. I could write much more but must close. farewell Dear Dear friends. You will not fail to write all of you the first opportunity. Father will write & mother also I hope, if it is but little.

---

[61] Unidentified. Likewise "Sister Dryer," "Brother & Sister Bridgeman," and "Aunt Phelps" mentioned in the postscript.

From your affectionate Daughter & sister   NARCISSA WHITMAN

P.S. Do not fail to give my love to Sister Dryer tell her I think of her often. Husband if he was here would unite with me in sending love to you all & other dear friends who are interested in us Brother & Sister Hull, Brother & Sister Bridgeman & our Amity friends. Aunt Phelps wished me to send her my journal in my own hand writing but I have not been able to coppy it for her. If you think best to favour her with a copy I shall be highly pleased for I love her & all our Onondaga friends. Tell me all you know about them when you write. Husband wish me to send a copy of my journal to Mother Loomis. I have done so, farewell.   NARCISSA WHITMAN

"AN UNHEARD-OF JOURNEY FOR FEMALES"

Now that the "unheard-of journey for females" overland to Oregon had been successfully completed, what was the verdict of those who were most involved? Since Marcus Whitman was the one who first conceived the idea, was he to be censured for a foolhardy undertaking, or was he to be commended for his sound judgment? Great risks were involved. Mrs. Satterlee, who with her husband had accompanied the Whitman party from New York State to Missouri, had died shortly after their arrival at Liberty. Might not one of the other missionary women have died before they got to Oregon? Of course Dr. Whitman had nothing to say about the poor physical condition of Mrs. Satterlee before she started on her journey, but neither was he consulted about the health of Mrs. Spalding. We know that Mrs. Spalding did become ill because of the exclusive meat diet for a portion of the overland journey and also because of the excessive fatigue of long hours of horseback riding. If she had died en route, would Whitman have been blamed for her death?

Of course, with the westward surge of American frontier life, the time would inevitably have come when someone would have taken a white woman over the Rockies. It was as impossible to keep the westward moving tide of humanity confined within the borders of the prairies as it would have been to sweep back the proverbial tide with a broom. To Dr. Marcus Whitman, however, belongs the credit of being the first to see the opportunity, of believing in its feasibility, of finding a couple to go with him and his bride, and finally proving that it could be done by doing it.

After it was all over and the participants were able to look back and evaluate their experiences, what was their judgment? Their opinions varied. Spalding, writing on July 8, 1836, from the Rendezvous to Secretary Greene of the Board commented on the diet of buffalo meat. "We have all endured it very well thus far," he wrote, "except Mrs. Spalding. Her health evidently suffers from its use. . ." And in the

same letter he wrote: "Never send another mission over these mountains if you value life and money." However, Whitman in his letter to
Greene written from the Rendezvous on July 16, was more optimistic.
"I see no reason to regret our choice of a journey by land," he wrote.
And he added: "In my own case & Mrs. Whitmans we are more than
compensated for the journey by the improvement of health." Whitman
confessed that the journey was ". . . somewhat fatiguing to Mrs.
Spalding." Writing from Fort Walla Walla on September 5, Whitman
reported: "Our Ladys are quite rested and in good health after the
journey. Mrs. Spalding has been quite well for the later part of the
way. . ." Gray, writing to his friend Ambler on September 9, gave
his testimony. "Mrs. Spalding's health and strength is improved beyond
all expectation. Mrs. Whitman has indured the Journey like a
heroine." [1] The fact that Gray returned east in 1837, was married, and
in 1838 took his bride over the same trail to Oregon, together with
three other newly-wedded couples, shows that he approved of the
venture.

While at Fort Vancouver Mrs. Whitman wrote to Mrs. Samuel
Parker on October 24. In this letter she commented as follows on the
overland journey: "Do you ask whether I regret coming by land? I
answer NO! *by no means*. If I were at home now, I would chose to come
this way in preference to a seven months voyage." Narcissa praised
the purity of the mountain air, its exhilarating effect on the system,
and the "healthful exercise of a horseback ride." "Never have I slept
more sweetly," she wrote, "than after a day thus spent." [2] And as
noted in her letter to her parents of November 1, as given above,
Narcissa felt that the overland route was much cheaper than if the
party had gone by sea.

No one could speak with more experience than could Samuel Parker
who made the journey out to Oregon by land and who returned by
sea. In a letter to Greene written from Honolulu on November 14,
1836, Parker discussed the merits of the two routes. "If I had known
[then] what I now do, I would rather have thrown myself upon the
mercy of the Blackfeet Indians, than to have come here." After endur-
ing the many inconveniences and hardships of a five-month voyage
around Cape Horn, Parker came to the conclusion that the overland
journey was much to be preferred. In a letter to Elkanah Walker, who
was a member of the 1838 reinforcement, Parker said: "A lady can go
with far more comfort by land than by sea." [3] After he had made the
overland journey, Walker wrote to Greene on October 15, 1838, and
said: "I believe that most of our company would, if they were to come
to this country again, & could, would prefer to come by water." [4] A. B.

---

[1] Hulbert, *Whitman*, I: p. 227.   [2] *Ibid.*, I: 237.
[3] Drury, *Walker*, 62.
[4] Drury, *Diaries and Letters of Spalding and Smith*, 89.

Smith, another member of the 1838 reinforcement, also strongly advised the Board against sending any more missionaries to Oregon overland. On February 6, 1840, he wrote: "Respecting the sending of missionaries across the continent, permit me to say that I hope it will never again be done. The more I think of our journey the more fully satisfied I am that it is improper for missionaries, especially females, thus to travel, certainly while there is access to the field by sea."[5]

In November 1840 the American Board commissioned two more couples for their Oregon Mission, the Rev. and Mrs. J. D. Paris and Mr. and Mrs. W. H. Rice. However, undoubtedly because of such adverse reports as those sent by Walker and Smith, the Board sent these four by sea. They reached the Sandwich Islands in May, 1841, where they were detained because of the discouraging reports of conditions in the Oregon Mission. It is interesting to note that the Methodist Church sent about seventy-five, including children, to its Oregon Mission during the years 1834-40. All went by sea except the five members of the Jason Lee party, all men, who crossed by land in 1834.

Contemporary writings of the members of the mission party of 1836 do not indicate that they fully appreciated the significance of their achievement. They were much more concerned about the physical hardships of the journey for women than about any impression it might make on contemporary society. Years later, Spalding looked back upon the coming of the first white women to Oregon and recalled the following: "The shrewd McKay as he met our little party leaving Green River to join his camp said referring to our ladies, 'There is something that Doct. McLoughlin cannot ship out of the country so easy'."[6]

Two women from the East at the Rendezvous! To McKay this was more than just an interesting incident. It was a portent of what was to follow. Women — mothers, wives, sisters, daughters — in unnumbered thousands were waiting for Oregon's door to open. Their coming would mean the establishment of homes, communities, schools, and finally government. The Hudson's Bay Company, with Dr. McLoughlin as its chief official in the Old Oregon country, could out-buy and out-sell and out-live all of its competitors in the fur business in that vast area, but here was a new commodity that would baffle counter-house methods. If Spalding's quotation is correct, then McKay was the first to realize the significance of the presence of the two missionary women at the Rendezvous. The power of the Hudson's Bay Company in Old Oregon had been successfully challenged. A new era in the history of Oregon had begun.

In 1840 the first immigrant family, consisting of Joel P. Walker, his

---

[5] *Ibid.*, p. 144.
[6] Spalding MS. File 201, p. 7, Whitman College Library.

wife, and five children, made the overland journey to Oregon.[7] In 1841 a party of twenty-four, including two families with little children, passed the Whitman station at Waiilatpu. "It was very pleasing," wrote Narcissa to her parents on October 6 of that year in referring to a mother with her six children, "to see such a mother with so many children around her, having come so far — such a dreadful journey." Narcissa knew because she had traveled the same route. By 1841 the gateway to Oregon was fully opened and all interested in the far west knew about it.

In reality the first great Oregon emigration came in 1843 when a train of about two hundred wagons with about one thousand people rolled through South Pass. Dr. Whitman was with that party on his way back to his mission station after his famous ride East the previous winter. Each year the numbers grew. In 1847 the Oregon Trail became the Mormon Trail when the handcarts of the Mormon pioneers, headed for the Great Salt Lake, were pulled over that same road. In 1849, at the time of the California gold rush, about twenty-five thousand made the long journey to California through this gateway. The Oregon Trail then became the California Trail. By the end of 1852, it is estimated that as many as one hundred thousand men, women, and children poured through this Pass in that one year.

Let the story be told again: years before the wagon trains of Oregonbound immigrants rolled through South Pass, two women, Narcissa Whitman and Eliza Spalding, led the way for their sisters who followed. They were the first white American women to cross the Rockies, the very first to undertake the "unheard-of journey for females."

---

[7] Drury, *Whitman*, 238. Drury, *Diaries and Letters of Spalding and Smith*, 37, erroneously stated that the first non-missionary women arrived overland in Oregon in 1841. The correct year is 1840.

Mrs. Whitman's Diary, December 1836 to March 1837

The following letter of Narcissa's to her mother may be considered as a continuation of her overland diary. It was first published, with over half of the letter omitted, in the Transactions of the Oregon Pioneer Association *for 1891. The full text appeared in the March 1937 number of the* Oregon Historical Quarterly *and subsequently appeared in Elliott's* Coming of the White Woman, 1836. *Here are Narcissa's first descriptions of the mission site at Waiilatpu which was to be her home for the next eleven years. The letter is filled with human interest incidents so characteristic of all of her writings. The letter is unsigned because on May 2 Narcissa continued with another letter which was added to the one here printed before both were mailed.*

WALLA WALLA   Dec 5th 1836

MY DEAR MOTHER   I have been thinking of my beloved Parents this evening, of the parting scene & the probability that I shall never see those dear faces again while I live. Sweet as it used to be, when my heart was full to sit down & pour into my mother's bosom all my feelings, both sad & rejoycing, now when far away from the parental roof & thirsting for the same precious privaledge, I take my pen & find a sweet relief in giving her my history in the same familiar way. Perhaps no one else feels as I do. It would be indeed a great satisfaction to me to have my mother know how I do from day to day what my employment & prospects are, but more especially the kind dealings of my heavenly Father towards us continually   .

We left Vancouver Thursday noon Nov 3rd in two boats. Mr McLeod myself & baggage in one & Mr and Mrs S in the other. We were well provided for in everything we could wish, good boats, with strong & faithful men to manage them. Indeed eight of them were Iroquois Indians from Montreal, men accostomed to the water from their child-hood & well acquainted with the dangers of this river. Mr McLeod's accompany us was as unexpected as desireable. He only came into Vancouver two days previous to our leaving from an expedition to the Umpaquai [Umpqua] south of the Willamut. It rained some that afternoon, also on the fourth & fifth. Sixth it rained all day, nearly, & the wind was very strong, but in our favour, so that we kept our sail up

most of the day. Our boat was well covered with an oil cloth. I succeeded in keeping myself dry by wrapping well in my cloak & getting
under the oil cloth. At night when a great fire was made our tents
pitched & the cloth spread for tea, all was pleasant & comfortable. I
roll'd my bed & blankets in my India Rubber cloak which preserved
them quite well from the rain, so that nights I slept warm & comfortably as ever. My fether bed was of essential service to me in keeping
my health during this rainy voyage, did not expect to get one when I
wrote from Vancouver.

On the morning of the Seventh we arrived at the Cascades made the
portage & breakfasted, had considerable rain. The men towed the boats
up the falls on the opposite side of the river. The water was very low &
made it exceeding difficult for them to drag the boats up in the midst
of the rocks, & noise of the foaming waters. Sometimes they were
obliged to lift the boats over the rocks, at others go round them to the
entire destruction of the gum upon them which prevents them from
leaking. It was nearly night before all was safely over the difficult
passage & our boats gumed ready for launching.[1]

8th   breakfasted just below the Dalls, past them without unloading
the boats. This was done by attaching a strong rope of considerable
length to the Stern of the boat, two men only remaining in it to guide
& keep it clear of the rocks, while the remainder & as many Indians as
can be obtained draw it along with the rope, walking upon the edge
of the rocks, above the freightful precipice. The little Dalls just above
these the current is exceeding strong & rapid & full of whirlpools. Not
recollecting the place particularly at the request of the bowsman I
remained in the boat being quite fatigued with my walk past the other
Dalls. It is a terrific sight, & a frightful place to be in, to be drawn
along in such a narrow channel between such high craggy perpendicular bluffs, the men with the rope, clambering sometimes upon their
hands & knees upon the very edge so high above us as to appear small,
like boys. Many times the rope would catch against the rocks & oblige
some one to creep carefully over the horrible precipice to unloose it
much to the danger of his life.

When my Husband came up in passing this place, their rope caught
in a place so difficult of access, that no one would venture his life to
extricate it for some time. At last an Indian ventured. When he had
ascended sufficiently to unfasten it he was unable to return & did not
untill he was drawn up by a rope. They had another accident which
threatened both the lives of some of them & the property & but for the
protecting hand of God would have been lost. While the men with
the rope were climbing up a steep & difficult ascent the rope lodged
upon a rock which held it fast & had it remained there untill all hands

---

[1] Elliott in a footnote at this point states that "Gum gathered from forest trees
and smeared on seams on bottom of the batteaux; it required frequent renewal."

had gained their point & commenced hauling, all would have been well, but one of the men above, prematurely shoved it off. The current took the boat down stream rapidly in spite of every effort to save it prostrating all hands upon the rocks & some of them were nearly precipitated down the precipice by the rope. The boat received no injury but was safely moored below the Dalls, on the opposite shore. Our husbands with the men obtained an Indian canoe & crossed to the boat thus they were preserved. It was just night as we succeeded in passing this difficult place in safety, for which we desired to be great-ful. Many boats have been dashed to pieces at these places & more than a hundred lives lost. The water was very low at this time which makes the danger much less in passing them. No rain today.

Thursday we made the portage of the Chutes & were all day about it. While on land had several heavy showers. Friday also was another soaking wet day, the night also. This was dreary enough. Saturday was much more pleasant no rain. We arrived at Walla W early Sab Morning in health with all our effects preserved to us mercifully.[2] I felt that I had great cause to bless & praise God for so seasonable return, & under such favorable circumstances. Husband came from our location on the 18th had nearly succeeded in makeing a comfortable place for me, but because of Mr Pambran earnest solicitation for me to remain a few weeks with his family I did not return with him. Mr & Mrs P are exceeding kind appear to feel that they cannot do to much to make us contented & happy here. In the mean time I am cheerfully engaged in teaching the wife & daughter to read. We consider it a very kind Providence to be situated near one family so interesting & a native female that promises to be so much society for me. She is learn-ing to speak the English language quite fast.

Mr & Mrs S left W W for their location on the 22d Nov. Mr Gray going with them to assist in building &c. This dear Sister goes very cheerfully to her location to live in a skin lodge untill her house is built & this too in the dead of winter, but she prefers it to remaining here & so should I.[3] Heard from Husband last week & of the death of Hinds a coulered man, who came with us from Rendezvous on account of his health being far gone with Dropsy. Already death has entered our house & laid one low.

Dec 8th   Received inteligence that Husband was coming tomorrow to remove our effects & myself to our new home. It is an agreeable thought to be so near a fixed location after journeying so long.

Dec 26th   Where are we now? & who are we that we should be thus blessed of the Lord. I can scarcely realize that we are thus com-

---

[2] The return trip up the Columbia took from November 3 to Nov. 19.

[3] Mrs. Whitman makes very few references to Mrs. Spalding in her diary or letters. Although so far as is known, no friction ever developed between the two women, yet no deep warm friendship seems to have existed.

fortably fixed & keeping house so soon after our marriage when considering what was then before us. We arrived here on the tenth distance twenty five miles from W W found a house reared & the lean too enclosed, a good chimney & fire place & the floor laid. No windows or door except blankets. My heart truly leaped for joy as I alighted from my horse entered and seated myself before a pleasant fire (for it was now night). It occurred to me that my dear Parents had made a similar beginning & perhaps more difficult one than ours.

We have neither straw bedstead nor table nor anything to make them of except green cottonwood all our boards are sawed by hand. Here my Husband with his labourers (two Owyhees from Vancouver & a man who crossed the mountains with us) & Mr Gray have been encamped in tents since the 19th of Oct. toiling excessively hard to accomplish this much for our comfortable residence during the remainder of the winter. It is indeed a lovely situation. We are on a beautiful level, a peninsula, formed by the branches of the W W river, upon the base of which, our house stands, on the S.E. corner near the shore of the main River. To run a fence across to the opposite river on the North, from our house this with the rivers would enclose 300 acres of good land for cultivation, all directly under the eye. The rivers are barely skirted with timber, this is all the wood land we can see, beyond them as far as the eye can reach plains & mountains appear. On the east a few rods from the house is a range of small hills [4] covered with bunch grass, a very excellent food for animals & upon which they subsist during winter even digging it from under the snow. Beyond these hills are the Blue Mountains. The history of our ride across them, I gave you in my letters from Vancouver. We are about half a days ride from them. There is more good land here for cultivation than at Mr. S. location, but he has the best timber & a plenty of it.

Friday the 16th Mr Pambran sent us a table & window sashes which he kindly offered to get made for us. The sashes were made with a crooked knife by a frenchman. I have taken the liberty to prime them & set some of the lights, & while engaged in it thought a great deal about Father, how handily he used to do such work, & could have wish him here to assist in many things difficult & perplexing to hands unacquainted & which he would accomplish with so much ease. How much work of every description is to be done on Mission ground & that too by but a few hands. When I came here there was no snow except in the Blue Mountains & the weather has been quite mild & pleasant. It commenced snowing on the 16th & fell about a foot & half deep & remains yet on the ground & it has been quite cold. Last Saturday all our windows were finished & put up. Now they are engaged in makeing partitions for two bed rooms & pantry.

---

[4] A granite shaft thirty feet high was erected as a memorial to the Whitmans on the brow of one of these hills in 1897.

Wieletpoo Jan 2 1837. Universal fast day.[5] Through the kind Providence of God we are permitted to celebrate this day in heathen lands. It has been one of peculiar interest to us, so widely separated from kindred souls, alone, in the thick darkness of heathenism. We have just finished a seperate room for ourselves with a stove in it, lent by Mr P for our use this winter. Thus I am spending my winter as comfortably as heart could wish, & have suffered less from excessive cold than in many winters previous in New York. Winters are not very severe here. Usually they have but little snow say there is more this winter now on the ground than they have had for many years previous & that the winter is nearly over.[6] After a season of worship during which I felt great depressure of spirits, we visited the lodges. All seemed well pleased as I had not been to any of them before.

We are on the lands of the Old Chief Umtippe who with a lodge or two are now absent for a few days hunting deer. But a few of the Cayuses winter here. They appear to seperate in small companies, makes their cashes of provision in the fall & remain for the winter, & besides they are not well united.[7] The young Chief Towerlooe is of another family & is more properly the ruling chief. He is Uncle to the Young Cayuse Halket[8] now at Red River Mission whom we expect to return this fall & to whom the chieftainship belongs by inheritance. The Old Chief Umtippe has been a savage creature in his day. His heart is still the same, full of all manner of hypocracy deceit and guile. He is a mortal beggar as all Indians are. If you ask a favour of him, sometimes it is granted or not just as he feels, if granted it must be well paid for. A few days ago he took it into his head to require pay for teaching us the language & forbid his people from coming & talking with us for fear we should learn a few words of them. The Cayuses as well as the Nez Perces are very strict in attending to their worship which they have regularly every morning at day break & eve at twilight and once on the Sab. They sing & repeat a form of prayers very devoutly after which the Chief gives them a talk. The tunes & prayers were taught them by a Roman Catholic trader. Indeed their worship

[5] Narcissa is here referring to a day of prayer and fasting appointed by the Presbyterian and Congregational Churches.

[6] The winter at Waiilatpu in 1836-37 was more severe than usual.

[7] The Whitmans were beginning to realize for the first time that the manner of life followed by the natives meant that they had to be constantly on the move in small bands in order to find food. This roving life made any consistent educational work on the part of the missionaries almost impossible.

[8] Cayuse Halket was one of several Indian lads sent by the Hudson's Bay Company from different tribes in the Pacific Northwest to a Church of England mission school at Red River, near what is now Winnepeg, Canada. In 1834 Halket returned home for a short visit with his people and then went back to the mission school, where he died some two years later.

was commenced by him.[9] As soon as we became settled we established a meeting among them on the Sab in our own house. Did not think it best to interfere with their worship but during the time had a family bible class & prayer meeting. Many are usually in to our family worship especially evenings, when we spend considerable time in teaching them to sing. About 12 or 14 boys come regularly every night & are delighted with it.

SAB JAN 29   Our meeting to day with the Indians was more interesting than usual. I find that as we succeed in their language in communicating the truth to them so as to obtain a knowledge of their views & feelings, my heart becomes more & more interested in them. They appear to have a partial knowledge of the leading truths of the Bible; of sin, so far as it extends to outward actions, but know [no] knowledge of the heart.

FEB 1st   Husband has gone to Walla W to day & is not expected to return untill tomorrow eve, & I am alone for the first time to sustain the family altar, in the midst of a room full of native youth & boys, who have come in to sing as usual.[10] After worship several gathered close arround me as if anxious I should tell them some thing about the Bible. I had been reading the 12th chap of Acts, & with Richards help endeavoured to give them an account of Peters imprisonment &c, as well as I could. O that I had full possession of their language so that I could converse with them freely.

FEB 18th   Anniversary of our marriage. I find it perfectly natural to suffer my thoughts to dwell upon scenes that transpired one year ago from the present time. One year since I have heard a lisp even of my beloved friends in Angelica, & who can tell how many are sleeping in their graves by this time. Ah! it would be like cold water to a thirsty soul indeed, to know how you all do. It is delightful weather now. The

---

9 We have many references to the Nez Perces and Cayuses observing certain forms of Christian worship before the arrival of the mission party of 1836. Some kept the "Sabbath" by remaining in camp on that day. Others had morning and evening worship in their lodges in which they sang hymns and repeated prayers. The question arises — where did these natives learn about Christianity? Some say they got their information from Catholic traders or from the Iroquois Indians in the employ of the Hudson's Bay Company, many of whom were Roman Catholics. Undoubtedly there was some communication of Christian truths from such sources but this would not explain the keeping of the "Sabbath" which was distinctly an evangelical Protestant emphasis. Some of the mountain men such as Jedediah Smith were known for their Christian faith. Possibly they had given some instruction. One of the most logical explanations is that the six or eight Oregon Indians taken to the Red River school as early as 1825 taught the basic principles of Christianity to their respective tribes upon their return. See Drury, *Diaries of Spalding and Smith,* 107, for the influence that Garry had on the Nez Perce "Delegation" of 1831. For a more detailed study of this, see Jessett's *Chief Spokane Garry.*

10 The complete trust that the Whitmans had in the Indians is here indicated. Narcissa was all alone during the absence of her husband except for the Indians.

birds sing sweetly & the frogs croak; familiar sounds these; the same I
used to hear in my native land. The Husbandmen are making arrangements for plowing immediately. The snow remained only about six
weeks upon the ground. Feb, so far, has been as warm and pleasant as
April at home, even more so.

In addition to my other conveniences we have now 3 chairs & a
bedstead & all our doors are made & hanging. These are exceedingly
comfortable although not of the finest order. My chairs two of them are
of my Husband making; with deer skin bottoms woven as the Fancy
chairs of the States are & very durable. Our bedstead is made of rough
boards & nailed to the wall, according to the fashion of the country.
Perhaps a more minute discription of our house is demanded. The
upright part is a story & half, faces the east. As I said before the leantoo only is enclosed. The siding is made of split logs fitted into groved
posts, & the spaces filled with mud. The roof is made of poles, first
covered with straw then with 5 or 6 inches of mud. The fire place &
chimney is of the same. The size of the whole building is 30 by 36
feet, the leantoo 12 feet between joints. My room is in the south end of
it, a small bedroom & pantry on the north end, and a very pleasant
kitchen in the middle. On the west side of the kitchen, is the fireplace
with a twelve lighted window on each side, & the outer door. At present the Indians have full liberty to visit the kitchen, but as soon as we
are able to prepare a seperate room for them they will not be allowed
to come in any other part of the house at all.

You will scarcely think it possible that I should have such a convenience as a barrel to pound my clothes in for washing so soon, in
this part of the world, & probably mine with Mrs. Pambran are the
only two this side of the Rocky Mountains. I am indebted to her for
mine; & she never knew the use of one untill I suggested it. I am not
without a dog and good cat even. My dog was a present from Mr.
McLeod. These may appear small subjects to fill a letter with, but my
object is to show you that people can live here, & as comfortably too
as in many places east of the mountains. A few lodges of Indians have
come to this place & the whole tribe will be here before many weeks.

MARCH 6th   SAB EVE.   To day our congregation has increased very
considerably in consequence of the arrival of a party of Indians during
the past week. A strong desire is manifest in them all to understand
the truth & to be taught. Last eve our room was full of men & boys,
who came every eve to learn to sing. The whole tribe both men women
& children would like the same privaledge if our room was larger &
my health would admit so much singing. Indeed I should not attempt
to sing with them, were it not for the assistance my Husband renders.
You will recollect when he was in Angelica he could not sing a single
tune. Now he is able to sing several tunes & lead the school in them.
This saves me a great deal hard singing. I have thought many times if

the singers in my Fathers family could have the same privaledge or were here to assist me in this work how much good they could do. I was not aware that singing was a qualification of so much importance to a missionary. While I was at Vancouver one Indian woman came a great distance with her daughter as she said to hear me sing with the children. The boys have introduced all the tunes they can sing alone, into their morning & eve worship, which they sing very well. To be at a distance & hear them singing them, one would almost forget he was in a savage land.

MARCH 30th   Again I can speak of the goodness & mercy of the Lord to us in an especial manner. On the evening of my birthday March 14th we received the gift of a little Daughter a treasure invaluable. During the winter my health was very good, so as to be able to do my work. About a week before her birth I was afflicted with an inflamatory rash which confined me mostly to my room. After repeated bleeding it abated very considerably. I was sick but about two hours. She was born half past eight, so early in the evening that we all had time to get considerable rest that night.

Mrs. Pambran had been with me two weeks previous to this & has been much out of health. She with my Husband dressed the babe. It would have made you smile to see them work over the little creature. Mrs P never saw one dressed before as we dress them having been accostomed to dress her own in the native stile. I was able to lend a helping hand & arranged the clothes for them &c. Between us all, it was done very well. She slept very quiet that night but the next night she cried very hard; all the reason of it was because she was hungry & we did not think to feed her soon enough. On the second day I dressed her alone sitting in the bed, & have ever since. I slept but little the first two nights, but since have got my usual sleep. She is a very quiet child both night & day, sleeps all night without nursing more than once sometimes not at all.

Thus you see Beloved Sisters how the missionary does in heathen lands. No Mother, No Sister, to relieve me of a single care, only an affectionate Husband, who was a Physition & nurse exceeds all I ever knew. He was excessively pressed with care and labour during the whole time of my confinement. Besides the attention I required of him, he had my washing & the cooking to do for the family. (Mrs. P had two children with her & on account of her ill health she could not give much assistance). During the same week we were thronged with company for the whole camp of Indians had arrived. Mr Gray spent several days with us at this time, also Mr Pambran & Mr Ermitinger [11] paid us a visit on Friday, left on Sat. All this with the care of 4 men & two boys that know little or nothing about work, just as the com-

---

[11] Francis Ermatinger, frequently in charge of Hudson's Bay Company's pack trains, often called at the mission stations.

mencement of plowing &c requires many steps for one man alone. It was a great mercy that I have been able to take the whole care of my babe & that she is so well & quiet.The Little Stranger is visited daily by the Chiefs & principal men in camp & the women throng the house continually waiting an opportunity to see her. Her whole appearance is so new to them. Her complexion her size & dress & all excite a deal of wonder for they never raise a child here except they are lash tight to a board & the girls heads undergo the flatening process.

I have not yet describe my babe to you. I think her Grand Mother would willingly own her as one of her number of babies, could she see her. Her hair is a light brown & we think will be like her Aunts Jane & Harriet. She is plump & large, holds her head up finely & looks about considerably. She weighs ten pounds.[12] Tee-low-kike, [Teloukaikt] a friendly Indian, called to see her the next day after she was born; Said she was a Cayuse Te-mi (Cayuse girl) because she was born on Cayuse wai-tis (Cayuse land). He told us her arrival was expected by all the people of the country. The Nez Perces, Cayuses & Walla Wallapoos Indians & now she had arrived it would soon be heard of by them all, & we must write to our land & tell our Parents & friends of it. The whole tribe are highly pleased because we allow her to be called a Cayuse Girl. We have beautiful weather this month. March here is pleasant as May is in New York.

[12] Narcissa was writing several weeks after the birth of her child.

At Waiilatpu

THE WHITMAN HOME

Complete detailed information regarding the first Whitman home at Waiilatpu is lacking. In his first letter to Secretary Greene from Waiilatpu, dated May 5, 1837, Whitman had the following to report regarding his house:

> Brother Gray & myself commenced to build at Wiiletpoo 14th Oct. The frame of my house is thirty by 36 built in a substantial manner with good chambers. The leanto only is finished making two bed rooms kitchen and pantry. We commenced house keeping the 10th Dec. The remainder of my house I intend to finish in the fall.

According to a scholarly report on the mission buildings at Waiilatpu made by Thomas R. Garth, archaeologist attached to the Whitman National Monument in 1948, Whitman planned a "New England-type saltbox house" to be a story-and-a-half high. Because of the lack of suitable timber at the mission site, Whitman and Gray found it necessary to resort to using adobes. The word "adobe" comes from the Spanish verb *adobar* meaning "to pickle." It was the descriptive name used for the sun-dried earthen or clay bricks used so extensively by the Spanish throughout the Southwest and also by the fur traders and the Hudson's Bay Company in the construction of some of their dwellings and forts along the Oregon Trail. Narcissa, in the entry in her diary for August 4, refers to the fact that parts of the building at Fort Hall were made out of "mud bricks." Thus the manufacture and use of adobe bricks were known to Whitman and Gray. Garth reports finding adobe walls eighteen inches thick in the excavated basement of the first mission house erected in the fall of 1836.

The house which Whitman and Gray began on October 14 was too large to be completed in time for the arrival of Narcissa, so a lean-to twelve feet wide was built along the thirty-six foot west wall of the house. This was made of split logs set in grooved posts. A large adobe fireplace and chimney were placed in the center of the west wall. The cellar which extended under the whole house was shallow under the lean-to. The roof was made out of poles covered first with the long tough rye grass, which still grows on the mission site, over which five or six inches of dirt or sod were laid. Such a roof had its disadvantages in very wet weather when large globules of mud would sometimes seep through into the room below. By the time Narcissa arrived on December 10, a floor made of hand-sawed lumber had been laid and perhaps the two partitions dividing off a room at either end of the lean-to were in place. The Whitmans used the room at the south end of the lean-to as their bedroom. The north room was the pantry and was also used as another bedroom when occasion required. Beds were made of boards fastened to the wall, "sink fashion" as Mrs. Eells later described them in her diary. A layer of grass, later corn husks when they became available, was placed over the hard boards and over this several blankets.

Available information does not indicate just how many windows were placed in the lean-to. Narcissa mentions a "twelve lighted window" on each side of the fireplace and also a window in the outer door. She says nothing about a window in either of the bedrooms. In the letter she began on December 5, 1836, to her mother, she refers to the fact that on December 16 Pambrun sent "a table & window sashes" and that all of the windows had been installed by the end of the month. Narcissa herself placed the thin window glass,[1] purchased at Fort Vancouver, into the individual frames within the sash. That first rude cabin to which Marcus Whitman brought his bride of ten months must have been very uncomfortable during the weeks before all of the window glass could be placed and the door hung. The winter of 1836-37 was unusually severe for that area. In Whitman's letter to Greene of May 5, 1837, he reported that snow began falling on December 16 and before the storm ceased a layer eighteen inches deep was upon the ground. Some of the snow remained for six weeks.

As for food, Whitman wrote:

> We feel we have passed a comfortable winter indeed; but still at my place we have eaten nine wild horses bought of the Indians at a cost of about $6. dollars each in goods. We have had a tolerable supply of flour corn butter & a little pork & venison & a few potatoes. We are now getting fish in small quantity but soon expect to get plenty of salmon of which I hope to salt a good supply.

On May 10, 1839, in another letter to Greene, Whitman reported: "We have killed and eaten twenty-three or four horses since we have been here." It is worthy of being mentioned again that the establishment of the missions of the American Board in Old Oregon would have

---

[1] Archaeological digging at the Whitman mission site has uncovered many pieces of this thin window glass. Samples may be seen in the museum at the Whitman National Monument. The glass is about one-half the thickness of the ordinary window glass used today.

been impossible without the assistance rendered to the missionaries by the Hudson's Bay Company. Such trading posts as those at Fort Vancouver and Fort Walla Walla were the shopping centers for the missionaries. The ships of the Company carried their freight from England and the States to Oregon. Sometimes letters to or from members of the Mission were carried overland across Canada by the Company's semi-annual express. And finally, when the tragedy of the massacre occured on November 29, 1847, it was the Hudson's Bay Company that ransomed the captives and transported them down to the Willamette Valley. The missionaries were fully aware of their dependence upon the good offices of the Hudson's Bay Company and were quick to express their appreciation. After Gray left the Mission in 1842, he developed a hostile feeling against the Company which finds expression in his *History of Oregon*.[2] This, however, was a later development. In general it may be said that without the prior establishment of the Company's posts in the Old Oregon country and the willingness of the Company to sell supplies, there would have been no Oregon Mission of the American Board.

When the spring of 1837 came, Whitman was so busy with his farm work that he had little time for anything else. Gray had left for the East. The natives were unaccustomed to such work as plowing so Whitman could not turn to them for help. He was able for a short time to get the services of two Hawaiians who had been brought to Oregon by the Hudson's Bay Company to serve as laborers. However, most of the gruelling labor of breaking the virgin sod with a walking plow drawn by teams of horses, mules, or oxen devolved upon him. In his letter of May 5, 1837, to Greene, Whitman reported that up to that date he had sowed two acres of peas, nine of corn, and was expecting to sow three more in corn. He planned to have two acres of potatoes, thus making sixteen acres under cultivation. No wheat could be sowed until the fall season.

The Whitman baby arrived on March 14, 1837. Of this further mention will be made later. During the winter of 1837-38, the Whitmans

---

[2] *Op. cit.*, pp. 153, 159. Gray became bitter in his hostility to the h.b.c. Regarding the dependence of the missionaries on the Company, he wrote: "To the disgrace of most of the missionaries, this state of absolute dependence and submission to the Hudson's Bay Company, or themselves, was submitted to, and encouraged." And again: "The Protestant missions were not dependent on the Hudson's Bay Company for supplies any more than the Sandwich Islands were, or the American Fur Company. If such were the fact, . . . the missionaries themselves and the Boards that sent them to Oregon must have been a set of foolish men, not competent to conduct the commonest affairs of life. The idea that seven men and two [sic] women should be sent to a distant wilderness and savage country, and no provisions made for their subsistence and future supplies, is one originated without a soul, a lie to produce effect, a slander upon common honesty and common-sense Christianity." Here is a good example of how Gray's prejudice warped his judgment.

took into their home two half-breed children. Of this also more will be said under the subsequent title of "Narcissa and Her Children." As time permitted, Whitman was also studying the language. No wonder he had so little time during the spring and summer of 1837 to work on his home. For the time being they lived in the lean-to. Only three letters of either of the Whitmans written in 1837 are extant. Two of these were written by Narcissa to her parents and the third is the letter Marcus wrote on May 5. Consequently we have no information as to their activities during the summer and fall of that year. Judging from scattered references in later letters, we may assume that Marcus was able to complete the building of his first house sometime in the late fall of 1837. When completed, this gave them more room in which to receive the natives for instruction and for religious services.

In the latter part of December, 1837, and the opening days of the following January, a warm "chinook" wind melted the snow that was lying deep on the slopes of the Blue Mountains. The little Walla Walla River became a surging torrent of water which spilled over its banks in a wild rush to join the Columbia. The rising water poured into the basement of the Whitman home. Some of the adobes which supported the main floor and the upper walls gave way. As a result a part of the upper wall began to sag. Narcissa, writing to her parents on April 11, gave details.

> On the eve of the 28th [December] the waters entered our cellar, the walls settled, the props gave away one after another, & for the whole night we were in the utmost anxiety, fearing the consequences to our whole house. Soon after dark our men & the Indians went to work diping out the water & throwing earth against the walls & continued all night long. In great mercy to us our house was preserved to us standing, although the wall is materially injured. Towards morning the water began to fall a little. We were obliged for several days & nights in succession to keep the water bailed out.

The Whitmans decided to move to safer ground. A new site was selected on a higher elevation eighty-six feet north of the original building. In a letter to Green dated May 8, 1838, Whitman wrote: "A second rise of water in March has so far damaged my house that I shall be obliged to build again this summer as the present one will not answer to finish. I intend to build of Dobies again with projecting roof & without a cellar on a place where I think there is no danger. . ." However, because of the pressure of many duties, little was done toward the erection of the new house before the arrival of the rein-forcement on August 29, 1838. The Whitmans were still living in their first home when four couples and a single man suddenly arrived — all of whom had to be housed for the coming winter either in the Spalding home at Lapwai or with the Whitmans at Waiilatpu. The demand for another house then became imperative.

On Saturday, September 1, 1838, the six married men held their first mission meeting.[3] The question of providing suitable living quarters received immediate attention. They voted to establish a new station in the vicinity of the falls on the Spokane River and that two couples should be in each of the three stations. The Walkers and the Eells were to live at the new northern mission; the Grays were to move to Lapwai to be with the Spaldings; and the Smiths were to remain at Waiilatpu with the Whitmans. Cornelius Rogers was free to go where he wished. He expected to spend much of his time studying the language and for the time being he was to live at Waiilatpu. This meant that until the northern station was opened, the Whitmans would be hosts to three couples and a single man. Or, in other words, the original Whitman house built for one family was to provide sleeping and eating accommodations for twelve including the Whitmans, their baby, and the two half-breed children in their care. Mrs. Walker was expecting to be confined in December. After that there would be another baby.

Whitman informed his colleagues about his plan to erect a new house and all agreed that work on it should commence at once. Whitman was to go to Fort Vancouver for supplies. In the meantime the men could begin with the manufacture of the adobes. These bricks measured 20 x 5 x 10 inches and required a suitable drying period in the hot sun before they could be used. Whitman left for Vancouver on September 17 and returned October 15. Mary Walker wrote in her diary on October 27: "Dr W's house is going up."

Whitman in a letter to Greene dated May 10, 1839, described the new house as being of the same style of construction, including the dirt roof, as that followed in the first house. According to this letter, the new building was to measure "nineteen by forty feet front & an ell of twenty-two by thirty." Of necessity, all boards needed for woodwork of floors had to be hand-sawed. This took time, as did the process of making the adobe bricks. On December 4, the Smiths were able to move into one of the completed rooms of the new house. This relieved the crowded conditions in the Whitman house to such an extent that it was possible for a corner of one of the larger rooms to be partitioned off to make a private bedroom for the Walkers. Mrs. Walker noted in her diary on December 5: "Moved into my new room. Think to find it very comfortable."

---

[3] Cornelius Rogers was never a full member of the Mission with voting privileges. Although Rogers became fluent in the Nez Perce language, he withdrew from the Mission in 1841. The mission meeting held in Sept. 1838 was the only time in the eleven-year history of the Mission when all were present, including the wives. The official business of the meeting was conducted by men only.

With the beginning of the winter rains in November or December, all major construction had to cease. Walker and Eells made their exploring tour from September 21 to October 12. They selected a desirable site at Tshimakain, "the place of springs," about twenty-five miles northwest of the present city of Spokane, but found it impossible to erect cabins and move their wives to the new location that fall. It was not until March 5, 1839, that the Walkers and Eells were able to leave Waiilatpu for Tshimakain.

The crowded and primitive conditions which existed in the Whitman home at Waiilatpu during the winter of 1838-39 developed situations which were most trying to all concerned. Personality difficulties had arisen among members of the 1838 reinforcement during their overland journey. After their arrival other little differences arose which sometimes involved the Whitmans. Narcissa grew up in a church where women were encouraged to pray in public. This in the opinion of Walker, Eells, and Smith was unbecoming. Women were to keep silent in the church. Thus in this little band of missionaries isolated in the wilderness, the wives could not join in audible prayer. Again, there was a difference of opinion regarding the use of fermented wine in the communion service. The Whitmans preferred grape juice. The New Englanders insisted on wine. And finally to aggravate the situation, Elkanah Walker chewed tobacco! This was a habit particularly offensive to Narcissa. As long as the beautiful fall weather remained, the men were busy out-of-doors, but when the rains commenced, they naturally remained indoors. Then when the thermometer dipped below freezing, all sought the warmth of the kitchen where a blazing fire in the big fireplace became a focal point of attraction.

Writing to her sister Jane, on May 17, 1839, Narcissa opened up her heart:

> We need help very much, and those who will pray, too. In this we have been disappointed in our helpers last come, particularly the two Revs. who have gone to the Flatheads. They think it not good to have too many meetings, too many prayers, and that it is wrong and unseemly for a woman to pray where there are men, and plead the necessity for wine, tobacco, etc.; and now how do you think I have lived with such folks right in my kitchen for the whole winter? If you can imagine my feelings you will do more than I can describe it.[4]

The compounding of tensions and difficulties arising out of the crowded conditions made life almost unbearable for Narcissa. The entries in Mrs. Walker's diary serve as little windows through which we can look, not only into the community life of the mission family

---

[4] *T.O.P.A.*, 1893, p. 122. Since the Spokane Indians spoke the same tongue as the Flatheads, they were often referred to by that name.

but also into the hearts of some of the individuals most involved.[5] A typical entry in Mrs. Walker's diary is that for December 4: "Mrs. W. in a sad mood all day, did not present herself at the breakfast table. Went out doors, down by the river to cry."

During the latter part of January, Marcus suggested to Narcissa that they take a short camping trip and live with the Indians. She welcomed the opportunity to get away even if it meant living in a tent with a baby not yet a year old, during the winter. "He had no difficulty to persuade me to accompany him," wrote Narcissa to Jane, "for I was nearly exhausted, both in body and mind, in the labour and care of our numerous family."

With the departure of the Walkers and the Eells for Tshimakain in March, 1839, life became more bearable. The Smiths were living in the completed part of the new house and the Whitmans could again be alone. The heavy demands of spring work in the fields kept Marcus busy during the spring and summer of 1839 so that little was done on completing the construction of the new house during that year. The Smiths moved to Kamiah in May, 1839, leaving vacant the quarters they had occupied at Waiilatpu. The Whitmans, however, continued to live in their first home. When the E. O. Halls [6] stayed at Waiilatpu in the fall of 1839, they occupied a room "in the house of Mr. Smith." [7]

In the fall of 1839 two missionary couples — Mr. and Mrs. Asahel Munger and the Reverend and Mrs. J. S. Griffin — arrived at the Whitman station. They were independent of any missionary board, although they may have had the promise of financial help from individuals or churches in the communities from which they came. The following year three more couples arrived, also on an independent basis. The presence of these five couples brought many difficulties to the members of the Oregon Mission of the American Board. The independent workers were destitute of the means to establish a mission station. They even lacked many of the necessities of life and thus became dependent

[5] Mrs. Walker kept the most complete diary of any member of the Mission. This runs to over a hundred thousand words and is included in the second volume of this work.

[6] E. O. Hall was a printer connected with the Hawaiian Mission of the American Board. He and his wife accompanied the mission press sent by the Hawaiian missionaries to Oregon in the spring of 1839. The Halls remained in Oregon for about a year. An invalid most of the time she was in Oregon, Mrs. Hall gave birth to a baby girl at Waiilatpu on Nov. 5, 1839.

[7] At the time the author was working on his biography of Marcus Whitman, he learned of the existence of a collection of about eighty letters written by various members of this Mission to the Walkers but was unable to gain permission to use them. Subsequently these were given by William Coe to Yale University where they are now available for study by qualified students. Upon examination the author finds that most of the letters deal with minor matters of Mission business. A letter from E. O. Hall, dated Dec. 3, 1839, to Walker contains the information here given.

upon the charity of the Whitmans and the Spaldings. For a time some of the men entered the employ of either Whitman or Spalding but within a few years all had moved on to the Willamette.

When Asahel Munger arrived at Waiilatpu in the fall of 1839, Whitman learned that he was an experienced carpenter and hired him to complete building the new house. Reporting on this in a letter to the Board on July 6, 1840, Whitman wrote: "I engaged him at eight dollars per month together with family supplies." The term of service was for six months but when March 1 came Whitman rehired him for another six month period.[8] Munger was able to make furniture, a spinning wheel, and the folding window blinds which Narcissa called "venetian blinds" in a letter to her parents. Writing to her father on April 30, 1840, she described the progress being made:

> A part of the house is nearly finished and will be a very comfortable and clean house to what this has been. Father cannot realize the difficulty and hardship we have had in getting what timber we must have for doors, floors, shelves, etc., for our house. No durable wood near us of any kind except alder, which we are trying to make answer for our tables, bedsteads, etc.[9]

Since Narcissa's father was a carpenter, he would appreciate their difficulties. Whitman had to go fifteen miles to the mountains to get large enough trees of the right kind which could be hand-sawed into boards. This was tedious work. Then the boards would have to be transported to the mission site on horseback. In a letter sent to her mother dated May 2, 1840, Narcissa included a drawing made by Munger of the floor plan of the new house. The house was "T" shaped. The top of the "T" was to be a story and a half high, about seventy-seven feet long and nineteen feet wide. This part would have four rooms including the Whitman's bedroom, a sitting room, a dining room, and an Indian room. The bottom of the "T" was to be a story high, about eighty feet long and twenty-two feet wide. This was to contain five rooms, including a kitchen, pantry, storeroom, bedroom, hen house, and a double privy at the end.

Actually the house was not built as originally planned. According to a floor plan of the mission house, drawn long after the massacre but based on information given by Mrs. Elizabeth Segar Helm, one of the survivors of the massacre, the top of the "T" included only three rooms.

---

[8] The Mungers spent the winter of 1840-41 with the Whitmans. By the spring of 1841 it was apparent that Munger was so badly deranged that he no longer could take care of himself. The Mungers went to Fort Hall in the summer of 1841 with the hope that they could be escorted to the States. However, when they got there, they learned that the Rendezvous had been abandoned so they were obliged to return to the Columbia River Valley. They then went to the Willamette Valley, where Munger committed suicide the following December.

[9] *T.O.P.A.*, 1891, p. 131.

They were the Whitman's bedroom, a large sitting room with a stairway to the half-story above, and a large Indian room. The bottom of the "T" contained the kitchen-dining room, two bedrooms, and a school room. An extension of this part of the building was being erected at the time of the massacre.[10] Members of the National Park Service staff stationed at the Whitman National Monument have determined that the top of the "T" measured 60'10" by 19'3", and the bottom of the "T", 80' by 22'. The overall length was 108 feet, including the double privy at the end of the "T". See illustration on page 149.

Narcissa, in her letter to her father of April 30, 1840, described the process of "smoothing, daubing, and whitewashing" the adobe walls of their new home as being "very tedious work and requires much time and labor." Marcus was unable to find any limestone. They were obliged, according to Narcissa's letter, "to burn clam shells, which we hope to make answer the purpose." From this they made their whitewash. Enough oil and paint were secured from the Hudson's Bay Company to paint all woodwork including floors and furniture. On the page containing Munger's drawing of the floor plan, Narcissa added: "We paint the wood work a light slate color; the front door, outside, green; the floors with yellow ochre; pantry shelves the same." Thus with the outside walls whitewashed and the outside woodwork painted green, the Whitmans did all they could to make their home look somewhat like a neat white New England house trimmed in green.[11]

Narcissa longed for a place which would give her more privacy than was possible in their first house. There she was constantly battling against the fleas which the Indians would leave behind them. In a letter to her mother dated May 2, 1840, she described her trials:

> Could dear mother know how I have been situated the two winters past, especially the winter before last, I know she would pity me. I often think how disagreeable it used to be to her feelings to do her cooking in the presence of men — sitting about the room. This I have had to bear ever since I have been here — at times it seemed as if I could not endure it any longer. It has been the more trying because our house has been so miserable and cold — small and inconvenient for us — many people as have lived in it.
>
> But the greatest trial to a woman's feelings is to have her cooking and eating room always filled with four or five or more Indians

[10] Archaeological research at the Whitman National Monument supports the view that the new construction at the east end of the Whitman home at the time of the Whitman massacre was for a larger room than indicated in Elizabeth Sager Helm's drawing. Evidence leads us to believe that the new addition included a store room, a hen house, an out-kitchen, and two privies.

[11] Mrs. Rowena Alcorn painted a picture of the Whitman home based upon the descriptions here given, which was reproduced in color as a frontispiece in Drury, *Diaries of Spalding and Smith.*

— men — especially at meal time — but we hope this trial is nearly done, for when we get into our other house we have a room there we devote to them especially, and shall not permit them to go into the other part of the house at all. They are so filthy they make a great deal of cleaning wherever they go, and this wears out a woman very fast. We must clean after them, for we have come to elevate them and not to suffer ourselves to sink down to their standard. I hardly know how to describe my feelings at the prospect of a clean, comfortable house, and one large enough so that I can find a closet to pray in.[12]

When the Indians were in the vicinity of the Mission, Marcus would conduct daily worship for them. During inclement weather these services were often held in one of the larger rooms of the first house. The Whitmans tried unsuccessfully to get the Indians to construct a meeting house of their own. Of this Narcissa wrote to her mother: "They said they would not do it, but would worship in our new house. . . We told them our house was to live in and we could not have them worship there for they would make it so dirty and fill it so full of fleas that we could not live in it." The Whitmans compromised by building a room in the new house, which measured about 20 x 20, known as the Indian room.

In May, 1840, Dr. and Mrs. Whitman rode to Tshimakain. Mrs. Walker gave birth to a daughter on May 24 and on the twenty-sixth they started their ride back home. As soon as they returned to Waiilatpu, the Whitmans moved into their new house, after having lived for about three and a half years in their first home. Writing to Walker on June 12, 1840, Whitman said: "We have got into our own new house at last." And in his report to the Board, of July 6, Whitman told of the work Munger had been doing finishing the house and making furniture. "Most of the wood work is painted," Whitman added, "Blinds for the windows are nearly finished." Narcissa gloried in the larger and cleaner rooms, and especially in the privacy which she could then enforce. But the Indians did not understand. In their lodges, they talked about the strange ways of the white woman and called her proud, haughty, and one who was far above them.

In a joint letter to the Board dated April 21, 1838, Whitman and Spalding requested two cook stoves and six "common box stoves." Years passed before the stoves arrived. Writing to a brother and sister on March 1, 1842, Narcissa boasted: ". . . we have a cooking stove,

---

[12] The Indians often brought fleas and lice into the house. In Narcissa's letter to her brother Edward of April 2, 1846, after thanking him for a box of useful items sent, she added: "I was in hopes of finding the one little article more that is needed more than most any other because it cannot be obtained here; namely, a pi-la-ain, as the Indians call it (louse trap). . . The finest combs cannot be obtained here, for that reason I was in hopes of finding one in the box."

sent us from the Board which is a great comfort to us this winter, and enables me to do my work with comparative ease, now that I have no domestic help." This means, therefore, that for about five years Narcissa had prepared the meals for her family over an open fire in the fireplace. The Spaldings also got a cooking stove but the Walkers and Eells at Tshimakain had no such luxury during their nine years' residence there.

The Whitman home at Waiilatpu was by far the most attractive and the most comfortable of any of the missionary houses erected at any of the stations of the Mission. A commentary on its excellence, in comparison with the other missionary dwellings, may be found in a letter Spalding wrote to the Board on October 15, 1842. By that time Spalding had been informed of his dismissal from the Mission. He then knew that several including Smith, Gray, and Rogers, had written letters of criticism regarding him to the Board. Even Whitman had once joined in the chorus of disapproval, and of this Spalding may have been aware. Be it said to Spalding's credit that he wrote no letters of criticism of his colleagues to the Board before he found it necessary to defend himself. When he did write the October 1842 letter, he was at a disadvantage in not knowing the nature of the charges against him. So in a long letter of over seventy-three hundred words, Spalding answered every imaginable criticism that might have been made. In this letter he wrote rather caustically about the Whitman home at Waiilatpu as follows:

> I am astonished that any body should let their eyes pass over the station at Waiilatpu with its mill, blacksmith shop & its large & commodious dwelling houses put up at great expense & with the aid of much hired help. One completed by an accomplished workman with large windows & green window blinds & richly painted doors, floors &c many nice tables, settees, &c &c, richly painted & varnished, servants &c., scores of cattle, horses, & hogs, without being at all alarmed for the future, but, as soon as the eye caught a glance of my old log-cabins, nothing could be seen but the germ of a costly establishment. . .

Whitman's first house at Waiilatpu remained standing for at least a year and a half after Marcus and Narcissa moved out of it. W. H. Gray began building a house at Waiilatpu for himself in the winter of 1840-41. This measured 32 x 40 feet and was a story-and-a-half high. The construction was similar to that of the two former houses — a frame made out of wood to hold the roof, and the walls made out of adobe bricks. The roof was constructed out of "slabs of dirt," probably grass sod, laid over the roof poles. In a letter dated April 8, 1845, Marcus commented on the fact that he had rebuilt his grist mill which had been burnt. He also emphasized his need for a sawmill. "It is necessary to have a saw-mill," he wrote, "as we are in want of conveniences, and our houses are to be roofed anew, as we have only dirt roofs at present. . ." This mill was built in the mountains about twenty miles distant from Waiilatpu.

Gray moved into his new house during the latter part of November, 1841, even though it was not fully completed. In a letter to Mrs. Walker dated January 24, 1842, Mrs. Whitman remarked: "The old house is entirely taken down & a blacksmith shop made of the dobies of it." [13] Thus the first building erected at Waiilatpu remained standing for over six years. Today visitors at the Whitman National Monument may see some of the adobes of the original basement wall in a section which has been exposed for tourists. The house Gray erected was sometimes called the mansion house or the emigrant house.

The inventory of the Whitman mission, made by Spalding after the massacre, included such items as six settees, two rocking chairs, twelve common chairs, three feather beds, tables, wash stands, clothes presses, two looking-glasses, bookcases, two spinning wheels, and venetian blinds (evidently the old fashioned folding wooden blinds.) [14] For a pioneer home so far removed from the centers of civilization, the Whitman home was indeed comfortable for that period. Much of the credit, of course, must go to Narcissa.

All of the soil under the second Whitman house has been sifted by archaeologists attached to the Whitman National Monument. Among the artifacts discovered were pieces of broken dishes and crockery, a few kitchen utensils including spoons, pieces of thin window glass of the type common to the Hudson's Bay Company, nails and similar items. In his report published in the *Pacific Northwest Quarterly*, 1950, Thomas R. Garth wrote: "Her [*i.e.* Mrs. Whitman's] refined taste is well expressed in her selection of chinaware, at least half of which is beautiful English pictorial wares — Spode, Staffordshire, Copeland and Garrett. . . There was very little plain undecorated earthenware or utility china. What must have been the everyday ware had an attractive blue border." [15]

The Whitman station at Waiilatpu became the largest and the most important of the several stations established by the Oregon Mission of the American Board. This was due not only to the initiative of Marcus Whitman but also to the demands placed upon the station during the latter years of its history by the annual fall immigration of Oregon-bound settlers. In a letter to her mother dated May 2, 1840, Narcissa commented upon the strategic location of their home. "We are emphatically situated on the highway between the states and the Columbia river," she wrote, "and are a resting place for the weary travelers,

13 Original in Coll. c.
14 The inventory was published in an appendix of Richardson, *The Whitman Mission*.
15 *Op. cit.*, p. 306.

consequently a greater burden rests upon us than upon any of our associates — to be always ready." And on October 9, 1844, she wrote again to her parents: "Here we are, one family, alone, a way mark as it were, or center post about which multitudes will or must gather this winter." Thus the Whitmans were called upon to provide food for the hungry, to give rest for the weary, and to minister to the sick.

In addition to the two main residences, the blacksmith shop, and the grist mill, there were a number of smaller buildings on the premises, the exact locations of which have not been determined. In one of his letters Whitman referred to ". . . out house such as Corn Cribs, & Granary, Harness house, Smoke & hen houses, double back house, Cow & Horse pen." [16] The Waiilatpu inventory lists seventy-five apple trees, a few of which were bearing, together with a nursery of peach trees, currants, and locust trees. Also at this time some 40,000 running board feet of lumber had been sawed and piled up. One-third of this amount had been hauled to the mission site. The balance was still at the saw-mill about twenty miles away in the Blue Mountains. One of the last letters Whitman wrote before his death was to S. N. Castle, editor of a paper published in Honolulu called *The Friend of Temperance and Seamen,* in which he stated his intention to build a school house for the children of the mission and a meeting house for the Indians. He also planned to assist the Indians in the erection of adobe houses for themselves.[17] Thus at the time of the massacre, Whitman was dreaming of increasing the physical facilities at Waiilatpu. The piles of lumber at the mill and on the mission site spoke eloquently of his intentions.

The inventory Spalding prepared of the property at Waiilatpu after the massacre included forty-six head of horses, ninety-two sheep, and two hundred and ninety cattle. Nothing was said about chickens though Whitman wrote about having hen houses and Mrs. Whitman once referred to a turkey house. Nor was there any mention of hogs. Spalding also listed "One farm of 30 acres, fenced, cultivated, ditched . . . $413.90." He placed the total evaluation of all listed items at $32,465.70. By modern prices the amount would be much larger as Spalding figured a cow to be worth $16.00 and a horse, $20.00.

Ever since the fall of 1843 when the first great immigration of about one thousand arrived, the Whitman station had become a haven for the sick, the weary, and the destitute. Waiilatpu was the first outpost on the Oregon Trail after the immigrants had crossed the Blue Mountains. The immigration of 1847 had left a larger residue of needy folk than usual. A virulent form of measles was carried to Oregon by the immigrants of 1847. This disease was raging among the Cayuses at the time of the massacre and had taken a heavy toll of lives, both children

16 Hulbert, *Whitman,* ii: p. 224.
17 *Op. cit.,* March 1, 1848.

and adults. Many of the immigrants were also afflicted with the disease and welcomed the opportunity to tarry at the Whitman station to rest and recuperate. For various reasons a number of immigrant families, together with some single men and women, numbering altogether fifty-six men, women, and children, were on the mission grounds on that fatal day of November 29, 1847. In addition there were two half-breeds, one of whom, Joe Lewis, was a trouble maker.

The Whitmans had reopened the school for mission children in the fall of 1847 with Andrew Rodgers, who had gone to Oregon with the 1845 immigration, as the teacher. In the school were the seven Sager children who had been left on the Whitman's doorstep by the immigration of 1844, five half-breed children, and Eliza Spalding. Thus there were sixteen in the Whitman family. This brought the total white or half-breed population of Waiilatpu on the morning of November 29 to seventy-four.

Never before had Waiilatpu been so crowded. The winter rains had started and naturally all sought the protection of a roof. Twenty-three, including the Whitmans and the school children, were lodged in the main mission building; twenty-nine had crowded into the mansion house; eight were living in the blacksmith shop; twelve were at the sawmill; and the two adult half-breeds were living in Indian lodges. Altogether there were twenty men, ten women, and forty-four children. At a little distance away were a number of lodges of the Cayuse Indians.

Had a stranger, one who had never heard of the Whitmans, visited Waiilatpu on the eve of the massacre he would have seen a busy self-contained community buzzing with activity. Although we do not know how many head of horses and cattle belonged to the immigrants, they probably numbered over one hundred. This would have brought the total head of livestock on the premises to over five hundred. There would have been six or eight covered wagons plus other wheeled vehicles about the grounds. He would have seen the fenced and irrigated fields, the orchard, the gardens, the corrals, the two large houses, the mill, the blacksmith shop, and the several smaller buildings. This stranger, after viewing the whole scene and noticing how many people were present, might well have asked: "What town is this?"

Someone would have replied: "Town? This is no town. This is the Whitman mission station."

"And who are the Whitmans?"

"They are Presbyterian missionaries serving under the American Board. Marcus Whitman is a doctor. He and his wife came out here in 1836 to Christianize and civilize the Indians."

"Who are all these people? Why are they here?"

"These people? O, they are immigrants most of whom arrived this year. They will be moving on as soon as they are able. Next year perhaps even more will cross the country to Oregon and again there will be many sick and destitute who will stop off here, thanking God for the Whitmans and this way-station on the Oregon Trail."

After reflecting on this information, the stranger might then have asked: "If the Whitmans came out to be missionaries for the Indians, why are they giving so much time and attention to the white people?"

The Cayuses were asking the same question.

NARCISSA AND HER CHILDREN

Marcus and Narcissa had but one child of their own, whom they named Alice Clarissa after her two grandmothers and also after two aunts. Marcus had a sister Alice and Narcissa had a sister Clarissa. At the time of the birth, March 14, 1837, Marcus was not only the affectionate husband, but also physician, nurse, and housekeeper. Mention has already been made of the excitement the arrival of the white child caused among the Cayuses. Among the visitors was Chief Tiloukaikt whom Narcissa referred to as a "kind, friendly Indian," but who, years later, was one of Dr. Whitman's murderers.

In November, 1837, Dr. Whitman was called to Lapwai to attend Mrs. Spalding upon the birth of her daughter. The question arose — should Narcissa remain alone at Waiilatpu with Alice Clarissa, then less than eight months old, or should she make the long one hundred and twenty mile trip to Lapwai with her husband on horseback. Narcissa decided to go. They left Waiilatpu on November 7 under the guidance of three Nez Perces whom Spalding had sent to help them in their travels. Whitman also took along a Hawaiian in his employ as further assistance. Spalding sent an Indian buffalo skin lodge for the Whitman's use. They met with cold rainy weather all the way. The second day out they traveled but six miles and the next morning they awoke to find two inches of snow on the ground. They arrived at Lapwai on the twelfth. A hint of the joy the two families experienced in being together again is found in the following quotation taken from Whitman's letter to the Board of the following March 12: "It was with no common emotion that we met after a year's absence & so far as Mrs. Spalding was concerned the year was spent without seeing any civilized friend after Brother Gray left the December previous." [1]

Eliza Spalding, the first white child born in the Pacific Northwest to live to maturity, was born on November 15, 1837. On Sunday, November 26, both Alice Clarissa and Eliza were baptized by Spalding who, on the same day, administered the sacrament of the Lord's Supper. The Whitmans started back to Waiilatpu on Saturday, December 2, taking a log canoe to Fort Walla Walla and then completing their journey by horseback. It took them a week to make the return trip.

---

[1] Gray seems to have spent the late winter of 1836-37 with the Spokane Indians. He returned to the States in the spring and summer of 1837 for reinforcements.

Mrs. Whitman was not only a mother, she was also a foster mother to sixteen or more boys and girls whom she and Marcus received into their homes at Waiilatpu for periods of a year or longer. Several of these children were half-breeds. The first of this number was Mungo Mevway, the son of a Hawaiian father and a native woman, who was about twelve or thirteen years old when he began living with the Whitmans sometime in December, 1837. He remained with the Whitmans until October, 1841, when he was sent to live with the Walkers at Tshimakain. Also, sometime during the winter of 1837-38, Margaret McKay, a teen-age daughter of Thomas McKay, arrived at the Whitman home.[2] In a letter Narcissa wrote to her parents on April 11, 1838, she referred to Margaret as being "a very good girl, for one who has had so few advantages, and renders me much assistance in my domestic duties." Margaret was still with the Whitmans at the time of the death of Alice Clarissa in June, 1839. In this same letter of April 11, Narcissa mentions a Sarah Hull who had spent most of the preceding winter in their home. Narcissa described Sarah's father as being "a very wicked, troublesome man."

In a letter to her sister Jane dated September 18, 1838, shortly after the arrival of the reinforcement, Narcissa proudly wrote about her little girl. "She is now eighteen months old, very large, and remarkably healthy." And Narcissa added: "She is a great talker. Causes her mother many steps and much anxiety. She is just beginning to sing with us in our family worship." After telling about other items of interest, including an account of the death of Mungo's father, Narcissa wrote:

> You see, Jane, Alice has come and laid her dirty hands on this letter, and given it a fine mark. I send it as it is, so that you may have some of her doings to look at, and realize, perhaps, there is such a child in existence.

The original of this letter was included in the collection of letters given by Narcissa's sister, Harriet, to the Oregon Historical Society. An imperfect transcription of the letter was published in the *Transactions of the Oregon Pioneer Association* for 1891. When the author was writing his *Marcus Whitman, M.D.*, he discovered that the original letter with the smudge made by the little girl's dirty hand was missing.[3] Years later he saw the letter in the Coe Collection at Yale University library. Just how the letter got into the Coe Collection is not fully known. The smudge mark may still be seen. Narcissa's statement is

---

[2] Thomas McKay was placed in charge of Fort Hall by the Hudson's Bay Company in 1838. He was ambitious to give his children the best education possible. One of his sons, William Cameron McKay, was sent to Scotland to study medicine. Since McKay, himself a halfbreed, was married to a native woman, the children had but one-quarter white blood.

[3] *Op. cit.*, p. 218.

still true. Here we may see evidence that "such a child" was once in existence.

In a letter to Mrs. H. K. W. Perkins, the wife of a Methodist missionary stationed at The Dalles, Narcissa on March 23, 1839, wrote about Alice: "She is a large, healthy and strong child, two years old the 14th of this month. She talks both Nez Perce and English quite fluently . . . and sings all our Nez Perce hymns and several in English." One of the hymns which she loved to sing to the delight of her parents was "Rock of Ages."

And then tragedy struck!

On Sunday morning, June 23, Alice asked that "Rock of Ages" be sung at family worship. They sang the first verse and then Alice said, "Mamma, should my tears forever flow." It was her way of asking for the second verse. When the Whitmans held worship for the Indians that noon, the hymn was again sung. A sorrowing mother later remembered these little details with nostalgic affection.

About two-thirty in the afternoon, Margaret began setting the table for their Sunday dinner. Both Marcus and Narcissa were reading. Later Narcissa had a dim recollection of Alice saying: "Mama, supper is almost ready; let Alice get some water." The child went to the table, got two cups, and left the room. A few minutes later, Narcissa sensed that Alice was missing and asked Margaret to look for her. Soon Margaret returned saying that she could not find her. Mungo then looked and quickly returned saying that he saw two cups in the river. As Marcus retrieved the cups, Narcissa with growing fear in her heart, hastily encircled the house, and then becoming alarmed hurried to the stream. Frantically the two scanned the waters of the river. They unknowingly passed the point where some roots of a tree held their little daughter under the water. Some Indians nearby were called and one plunged into the stream and found the body. Hurriedly and with all the skill he could summon, Marcus tried to bring back life, but his efforts were in vain. Finally, with leaden hearts, they were obliged to admit the dreadful fact. Alice Clarissa was dead.

A messenger was sent at once to notify the Spaldings and the Halls at Lapwai. He rode the one hundred and twenty miles in twenty-five hours. Hall left at once on horseback for Waiilatpu and by riding all night covered the distance in twenty-four hours. Spalding, however, because of an injury suffered from a fall, was unable to ride so far. Consequently he, his wife, and little girl, left Lapwai by canoe on Monday evening. They arrived at Fort Walla Walla on the following Wednesday evening and the next day rode out to Waiilatpu. A grave had been dug, perhaps near that of the colored man, Hinds, who had died in December, 1836.[4] The funeral service was held on Thursday

---

[4] The exact location of the grave of Alice Clarissa has not been determined.

afternoon, June 26. Spalding took for his text, II Kings 4:26: "Is it well with thee? Is it well with thy husband? Is it well with the child?" Only a few were present. In addition to the missionaries, there were Mr. Pambrun and a few Indians.

Shortly before the death of Alice, dissensions within the missionary circle had become so tense that the Whitmans were on the point of withdrawing from the mission. The loss of the Whitman child, in which the Spaldings sincerely sympathized, was the cause of bringing about a better feeling between the two couples. Narcissa, in a letter to her father dated October 10, 1840, commented on her husband's feelings:

> He felt as if he must leave the mission, and no doubt would have done it, had not the Lord removed from us our beloved child. This affliction softened his feelings and made him willing to suffer the will of the Lord, although we felt that we were suffering wrongfully. The death of our babe had a great affect upon all in the mission; it softened their hearts towards us, even Mr. S's for a season. I never had any difficulty with his wife. . .

The Spaldings remained at Waiilatpu until July 4. They persuaded the Whitmans to return with them to Lapwai. The Whitmans did so and stayed for a few days. They were back in their lonely home by Friday, the nineteenth. The Doctor was then called to Tshimakain to attend Mrs. Eells who was seriously ill. Narcissa was reluctant to have him go but this was the price she paid for being a doctor's wife. "It was then," wrote Narcissa to her mother, "that I fully realized the full reality of my bereavement."

Narcissa's letters to her parents following the death of Alice carry many references to her sorrow. The following, taken from her letter of September 30, 1839, to her father, is typical:

> I would describe to you, if I could, her bright, lively appearance on Sabbath morning, the day of her death. She had always slept with me until just a week before her death, and that night she proposed, of her own accord, to sleep on the mat on the floor. This gave me a very strange and singular feeling, for I never could persuade her to live away from me, not even in her father's arms, before, and I could not divest myself of the feeling that she was laid away for the grave. It being very warm, and because she preferred it, I let her sleep on the floor all night — but did not sleep much myself. Ever after this, I made a bed for her by the side of mine, where I could lay my hand upon her. When I used to take her into the bed with me, she would lie a little while and then wish to go back again. Thus she gradually went out of my arms to the grave, so that I should not feel it so severely as if torn from them at once.

In the fall of 1840 a small band of former trappers together with a couple of immigrant families succeeded in taking the first wagons over the Blue Mountains on their trek into the Willamette Valley. In the party was the well-known mountain man Joe Meek who was at the Rendezvous in 1836 and who is reported to have never lost an opportunity to ride alongside Mrs. Whitman "entertaining her with stories of Blackfeet battles, and encounters with grizzly bears." [5] Meek had a Nez Perce wife who deserted him, leaving him with a little girl two years old. While in the mountains, Meek had read Porter's *Scottish Chiefs* and had admired the character of Helen Mar. So he bestowed that name on his daughter.[6] Meek urged Mrs. Whitman, for whom he had great respect, to take his little girl and give her a Christian upbringing. Narcissa found the child to be in a deplorable condition. She was dirty, half-starved, and her body covered with lice. She was also stubborn and fretful. Undoubtedly there was some hesitation to accept the responsibility, but if so there was also the memory of her own little girl. Could this dirty sullen little creature fill the void left by Alice Clarissa?

Nard Jones, in his fine interpretive study of the Whitmans, *The Great Command,* makes the following suggestive comment: "It must have been on this day, above all others, that Whitman looked at Meek, and the pitiable child, and Narcissa — and out of the window at the battered wagons in the mission yard — and knew that Oregon was a foreign mission no longer." [7] Each fall, thereafter, other children were accepted into the Whitman household until at the end of 1844 there were at least eleven. As the number of her foster children grew, Narcissa found it increasingly difficult to give time to such distinctly missionary duties as teaching in an Indian school. Almost imperceptibly the transition took place so that by the fall of 1847, she was giving all of her time to the multitudinous duties connected with running her house and raising her children.

In the fall of 1841 another famous mountain man, Jim Bridger, visited the Whitman station and persuaded Narcissa to take his six-year-old Mary Ann into her home. She too was the daughter of an Indian woman. In a letter to her parents dated October 6, 1841, Narcissa confided: "My two little girls are a comfort to me." Again on March 2, 1842, Narcissa's heart was touched with compassion when two Indian women brought to her "a miserable looking child, a boy between three and four years old." In a letter of that date directed to Jane and Edward, Narcissa described him:

His father is a Spaniard and is in the mountains. It has been living with its grandmother the winter past, who is an old and

[5] Victor, *River of the West,* 204.

[6] *Ibid.,* p. 238.   [7] *Op. cit.,* p. 235.

adulterous woman and has no compassion for it. . . The care
of such a child is very great at first — dirty, covered with body
and head lice and starved.

The little boy had been made the butt of cruel jokes. Narcissa wrote
that some older Indian boys had shaved a strip as wide as a finger
"from ear to ear, and also from his forehead to his neck, crossing the
other at right angles," in order to make him look ridiculous. He had
been pushed into the fire and had suffered a burn on one foot. It is
reported that the last name of his father was Cortez.[8] Narcissa, however, remembered a schoolmate of hers at Prattsburg, by the name of
David Malin, who had become a Presbyterian minister. The missionaries of both the Methodist and the American Boards often
bestowed names of famous people or of friends on the natives. This is
what Narcissa did when she gave the forlorn half-breed Spanish lad
the name of David Malin. He quickly became devoted to his foster
mother.

When Marcus Whitman was east during the spring of 1843, he
visited in the home of his younger brother, Samuel, at Rushville, New
York. Samuel's wife had died the previous fall leaving four children of
whom Perrin, then in his thirteenth year, was the oldest. Marcus, no
doubt remembering how his mother had been left a widow with five
small children and of how he had gone to live with relatives, suggested
that Perrin return with him to Oregon. The idea was so startling, for
Oregon was so far away, that it took three days of discussion before
Samuel gave his reluctant consent. Years later Perrin remembered that
his Uncle Marcus had promised him a gun, a saddle, and a donkey.

Perrin went out to Oregon with his uncle in the 1843 emigration and
Narcissa received him into her home as another son. Perrin was the
only relative of either Marcus or Narcissa who ever went to Oregon
during their lifetime. Since Perrin was said to have closely resembled
his uncle and since no portrait was painted or photograph taken of
Marcus, Perrin's likeness was sometimes used in idealized pictures of
his famous uncle.[9] After his arrival at Waiilatpu, Perrin had such close
associations with the Indians that he quickly picked up the language.
This qualified him to serve as a government interpreter in later years.

Also in the fall of 1843 two motherless girls, Emma and Ann Hobson,
ages six and thirteen, who with their father had gone to Oregon with
the immigration of that year, were left with the Whitmans. This
brought the total number of children in the Whitman home to six. In
a letter to her friend, Mrs. L. L. Brewer of the Methodist Mission,
dated January 30, 1844, Narcissa confessed that she was "unwilling to

---

[8] Clarke, *Pioneer Days*, ii: p. 521.

[9] The statue of Marcus Whitman, formerly on the Witherspoon Building, Philadelphia, but now in storage, was modeled after the likeness of Perrin Whitman.

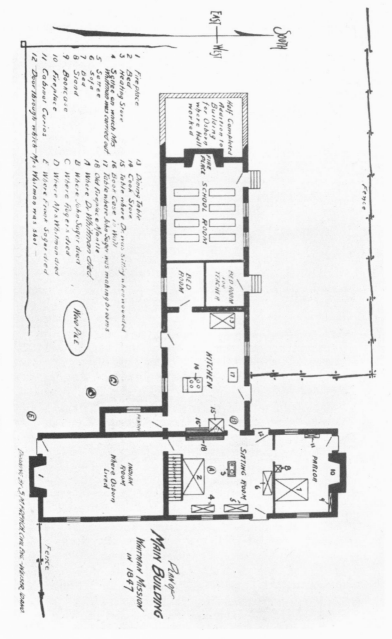

FLOOR PLAN OF THE WHITMAN HOME AT WAIILATPU

As described to the artist by Mrs. Elizabeth Sager Helm, one of the survivors, who was ten years old at the time of the massacre. Another drawing of the floor plan was given by Mrs. Whitman in a letter to her parents, dated May 2, 1840, which appeared in the *Transactions of the Oregon Pioneer Association* for 1891. The two plans are very much the same except the latter one shows fewer but larger rooms. See text pages 129-142. From Miles Cannon, *Waiilatpu, Its Rise and Fall.*

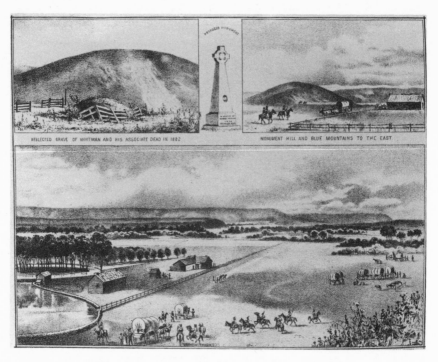

WAIILATPU AND THE VALLEY TO THE WEST
The earliest drawing of the mission site known to have been published.
The buildings, left to right, are the grist mill, emigrant house, black-
smith shop, and Whitman home. From Evans, *History of Pacific Northwest*.

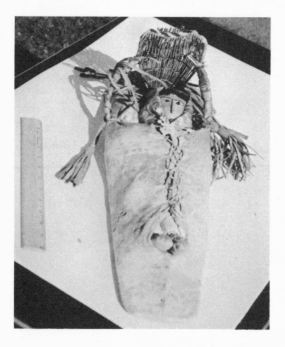

INDIAN DOLL
Once owned by Elizabeth Sager
at the Whitman Mission.
See text page 154.

increase my family," but when the girls pled so urgently to stay with her, she found she could not refuse. Emma went to live with the Walkers at Tshimakain in April, 1844, and remained there until the following March when both girls were sent to the Willamette Valley, probably to be reunited with their father.

The immigration of 1844 left the seven orphan Sager children with the Whitmans. Henry Sager with his wife and six children — John, aged 14; Francis, 12; Catherine, 9; Elizabeth M., 7; Matilda Jane, 5; and Hannah Louise, 3 — left the Missouri frontier in April, 1844, for Oregon. His wife, who was then about to give birth to another child, did not want to go. With prophetic insight she declared that she would never be able to make the journey. In the latter part of May she gave birth to a baby girl who was later named Henrietta.

A series of misfortunes followed the Sagers across the country. At Fort Laramie, Catherine fell under the wheel of a moving wagon and suffered a broken leg. A kindly German doctor who was also migrating to Oregon, Dr. Dagen, set the leg and thereafter took a special interest in the Sager family. Henry Sager died on August 27 when the party was encamped on the bank of the Green River. Before his death, he committed his family to the care of William Shaw, the captain of that section of the wagon train in which the Sagers were travelling, and requested that he take the children through to Dr. Whitman's mission. Various men of the wagon train assisted in driving the Sager wagon. About a month after the father died, Mrs. Sager died in the vicinity of what is now Twin Falls. The little infant Henrietta was given into the care of another woman of the company. Somewhere along the way the four-wheeled wagon was reduced to a two-wheeled cart.

On October 25 Captain Shaw, Dr. Dagen, and the seven Sager children reached the Whitman mission. Years later Catherine Sager Pringle wrote her reminiscences of the event from which account the following is taken:

> We reached the station in the forenoon. For weeks this place had been a subject of our talk by day and formed our dreams at night. We expected to see log houses, occupied by Indians and such people as we had seen about the forts. Instead we saw a large white house surrounded with palisades [*i.e.* a picket fence.]
> . . . We drove up and halted . . . Captain Shaw was in the house conversing with Mrs. Whitman. Glancing through the window, he saw us, and turning to her said: "Your children have come; will you go out and see them?" . . . Here was a scene for an artist to describe! Foremost stood the little cart, with the tired oxen that had been unyoked lying near it. Sitting in the front end of the cart was John, weeping bitterly; on the opposite side stood Francis, his arms on the wheel and his head resting on

his arms, sobbing aloud; on the near side the little girls were huddled together, bareheaded and barefooted, looking at the boys and then at the house, dreading we knew not what. By the oxen stood the good German doctor, with his whip in his hand, regarding the scene with suppressed emotion.

Thus Mrs. Whitman found us. She was a large, well-formed woman, fair complexioned, with beautiful auburn hair, nose rather large, and large gray eyes. She had on a dark calico dress and gingham sunbonnet. We thought as we shyly looked at her that she was the prettiest woman we had ever seen.[10]

Captain Shaw asked Narcissa if she had any children of her own. Pointing to the grave of Alice Clarissa, she replied: "All the child I ever had sleeps yonder." Both Marcus and Narcissa were somewhat overwhelmed at first by the prospect of adding seven more to their family. Marcus suggested that perhaps the little baby could be given over to the care of somebody else and Narcissa once considered whether or not they should keep only the girls. Finally they agreed, it was to be "all or none."

Narcissa made several references to the Sager children in her extant letters. Writing to her sister Jane on April 2, 1846, she said:

> I believe I have written very few letters since the doctor returned. My health has been so poor, and my family has increased so rapidly, that it has been impossible. You will be astonished to know that we have eleven children in our family, and not one of them our own by birth, but so it is. Seven orphans were brought to our door in Oct., 1844, whose parents both died on the way to this country. Destitute and friendless, there was no other alternative — we must take them in or they must perish. The youngest was an infant five months old — born on the way — nearly famished and but just alive; the eldest was 13 — two boys and five girls; the boys were the oldest. The eldest daughter was lying with a broken leg by the side of her parents as they were dying, one after the other. They were an afflicted and distressed family in the journey, and when the children arrived here they were in a miserable condition.

And in a letter to her sister Harriet written April 13, Narcissa wrote concerning the baby: "She arrived here in the hands of an old filthy woman, sick emaciated and but just alive. . . The old woman did the best she could, but she was in distressed circumstances herself, and a wicked disobedient family around her to see to." [11]

---

10 Clark, *Pioneer days*, II: p. 508.

11 A fictionized and highly fanciful account of the Sager children making the 500-mile trip from Fort Hall to Waiilatpu, "unaccompanied," by Honoré Willsie

Long before the Sager children had arrived, Narcissa had thought about the coming of foster children into her home as an act of Providence. In a letter to her sister Jane written on March 1, 1842, she had commented: "The Lord has taken our own dear child away so that we may care for the poor outcasts of the country." Her health about which she despaired in 1841-43 seemed to improve after the beginning of 1844. The multitudinous duties connected with caring for so many children in a pioneer home in the wilderness meant that she had less time for herself and for writing.

Whitman visited Oregon City in June, 1845, when he was made the legally appointed guardian of the Sager children. Three of the Sager girls later wrote their reminiscences or dictated them to others.[12] These show that they spent three happy years in the Whitman home at Waiilatpu. Matilda remembered: "Mrs. Whitman taught us the love of flowers. We each had a flower garden, which we had to weed and care for." Occasionally the family would pack a lunch and go on a picnic. There were frequent horseback rides. Mrs. Whitman, in a letter to her sister Harriet dated April 13, 1846, told: "Every one of my girls go to the river all summer long for bathing every day before dinner, and they love it so well that they would as soon do without their dinner as without that." And again in the same letter: "We sleep out of doors in the summer a good deal — the boys all summer. This is a fine, healthy climate."

Due attention was given to religious instruction. There was daily family worship with Sunday School and church service on Sunday. In the absence of a minister, Dr. Whitman would read a sermon although some of the immigrants remembered him "preaching" both in English and to the natives in Nez Perce.

In a letter to Jane and Edward dated March 1, 1842, Narcissa told of making "two rag babies" for Helen Mar and Mary Ann. She wrote:

> They have a great disposition to take a piece of board or a stick and carry it around on their backs, if I would let them, for a baby, so I thought I would make them something that would change their taste a little. You wonder, I suppose, what looking objects Narcissa would make. No matter how they look, so long as it is a piece of cloth rolled up with eyes, nose, and mouth marked on it with a pen, it answers every purpose. They caress them and carry them about the room at a great rate, and are as happy as need be.

Morrow appeared in *Cosmopolitan* for Jan. 1926; was reprinted in *Reader's Digest,* Dec. 1940, and again in Aug. 1960, under the title "Child Pioneer." Such wide publicity in such reputable magazines has given this distorted account of the Sager children a tenacious hold in the public mind.

[12] They were Catherine, Elizabeth, and Matilda. For a detailed review of their reminiscences see Drury, *Whitman,* 456.

One of the choice relics recently presented to the museum of the Whitman National Monument is an Indian papoose doll, properly bound up in dressed deer skin on a papoose board, which originally had been given to Elizabeth Sager by an Indian woman. The doll passed to Elizabeth's daughter Myra who specified that upon her death it should go to the museum. The cradleboard is twenty-three and one-half inches long and the doll measures thirteen and one-half inches. The cradleboard is made of willow covered with the same soft dressed deer skin used for the doll. The hair is wool from a black sheep and the eyes are trade beads. The head covering or shawl is of colored cotton cloth. There is a sunshade seven and one-half inches long over the head of the doll. Here we have not only a demonstration of the way the Indians cared for their babies, but also one of the actual toys that delighted one of Narcissa's girls. See illustration on page 150.

Sharing with Narcissa in the responsibilities of caring for the children was Marcus who fully approved of having so many foster children brought into the home. On June 3, 1845, while in the Willamette Valley on business, Whitman appeared before Probate Judge J. W. Nesmith at Oregon City and was appointed the legal guardian of the Sager children. Years later three of the older children wrote their reminiscences. Each told of the closely-knit family life in which Marcus and Narcissa were called "Father" and "Mother."

"IT WAS HER MISFORTUNE"

Following the massacre of November 29, 1847, which took the lives of Marcus and Narcissa Whitman, Miss Jane Prentiss, a sister of Narcissa's, wrote to the Reverend H. K. W. Perkins asking: "Why did the Indians kill my sister and her husband who had done so much for them?" Few could have answered such an inquiry out of a more intimate knowledge of both Marcus and Narcissa Whitman than Perkins. When Marcus was on his eastern journey, Narcissa spent the winter of 1842-43 with Mr. and Mrs. Perkins at their mission station at Waskopum, or The Dalles. Marcus had been a frequent visitor in the Perkins home in his travels to and from the Willamette Valley.

Perkins replied on October 19, 1849. In his frank and deeply penetrating analysis of the Whitmans, Perkins maintained that neither was fitted for the life of a missionary. He wrote:

> The truth is Miss Prentiss your lamented sister was far from happy in the situation she had chosen to occupy. . . I should say, unhesitatingly that both herself & husband were out of their proper sphere. They were not adapted to their work. They could not possibly interest & gain the affections of the natives. I know for a long time before the tragedy that closed their final career that many of the natives around them looked upon them suspi-

ciously. Though they *feared* the Doctor they did not *love* him. They did not love your sister. They could appreciate neither the one nor the other.

The Doctor I presume you knew familiarly. And *knowing him* as *I knew him* you would not need to be told that an Oregon Indian & he could never get along well together. It was "the last place," to use a familiar phrase, that he ought to have occupied. And first . . . he cared for no man under heaven, — perfectly fearless & independent. Secondly he could never stop *to parley*. It was always *yes* or *no*. In the 3d place he had no sense of *etiquette* or personal dignity — manners, I mean. 4. And in the fourth place he was *always at work*. Now I need not tell you that he & an Indian would never agree.[1]

Perkins then dwelt on Whitman's interest in the white settlers. "Dr. Whitman . . . never identified himself with the natives as to make their interests *paramount*." Whitman felt, according to Perkins, that the Indians could never stand up against the aggressiveness of the white man, that the rich valleys would inevitably be settled by an industrious people, and that "he was willing meantime to do what he could incidentally, for the poor, weak, feeble doomed Oregonians." In these respects Whitman was a realist, a prophet. Any alert person who knew what had happened to the Indians in the eastern part of the nation would have come to the same conclusion. The trouble was that the natives began to suspect that Whitman was more interested in the white man than in them.

In further comment about Narcissa, Perkins wrote:

That she felt a deep interest in the welfare of the natives, no one who was at all acquainted with her could doubt. But the affection was manifested under false views of Indian character. Her carriage towards them was always considered *haughty*. It was the common remark among them that Mrs. Whitman was "very proud." . .

Mrs. Whitman was not adapted to savage but *civilized* life. She would have done honor to her sex in a polished & exalted sphere. The natives esteemed her as proud, haughty, as *far above them*. No doubt she really seemed so. It was her *misfortune*, not her *fault*. She was adapted to a different destiny. She wanted something exalted — communion with mind. She longed for society, *refined society*. She was intellectually & by association fitted to do good only in such a sphere. She should have been different situated. . .

---

[1] The original Perkins letter is at Whitman College, Walla Walla. The words in italics are underlined in the original.

She loved company, society, excitement & ought always to have enjoyed it. The self-denial that took her away from it was suicidal. Perhaps, however, more good was accomplished by it than could have been accomplished by pursuing a different course. Certain it is that we needed such minds to keep us in love with civilized life, to remind us occasionally of *home.* As for myself I could as easily have become an Indian as not. . . I could gladly have made the wigwam my home for life if duty had called. But it was not so with Mrs. W. She had nothing apparently with them in common. She kept in her original sphere to the last. She was not a *missionary* but a *woman,* an American highly gifted, polished American lady. And such she died.

Undoubtedly Jane Prentiss was both shocked and hurt when she read this letter. If she wished, she could have turned to some of Narcissa's letters to find therein ample confirmation for all that Perkins had said. Repeatedly Narcissa had referred to her husband as being "a courageous man," and as one who had "amazing energy of thought and action." Once she wrote of him as being "a bundle of thoughts"[2] and on April 15, 1847, she wrote: "A head and heart more full of benevolent plans, and hands more ready in the execution of them for the good of the poor Indian and the white population of the country, you have probably never seen." But according to Perkins, this very industry and energy had built a barrier between the doctor and the natives.

If Jane took the time to reread all of her sister's letters, she would have noted a gradual shifting of emphasis on the part of Narcissa from that which was native-centered to that which was home-centered. In the early months and years of Narcissa's residence at Waiilatpu, her letters reflect her enthusiasm for missionary work. The Indians were friendly and receptive. In her letter which was begun on December 5, 1836, she tells of having the lean-to filled with "native youth & boys who have come in to sing." At that time she was using Richard as an interpreter as she read and explained chapters of the Bible. Since Narcissa did not then know the native language, any singing done by the group must have been by the use of English words which were meaningless to them.

At first there was some discussion among the missionaries as to whether or not they should teach the natives English and give instruction in that tongue or whether the missionaries should themselves learn the Nez Perce. Within a year or so, they decided that it was easier for them to learn Nez Perce, difficult as that was, than to expect a whole tribe to learn English. In a letter to her parents dated April 11, 1838, Narcissa wrote: "We shall soon commence teaching them to

---

[2] References taken from Narcissa's letters of March 1, 1842, Oct. 9, 1844, and Nov. 3, 1846.

read their own language, for I have just finished copying a book of seventy-two pages, which Mr. Spalding intends to send to the Sandwich Islands to get it printed. . ." If the book were sent to the Islands, we have no proof that it was ever printed. But here is evidence that a beginning had been made to reduce the Nez Perce language to writing and that the Whitmans were using this hand-written primer in their school at Waiilatpu. In this same letter Narcissa wrote: "We have had a school for them for about four months past & much of the time our kitchen has been crowded."

In September 1839 T. J. Farnham and three associates called at the Whitman station. In 1848 Farnham published his *Travels Across the Great Western Prairies*, in which he gave a detailed description of Waiilatpu. He paid the following tribute: "Mrs. Whitman is an indefatigable instructress." [3] The periodic migrations of the natives for food meant that there could be no regular sustained attendance in school. In his report to Greene dated March 27, 1840, Whitman wrote: "For three months during the winter our school averaged ten scholars & was taught by Mrs. Whitman. Since it has been increasing at present it consists of from thirty to fifty & so far as we can both of us employ ourselves in teaching." Members of a United States Naval Exploring Expedition visited Waiilatpu in the summer of 1841. Joseph Drayton, one of this number, wrote that the Whitmans had one hundred and twenty-four on their school rolls but that the average attendance was only twenty-five.[4] Drayton noted that Whitman had induced a number of the Indians to cultivate garden plots of their own.

Narcissa tried to teach the Cayuse women to spin, weave, and knit but had little success. In a letter to Mrs. Parker dated July 25, 1842, she said: "The Kayuse ladies are too proud to be seen usefully employed." Among the Walla Walla Indians, a tribe related to the Cayuses who also came within the influence of the mission, Narcissa reported that there was one woman who had learned to spin and weave and that a few others knew how to sew.

In a long letter to her parents dated October 6, 1841, we find evidence of a growing discouragement in Narcissa's heart. Regarding the attitude of the natives, she wrote: "It is difficult for them to feel but that we are rich and getting richer by the houses we dwell in and the clothes we wear and hang out to dry after washing from week to week, and the grain we consume in our families." And she confessed: "The missionary work is hard, up-hill work, even the best of it. There are no flowery beds of ease here."

In this same letter Narcissa referred to her ill health. "My health has been poor for more than a year past," she wrote, "and my many bodily infirmities doubtless causes my gloomy moments and unfits me

[3] *Op. cit.*, pp. 147 ff.
[4] Wilkes, *Narrative of U.S. Exploring Expedition*, IV, p. 399.

for reading and reflection many times." She mentioned her weak eyes. "I am obliged to use my spectacles while writing, or I could not write so much. When my health is poor my eyes are very weak." [5] Writing to her husband on October 4, 1842, just after he left on his famous ride to Washington and Boston, Narcissa said: "I intended to have spoken to you about purchasing one or two pair of spectacles. Perhaps you will think of it." We have no evidence to show that her husband ever received the letter. Buying a pair of spectacles in those days meant little more than buying a pair of magnifying glasses set in a frame.

Narcissa suffered considerably from ill health during the years 1840-44. In a letter to her parents dated April 12, 1844, she said: "My beloved parents need not be surprised should they hear about my death soon. Ever since the fall of 1840, the sickness I had at that time, I have been declining." The Whitmans had only one child of their own. There is some evidence in the letters of Narcissa to indicate that she suffered from some female disorder which might have explained why they had no more children.

In the closing years of Narcissa's life at Waiilatpu, she had neither the time nor the strength to carry on those activities such as teaching in the Indian school which characterized her earlier years. Added to these facts was a growing despondency and at times a feeling of repugnance towards the natives. Concerning all of this Perkins wrote: "Her hopes of success also, were very much weakened and melancholy musings occupied her more than at first setting out in missionary life." Thus a combination of circumstances and attitudes accounted for Narcissa's withdrawal from the natives. Perkins summed up the Indians' point of view when he wrote that the natives considered her to be proud and haughty.

Dr. Whitman was frequently called away on professional visits. Because of the long distances to be covered and the slowness of travel on horseback, he would occasionally be gone for weeks at a time. Narcissa was often left alone with the children at Waiilatpu. In a letter to Jane and Edward dated March 1, 1842, Narcissa mentioned the fact that her husband had been called "to go on a professional visit to Brother Walker's." And then she wrote: "Jane, I wish you were here to sleep with me, I am such a timid creature about sleeping alone that sometimes I suffer considerably, especially since my health has been not very good."

On September 9, 1842, Dr. Elijah White arrived at the Whitman mission with a letter from Greene of the American Board.[6] As a result

---

[5] In a letter to her parents dated Feb. 7, 1843, Narcissa wrote: "My eyes are almost gone — my poor health affects them materially and writing is very injurious to me. I can neither read, write or sew without spectacles, the most of the time, and sometimes with them I suffer considerable pain." *T.O.P.A.*, 1891, p. 171.

[6] See diary of Mrs. W. H. Gray, under same date, in this volume, page 263.

of many letters of complaint which had been sent to the Board by Smith, Gray, and Rogers, the Board at its spring meeting of that year had taken the drastic action of dismissing the Spaldings and of closing both the Lapwai and the Waiilatpu stations. The Whitmans were directed to move to Tshimakain. During the interval of about two years which extended between the writing of the letters of criticism and the arrival of the order in Oregon, the situation had greatly changed. The Smiths and Rogers had left the mission. The Grays were on the point of doing so. Spalding and Whitman had reconciled their differences. By the fall of 1842 it was very clear to Whitman that his station was strategically located on the Oregon Trail. Of all places Waiilatpu should be the last to be closed.

A mission meeting was hastily called for September 26. Whitman proposed that he go East to intercede with the Board to keep Spalding, and not to close the two southern stations. With some reluctance Walker and Eells consented. Of course Spalding approved. Whitman left on October 3 and after one of the most dramatic rides in American history reached Boston about April 1. En route to Boston, Whitman visited Washington, D.C., where he undoubtedly saw some high government officials and where he wrote out a proposed bill to be introduced into Congress which would have established some forts along the Oregon Trail.[7] Later, Spalding, building on half-truths and hesitating to say anything about his own dismissal, claimed that the primary purpose of Whitman's ride was to go to Washington to prevent the United States from signing away any of its rights to Oregon. Whitman, with his nephew Perrin, returned with the immigration of 1843.

Before leaving Waiilatpu, Whitman instructed Gray to find someone to go to the mission to stay with his wife and children and to take care of the property. However, Gray and his family left Waiilatpu the day after Whitman started east leaving only a Hawaiian in the house with Narcissa and the children. On the night of October 6, Narcissa was awakened by the sound of someone trying to enter her bedroom. She jumped from her bed and succeeded in closing the door and fastening the latch but the intruder was able to push the door partly open again. Narcissa called for John, the Hawaiian, and the ruffian, becoming alarmed, ran. She lit a candle and returned to her bed, trembling and cold. But she could not rest. She described the harrowing experience in a letter to her husband written a few days later. The intruder is believed to have been Tamsucky, a sub-chief under Tiloukaikt, who played a leading role in the massacre.

When the incident became known to Archibald McKinley, then in

---

[7] In a letter to the Sec. of War, J. M. Porter, which Whitman sent with his copy of the bill, he suggested the establishment of a pony express. He felt that the mail could be carried from the Missouri frontier to the mouth of the Columbia in forty days. Drury, *Whitman*, 312.

charge of Fort Walla Walla, he insisted that Narcissa leave Waiilatpu. On October 11, McKinley drove out to Waiilatpu in a wagon and took Narcissa and the three half-breed children who were with her back to the fort. Narcissa spent most of the time during the absence of her husband with Methodist missionaries at The Dalles and in the Willamette, having Helen Mar and Mary Ann with her. David Malin was left at the fort. "I think her stay with us," wrote Perkins to Jane Prentiss, "including her visit to the Willamette the pleasantest portion of her Oregon life." (See illustration at page 168.)

After her husband's return from his famous ride and after the arrival of the Sager children in the fall of 1844, we find Narcissa giving even less time to distinctly missionary activities and more time to the needs of her family. Her health showed some improvement. To some extent her love for company was satisfied by the numbers of immigrants who stayed at Waiilatpu, sometimes for an entire winter, following each year's incoming tide. The presence of so many white and half-breed children on the mission grounds made a school imperative. The Whitmans succeeded in hiring a teacher from the incoming migration each year beginning with the fall of 1844. The Walkers sent their oldest son, Cyrus, to the school during the winter of 1845-46 and the Spaldings sent Eliza. The next year the Spaldings sent both Eliza and their little boy Henry. In addition, the Whitmans sometimes received half-breed children from Fort Walla Walla. At the time of the massacre, two Manson boys from the Fort were in their home. In her letter to her mother written on November 3, 1846, Narcissa stated: "We set the table for more than twenty every day three times — and it is a pleasing sight."

Narcissa's last extant letter to her mother, dated July 4, 1847, carried sections written during the latter part of August when the large immigration of that year had begun to stream by the Whitman home. She included this penetrating observation: "The poor Indians are amazed at the overwhelming numbers of Americans coming into the country. They seem not to know what to make of it."

"Amazed" was hardly the right word. Narcissa should have mentioned the resentment of the Indians. The immigrants' covered wagons parked in the Whitman's front yard and the Cayuses' tepees pitched a little farther away in the rear of the Whitman home were symbols of two contending forces struggling for the possession of the land. The Whitman mission happened to be in the center, in the vortex of a cyclone of fear, superstition, and finally of murder.

When the small band of revenge-seeking Cayuses let loose their fury on that tragic morning of November 29, 1847, they centered their attention first on Marcus and Narcissa Whitman. To the inflamed minds of the murderers, who couldn't understand the forces at work in the great immigration of white people to Oregon or the mystery as to why measles would kill the red man and spare the white, to them the Whitmans were somehow and in some way the cause of all their misfortunes.

The act was that of a small group, but the consequences were as irrevocable as though the whole tribe were involved.

Paraphrasing slightly the statement of Perkins — it was *their* misfortune and not *their* fault.

THE TRAGEDY AT WAIILATPU

The causes of the massacre which began at Waiilatpu on Monday afternoon, November 29, 1847, and which took the lives of Marcus and Narcissa Whitman and twelve others are many and complex. To begin with there were social and economic reasons. All of the Indians in the upper Columbia River country were showing increasing signs of restlessness after the great immigrations of white people began to pour into their country. A number of individual cases of insult against the missionaries and even against the Hudson's Bay men had taken place. In some instances the Indians resorted to violence. The Cayuses, through whose country the Oregon Trail ran, were naturally among the first to become aroused. As early as 1844 Dr. McLoughlin had warned Whitman about the danger of remaining in the Cayuse country and had advised him to move to the Willamette Valley. Marcus had talked about this with Narcissa but both felt that duty demanded that they should remain.

The winter of 1846-47 was unusually severe all along the north Pacific Coast. This was the winter in which the Donner party was trapped in the snows of the high Sierras, when about one-half of a party of ninety-one perished. All who owned cattle or horses in the upper Columbia River country suffered a heavy loss that winter as it was the custom to let the livestock fend for themselves without shelter. The Nez Perces are reported to have lost one-half of their total stock of horses. The Cayuses suffered a similar loss. The severe winter took its toll of wild game which in turn meant that the natives had more difficulty in finding food. It seemed that even Nature herself was conspiring to arouse feelings of restlessness in the hearts of the Indians.

The coming of the Roman Catholic missionaries into the Nez Perce and Cayuse country, beginning about 1838, was a disturbing factor as it introduced the spirit of religious rivalry among the natives. The Protestant missionaries habitually referred to the Pope as "the man of sin." Whitman was greatly disturbed in the fall of 1847 to learn that the Roman Catholics were establishing a mission on the Umatilla River about twenty-five miles from Waiilatpu. Many of the Indians were astute enough to play one religious group against the other hoping thereby to reap some advantage.

By the fall of 1847, as Perkins pointed out, Marcus and Narcissa Whitman had lost the confidence and goodwill of the natives. The Indians had become jealous of the material prosperity of the missionaries. They became suspicious of what they considered to be too much attention given by the Whitmans to the incoming immigrants. Perkins wrote: "They looked upon the Doctor & wife as not missionaries to them but to the Americans."

Another complicating factor was the nefarious influence of two half-breeds who were at Waiilatpu at that time. They were Joe Lewis and Nicholas Finley. Lewis arrived at Waiilatpu in the fall of 1847 in a destitute condition. Whitman gave him some clothing and made arrangements for him to continue his travels by assisting in driving an immigrant's team. However, within a few days Joe was back at Waiilatpu and there was nothing that Whitman could do about it. Reports soon reached Whitman's ears that Joe was stirring up trouble. Gray, in his *History of Oregon,* wrote: "He was seen several times approaching the windows with a gun, but when Mrs. Whitman would ask, 'Joe, what do you want?' he would run away." [1]

Nicholas Finley, a half-breed Frenchman and a former employee of the Hudson's Bay Company, was of the same stamp. According to a statement in the report of the massacre written by Spalding on April 6, 1848, for Narcissa's parents, Finley was one of the ringleaders of the tragedy. Spalding wrote: "The half-breed Finley was camped near the station, and in his lodge the murderers held their councils before and during the massacre." [2] Too much emphasis can not be placed on the baneful influence of these maladjusted half-breeds in precipitating the massacre.

And finally, the proverbial straw that broke the camel's back, was the outbreak of a virulent form of measles which had been introduced by the immigration of 1847. Many of the white children were stricken with the disease and some died. However, the death toll was far greater among the natives, where both adults and children were stricken. The Indians suffered especially because they had no previous immunity against the disease. To the suspicious minds of the natives, the very fact that more Indians were dying than white people was clear evidence that Joe Lewis' assertion regarding Dr. Whitman was true. Joe claimed that he had once overheard Whitman and Spalding plotting to poison the Indians in order to get their land and their horses.

William McBean, who was in charge of Fort Walla Walla at the time of the massacre, in his first report of the tragedy laid great emphasis on the outbreak of measles as being perhaps the main cause. He wrote: "I presume you are well acquainted that fever and dysentery has been raging here, and in this vicinity, in consequence of which a

---

[1] *Op. cit.,* p. 468.
[2] *T.O.P.A.,* 1893, 102.

great number of Indians have been swept away, but more especially at the Doctor's place where he attended upon the indians, about 30 souls of the Cayuse tribe died. . ." [3] Mrs. L. W. Saunders, one of the survivors, stated in her reminiscences that Dr. Whitman buried three of the children of Chief Tiloukaikt on the morning of the twenty-ninth.[4] The Indians in the vicinity of Waiilatpu had a superstition, common among primitive peoples, which dictated that if a te-wat (an Indian medicine man) could not cure a patient, then the relatives of the dead patient could kill the te-wat. A number of te-wats had been killed during the eleven years the Whitmans had lived at Waiilatpu.[5] It seemed so reasonable to the Indians: here was a white te-wat who could not cure a white man's disease — therefore, he must die.

Spalding arrived at Waiilatpu on Monday, November 22, just a week before the massacre began, with his ten-year-old daughter, Eliza, who was to enter the school. Spalding was impressed with the large number of Indians who were sick with measles and dysentery. On Saturday, Whitman was asked to visit some sick Indians on the Umatilla. Spalding accompanied him. The night was stormy. As they rode through the rain, they were reminded of the fact that they had followed the same trail more than eleven years previous on their first entry into the valley. They also talked about the threatening attitude of some of the Indians. And Spalding later remembered that Whitman said: "But my death will probably do as much good to Oregon as my life can." [6]

On Sunday afternoon, when Whitman and Spalding were in the lodge of Stickus,[7] who was one of the most faithful friends of the Whitmans, Stickus warned the Doctor of what Joe Lewis was telling. He advised Whitman to go away "until my people have better hearts." [8]

---

[3] See letter of McBean, Nov. 30, 1847, in *Oregon Spectator*, Dec. 10, 1847.

[4] Mrs. Mary Saunders, *The Whitman Massacre*. Quotations from this work are found in Drury, *Whitman*, p. 399.

[5] Drury, *Whitman*, p. 395. "McKinley also informed Dr. Tolmie that he considered the Cayuse and the Walla Walla Indians to be the most superstitious of any of the coast tribes, and added: 'They shot seven of their own medicine men by the fort during my five years' stay there, and probably over three times that number altogether.' "

[6] The author's chapter on "The Massacre" in his *Whitman* goes into more detail regarding what happened to all concerned than can possibly be given here. Also in that chapter he has documented material that has been used here without documentation.

[7] Stickus, although never baptized nor a member of the First Presbyterian Church of Oregon, which had been organized on Aug. 18, 1838, showed more evidence of knowing what it meant to be a Christian than any other native in the vicinity of the Whitman mission. Only one of the Cayuses, Five Crows or Hezekiah, had been received into the church. Although he did not take part in the massacre, neither did he seem to have done anything to prevent it. After the massacre he took Lorinda Bewley to his lodge to be his wife.

[8] Clarke, *Pioneer days*, II, p. 529.

The warning made Whitman feel that he must hasten back even if it meant travelling on Sunday. Spalding remained at the Umatilla and thus escaped being caught in the massacre.

Whitman got back to Waiilatpu late Sunday night. Narcissa, who had been reluctant to see her husband go to the Umatilla, was deeply relieved to have him home. Marcus told her what Stickus had said. The two spent a sleepless night. In the morning, Narcissa did not go to the breakfast table but remained in her room. One of the Sager girls carried some food in to her and remembered seeing her seated in a chair with her face in a handkerchief, weeping. Narcissa took the food, motioned the child to leave, but did not eat.

There were three very sick children in the Whitman home, Helen Mar Meek, Louise and Henrietta Sager. The usual day's duties were carried on. The Doctor made his rounds of the sick and attended an Indian funeral. The school opened at nine o'clock as usual with L. W. Saunders, one of the immigrants, as the teacher. A beef was driven in to be slaughtered. This seemed to have attracted the attention of many of the Indians, who loitered around with guns and tomahawks concealed under their blankets. Noon came and the Whitman family partook of their midday meal. After lunch Francis Sager shot the beef and several of the men of the immigration started to dress the carcass. In the house, Narcissa was bathing Elizabeth Sager in a tub in her bedroom.

About two o'clock, while Dr. Whitman was seated on a settee in his living room reading, there came a knock on the door leading into the kitchen. Mrs. Whitman answered the call and turning to the Doctor said: "Doctor, you are wanted." In the kitchen was Chief Tiloukaikt who asked for some medicine. As Whitman opened the door to go into the kitchen, Tiloukaikt tried to force his way into the sitting room, but Whitman pushed him back. The Doctor closed the door and turned to the medicine closet under the stairway to get what was needed. As he went into the kitchen, he warned Narcissa to lock the door behind him.

Elizabeth remembered how they heard loud words between the Indians and the Doctor. Then there was the sound of a gun being fired! Narcissa cried out in alarm: "The Indians will murder us all!" The frightened child climbed out of the tub and began to run naked from the room. Narcissa hastily called her back and assisted her in dressing. In the meantime Mary Ann Bridger was in the kitchen and saw what had taken place. John Sager, who was just recovering from the measles, was seated in the kitchen winding some twine which was to be made into brooms. While the doctor was giving the medicine to the Chief, Tomahas sneaked around behind Whitman and struck him a blow on the head with a tomahawk. Whitman was knocked to the floor but managed to get outside in a desperate effort to escape. One of the Indians shot him and Tiloukaikt struck the doctor repeatedly on the head and in the face with his tomahawk.

When John Sager saw what was happening, he attempted to draw a pistol. A watchful Indian saw what he was attempting to do and shot him. It was then that Mary Ann climbed out of a window and ran around the end of the building to the west entrance of the sitting room, crying out: "The Indians are killing Father and John!" The outburst of gunfire in the kitchen was the signal for other Indians to kill the men engaged in butchering. Mrs. Whitman rushed out to see what could be done to help her stricken husband. With the help of some women, she was able to half-carry and half-drag Marcus into the sitting room and lay him on a settee. Narcissa tried to talk with him but he answered only in monosyllables. "Do you know me?" she asked. He whispered "Yes." "Is there anything I can do to stop the bleeding?" A weak "No." Narcissa, however, tried to stanch the bleeding with a towel and by the application of some ashes taken from the stove.

Andrew Rodgers, who had been at the river, burst into the room shouting that he had been chased by the Indians. Seeing Dr. Whitman prostrate and bleeding, he asked if he were dead. Marcus was still conscious enough to answer "No." He then seemed to lapse into unconsciousness. Narcissa, desperately seeking for an explanation of the outbreak, cried: "I am a widow! I am a widow! That Joe! That Joe! He has done it all." About that time Nathan Kimball, one of the men engaged in butchering, entered with a bleeding arm. He exclaimed: "The Indians are killing us. I don't know what the damned Indians want to kill me for, I never did anything to them. Get me some water." Elizabeth, who was standing near, was shocked to hear Kimball, a very religious man, use such a profane word as "damn." She giggled, half expecting Narcissa to rebuke him, but nothing was said.

There was more gunfire outside. Elizabeth looked out of a window and saw the Indians shooting at Mr. Saunders, one of the immigrants. She cried in excitement: "Mother, they are killing Mr. Saunders." Narcissa, looked out of the window which was in the upper part of the door leading from the sitting room to the yard and saw Joe Lewis. She cried out to him: "Is it you, Joe, who are doing this?" It was then that a young Indian by the name of Frank Escaloom, who was standing on the steps leading into the schoolroom, raised his gun and fired at Mrs. Whitman. The bullet entered "under her left arm." [9] She screamed, fell to the floor, but soon staggered to her feet again. Some of the women helped her to a chair. She began to pray aloud that God would protect the children and that her mother would be given strength to bear the news when she heard of her death.

[9] Matilda Sager Delaney, *A Survivor's Recollections*, p. 16, states that Mrs. Whitman was wounded "under her left arm," whereas Spalding in his letter to Judge and Mrs. Prentiss says that she was shot "in her right breast." *T.O.P.A.*, 1893, p. 99.

The Indians were breaking windows and beginning to loot. Rodgers suggested that all go upstairs. The party then included Rodgers and Kimball, both of whom were wounded; Mrs. Hayes, Mrs. Hall, and Lorinda Bewley, all of the immigration of that year; Mary Ann Bridger, Helen Mar Meek, and all of the Sager girls except Matilda who was still in the schoolroom; and Mrs. Whitman. The three sick girls had to be carried up. No effort was made to move Dr. Whitman who was still lying unconscious on the settee.

The Indians broke into the sitting room and were about to rush upstairs when they suddenly became very docile as they saw the muzzle of a gun pointed at them. Rodgers had found an old broken gun in the upstairs room. Although it was useless, the Indians were unaware of that. For a time they stayed away from the stairway. Mrs. Whitman was laid out on one of the beds. She was bleeding profusely and soon the bed clothing was stained with her blood. The timing of the events of the afternoon is hard to reconstruct as the accounts are confused and sometimes contradictory. Spalding says that the group in the upstairs bedroom remained there "till near night." Then an Indian by the name of Tamsucky, possibly the very one who had tried to break into Narcissa's bedroom in October, 1842, promised them immunity if they would descend. Catherine recognized him as the one who had killed Mr. Saunders and warned her mother. However, Tamsucky was so persuasive that Mrs. Whitman trusted him. They all descended to the room below, except Kimball who remained in hiding.

Narcissa was so weak from the loss of blood that she had to be helped in going downstairs. She was laid on the second settee in the living room. Elizabeth Sager noticed and long remembered that her mother "averted her face from the Dr. who was still breathing." Again the record of the sequence of events is confused but it seems that all were ordered into the Indian room adjacent to the Whitman's living-room. Here there was some debate among the Indians as to whether or not they should kill all the women and children. Eliza Spalding, who understood the native language, heard and remembered much of the conversation. The moderate element won out in their plea to spare the women and the children, except for Narcissa Whitman.

The order was given for her to be carried out of the Indian room. Rodgers was directed to carry one end of the settee, even though one arm was helpless because of his wound, and Joe Lewis took the other end. After taking a few steps outside the doorway, Joe dropped his end. A number of Indians then began to fire at Mrs. Whitman and Rodgers. Both were hit several times and both were mortally wounded. One of the Indians took his whip and slashed Mrs. Whitman across the head and face and turned over the settee dumping her into the mud of an irrigation ditch that flowed thereby. During the first part of that night, the frightened children who had returned to the upstairs

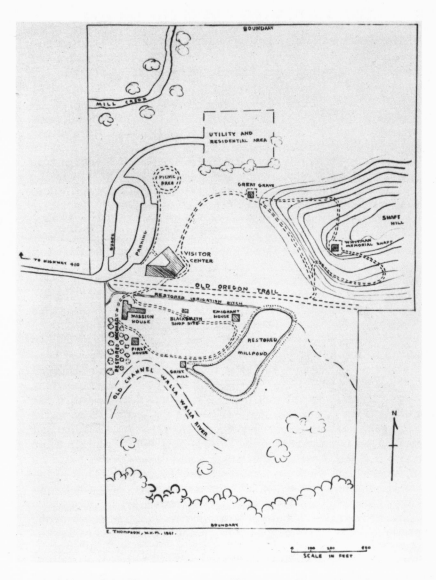

MAP OF THE VICINITY OF THE WHITMAN NATIONAL MONUMENT

This sketch map of the mission site was made on the basis of archaeological discoveries by Thomas R. Garth after the site became a national monument. In addition to the five buildings shown here, the site contained some other structures as granaries, smoke-house, wood-house, mill-shelter, etc. The Coe Collection in Yale Library contains a letter from W. H. Gray, 1842, which shows a series of parallel irrigation ditches from the main ditch toward the river. The Walla Walla River has changed its course and today flows several hundred feet distant.   From the Report of the Monument's Archaeologist.

THE DALLES MISSION AS PAINTED BY W. H. TAPPAN, 1849

Also known as Waskopum, here Mrs. Whitman spent the winter of 1842-43, while her husband was on his Eastern trip with the Methodist Perkins. Courtesy, Oregon Historical Society, owner of the painting.

THE GREAT GRAVE AT WAIILATPU

The slab covers the remains of thirteen of the victims of the Whitman massacre. The body of Peter D. Hall, reportedly drowned while attempting to go to the Willamette Valley for help, was never found. The vertical monument marks the grave of the W. H. Grays whose bodies were moved here in 1916. Courtesy of Whitman National Monument, Walla Walla.

TILOUKAIKT

TOMAHAS

Murderers of Dr. Whitman, from Paul Kane paintings. Courtesy of Royal Ontario Museum, Toronto.

bedroom and the members of the Osborn family who were hiding under the floor of the Indian room heard the dying groans of Mrs. Whitman and Rodgers until a late hour. Then all was still.

Shortly after Narcissa and Rodgers were mortally wounded, Francis Sager, who had been hiding in the attic of the schoolroom and who had come out of his hiding place, was dragged out of the house and shot by Joe Lewis. When darkness finally came, nine were either dead or dying. In addition to Dr. and Mrs. Whitman, the two Sager boys, and Andrew Rodgers, two men of the immigration were also killed that day. They were Jacob Hoffman and Walter Marsh. Two more, Isaac Gilliland and Nathan Kimball, were wounded. Gilliland died in the early hours of the next morning. Kimball remained hidden in the upstairs bedroom until the next day when he was discovered and killed. James Young was murdered on November 30. Two more men were killed on December 5, Crocket Bewley, and Amos Sales. This brought the total, counting Peter Hall who tried to carry news of the massacre to the Willamette Valley and disappeared, to fourteen.

About three o'clock in the morning of Tuesday, November 30, Elizabeth Sager was awakened out of her sleep by Kimball who wanted her to help him bind up his arm. Kimball told her to take a sheet from the bed and tear it into strips. Elizabeth hastened to remonstrate: "Mother would not like to have the sheets torn up." Kimball replied: "Child, don't you know your mother is dead, and will never have any use for the sheets?" [10]

The bodies of Marcus and Narcissa Whitman, Andrew Rodgers, and Frank Sager lay outside the door of the Indian room until Wednesday before the Indians would allow their burial. Finally Joseph Stanfield, a French Canadian who was at Waiilatpu at the time, was permitted to dig a grave and bury the victims. Father Brouillet assisted in the burial.

Perrin Whitman escaped the massacre because he happened to be at The Dalles at the time. Spalding also escaped, being warned by Father J. B. A. Brouillet shortly before he reached Waiilatpu on December 1. One of the survivors, W. D. Canfield, who was wounded, managed to travel the one hundred and twenty miles to Lapwai by foot to warn Mrs. Spalding. She, becoming alarmed about the safety of her husband and her daughter, sent Timothy and Grey Eagle to attempt their rescue. They arrived at Waiilatpu on the fifth of December. Somewhere along the trail the two Nez Perces unknowingly passed Spalding, who was making his way back to Lapwai on foot, possibly away from the main trail, his horse having gotten away from him during the first night. The Indians at Waiilatpu refused to let Eliza return with the friendly Nez Perces.

---

[10] Clarke, *Pioneer Days*, II, p. 537.

On December 5 Louise Sager died. Before her death, faithful Timothy, who of all the converts was the most sincere, knelt by her bedside and prayed. Three days later Helen Mar Meek died also. The captives were rescued by the Hudson's Bay Company on December 29 and taken to Fort Walla Walla. The Spaldings were escorted to the Fort on January 1. Ogden with the men, women, and children left for Fort Vancouver on January 2. There was one exception. For some reason it was decided not to take David Malin. One of the Sager girls remembered the forlorn eight-year-old boy standing on the river bank at Fort Walla Walla as the boats pulled away crying as though his heart would break. The four surviving Sager girls and Mary Ann Bridger found foster homes in the Willamette Valley. Mary Ann died the following March.

The Whitman massacre brought the story of Waiilatpu to a sudden and tragic end. Because of the tragedy, the work at Lapwai and Tshimakain had to be abandoned. Desolation ruled at Waiilatpu. A small band of resentful Cayuses burned the mission buildings and even cut down the fruit trees. The gardens and fields lay neglected. The tall rye grass spread through what were once plowed fields, gradually covering up all traces of the white man's industry. For years the mission site was nothing more than an abandoned cemetery in the primeval wilderness.

In 1860 the Reverend Cushing Eells bought the site from the American Board for one thousand dollars. He was then active in promoting Whitman Seminary in Walla Walla. Eells built a frame house on the site of Whitman's second home, where he and his wife lived for twelve years, or until their house was burned on May 28, 1872. Charles Moore purchased the site in 1872 and built a house where the Eells home had stood. In 1912 this was moved about six hundred and fifty feet away, where it still stands, and a fourth house was erected on the site by Marion Swegle. This stood until 1936 when it was torn down at the time the National Park Service established the Whitman National Monument. It is hoped that some day in the near future replicas of the main mission buildings, as they existed at the time of the massacre, may be constructed on the original sites so that the thousands of tourists who annually visit the Monument may the better visualize how the Whitmans and their associates lived.

Mrs. Henry Harmon Spalding

Eliza Hart Spalding

The memory of Eliza Hart Spalding's kindly spirit and deep devotion has continued in the Nez Perce country for more than one hundred years. The author has frequently heard testimonies of praise of her, from Nez Perces who felt inclined to criticize her husband but who joined enthusiastically in commending her. On August 10, 1849, Robert Newell [1] wrote a report regarding the different Indian tribes living south of the Columbia River. In the section dealing with the Nez Perces he wrote: "Mrs. Spalding also they speak much about and say that have lost *a good woman that took so much pains to learn them.*[2] Of the six women who were in the Oregon Mission of the American Board, no one was more successful in her work for the natives and consequently more beloved than Mrs. Henry Harmon Spalding of Lapwai.

Eliza Hart was born at what is now Berlin, Connecticut, on August 11, 1807, the oldest child of Levi and Martha Hart. There were two other daughters and three sons in the family. The Hart family belonged to pioneer stock. Stephen Hart, the progenitor of the American line, came to the colonies in 1652. Eliza's father had the title of "Captain" which may have referred to some connection with the state militia. He was described by Gray in his *History of Oregon* as being "a plain substantial farmer."[3] In 1820, when Eliza was thirteen years old, the Hart family moved to a farm near Holland Patent, Oneida County, New York. There Eliza's parents made their home until they died.

Little is known of Eliza's youth and early education. We know that she received good training in all of the arts and crafts associated with a farm home. She knew how to spin and weave; how to make soap, candles, butter, and cheese; and how to cook over an open fire in a fireplace. She also had some modest skill in drawing and painting.

---

[1] Robert Newell was formerly a mountain man who met the Spaldings and the Whitmans at the 1836 Rendezvous. He was a member of the party which included Joe Meek, that migrated to the Willamette Valley in the fall of 1840. In the summer of 1849 he was appointed a subagent for Indian Affairs in Oregon Territory.

[2] Johansen, *Robert Newell's Memoranda*, 151. Italics the author's.

[3] *Op. cit.*, p. 110.

According to a family tradition, she attended Chipman Female Academy in Clinton, about twenty miles from her home. It is also reported that she taught school for a time.[4]

On August 20, 1826, when nineteen years old, Eliza joined the Presbyterian Church of Holland Patent on confession of faith. She had a deep religious nature, bordering at times upon the mystical. She knew in Whom she believed and why. There never seemed to be any doubt in her mind on that point. Her whole life after she joined the church was characterized by a complete surrender to what she thought to be the will of Christ.

Sometime during 1830, when Eliza was about twenty-three, she received a letter from a friend in Prattsburg, Steuben County, New York, telling of Henry Harmon Spalding, twenty-seven years old and a student at Franklin Academy in Prattsburg, who wanted to correspond with a pious young lady. Evidently the correspondence which ensued was pleasing to both, for when Henry completed his work at Franklin Academy in the summer of 1831, he enrolled at Hamilton College in Clinton. This placed him in the vicinity of Eliza's home and perhaps of her school if she were then teaching. We assume that they met for the first time that summer or fall.

Henry was not happy at Hamilton College. As a student for the ministry, he was receiving financial aid from the American Education Society.[5] In November, 1838, Henry began a diary. Looking back upon his experience as a junior in Hamilton College, he wrote: "But the hostile spirit against Education students made it necessary for myself & some others receiving aid of Am Ed Soc to change our relations." Consequently Spalding transferred to Western Reserve College at Hudson, Ohio. He returned to Prattsburg for a visit in the fall of 1832 and commented in his diary that he traveled "as far East as Utica." This is rather significant. Utica was the county seat of Oneida County, in which Holland Patent was located. And also Utica was the point where Henry would have left the canal boat to go to Holland Patent if he had traveled from Ohio by water. All evidence points to the fact that sometime during this visit Henry proposed marriage to Eliza and was accepted.

Although positive evidence is lacking, it appears that when Henry returned to Western Reserve College in the fall of 1832, Eliza went back with him. On September 14, 1833, Henry addressed a letter to Captain and Mrs. Levi Hart in which he requested permission for the two to be married at Hudson rather than return to the home of the bride for the ceremony. Eliza appended a note in which she wrote:

---

[4] Drury, *Spalding* gives more detail regarding the early life of Mrs. Spalding. The author has drawn upon his former work for some material used in this chapter.

[5] The American Education Society was supported by the Presbyterians and the Congregationalists for the purpose of helping promising young men prepare for the gospel ministry.

I trust, dear parents, that you will not hesitate to grant the request Mr. Spalding has now made although you have had but a slight personal acquaintance with him. I am happy to inform you that I have found in him a kind and affectionate friend, one in whose society I should consider it a high privilege to spend the days of my earthly pilgrimage.

I shall expect that your affectionate minds (in view of what we now anticipate by your consent) will be relieved from many anxious thoughts concerning my welfare. I presume you do not question the object which induced me to break away from your fond embrace and consent to accompany a stranger, to a land of strangers. If I am not deceived respecting the motive which led me to take this step it was to seek those qualifications which are requisite in order to become prepared for usefulness in the service of my Redeeming Lord.[6]

From the reference to seeking "those qualifications which are requisite," we may assume that Eliza had attended some school in Hudson during 1832-33 when Henry was studying at Western Reserve College. Henry in his letter to her parents mentioned the fact that he and Eliza, if married, planned to go to Cincinnati where Lane Theological Seminary was located. Henry wrote:

We can be pleasantly situated at Cincinnati and I can pursue my studies in connection with the Seminary, and Sister in connection with a ladies' school, or should she think best, recite daily to me as she now does during this vacation. I hear her twice a day. She is making rapid progress in algebra and astronomy.

Parental permission for the marriage was evidently granted for the wedding took place in the chapel of Western Reserve College on Sunday evening, October 13, 1833. Henry was then nearly thirty years old, she was twenty-six.

Having been graduated from the College on August 28 preceding, Henry was ready for his theological course. Lane Theological Seminary, a Presbyterian institution, first opened its doors in the fall of 1833 with the famed Dr. Lyman Beecher as its President. Henry Spalding was a member of the first entering class of forty-two.

Marriage had somewhat complicated Spalding's financial situation. No longer was he eligible for aid from the American Education Society which operated on the principle that if a theological student felt rich enough to get married, he no longer needed financial assistance from

---

[6] The letters addressed to Eliza's parents or to her sister, Lorena, from which quotations used in this chapter were taken, were secured by the author in the summer of 1934 from Mrs. Henry Hart Spalding, a daughter-in-law of Henry and Eliza Spalding. A list of Spalding letters with locations is given in an appendix of Drury, *Spalding*.

the church. Henry and Eliza were on their own. They tackled their problem resolutely. Henry rented a house in Cincinnati and bought a good milch cow. Eliza opened a boarding house, charging three dollars a week for meals. In addition to carrying on his studies at the Seminary, Henry worked in a printing shop, earning three dollars a week.

On March 31, 1834, Eliza wrote a long letter to her sister Lorena, to which Henry added a postscript giving the following information:

> Three of our six presses have stopped which has thrown us out of half of our labor. Consequently, half of our $3 a week. Consequently, three of the six boys that rolled for the presses have left boarding with us. This is the reason why I have given up the idea of Mrs. S. visiting her friends this fall. We would have raised the money very easy, $3 a week at printing, and about $3 clear by boarding. But now we can only comfortably meet our expenses.
>
> Mrs. S. is inclined to teach this season. Our circumstances do not demand it. She thinks she can be doing more good, and at the same time, pursue her regular studies. You may suppose, and justly, that much of her time is taken up in her domestic concerns. She does much work in a short time, as probably you already know. But our boarders are boys not requiring so much care. We have an excellent cow which furnishes milk and butter in abundance, have no tea, coffee or sweet cakes.

Eliza in her two thousand-word letter to her sister goes into more detail regarding the prospect of teaching:

> We have three boarders, but shall dismiss them soon if I conclude to engage in teaching school this season, as I have at present some expectation of it. I have been applied to by a number of the ladies in this society to open a select school here, but was unwilling to accept of the terms they proposed, and consequently declined their offer. I have another in view, at Cummingsville, a small village about five miles distant from this place; I have received some particular information concerning it, and am pleased with the prospect. This school generally averages about forty scholars and the principal manager of the school has resolved to pay $4 a scholar for the term of six months if he can procure a teacher who will answer their demand, and I am inclined to think that it will not require a first rate teacher to satisfy their demand — from what I can learn respecting schools, generally, in this region; they are in a deplorable condition, conducted without much order or interest.

Forty scholars at four dollars each would have realized one hundred and sixty dollars, or $26.66 for each of the six months involved. Information is lacking as to whether or not Eliza took the school. The evidence is clear that she was doing her part to help make ends meet. When Spalding submitted his application for an appointment under the American Board, he looked back upon the two years spent at Lane Theological Seminary and wrote:

> In the course of study sometimes I used the axe, sometimes the saw & sometimes the press. By this means & the aid above mentioned I met all my expenses, secured good health, and regained a firm constitution, & what is more importance God has given me a companion that knows how to "spin" even in these days, in my opinion well calculated for the work we presume to contemplate.

Eliza found time in addition to her busy household duties to join her husband in the classroom. In her long letter to her sister of March 31, 1834, she wrote:

> I am now pursuing Greek and Hebrew studies. I take the same lessons that Mr. S. does in the Greek testament, and in the Hebrew Bible. I am quite pleased with these studies, but find the Greek grammar rather perplexing. I generally attend Dr. Beecher's lectures on theology, Saturdays, from the hours of ten to twelve, which are very interesting and profitable.

The Spalding home became a center for the students of the Seminary who were planning to become foreign missionaries. In her letter to her sister, Eliza wrote:

> Five students, together with one female (who is the intended of one of this little number), have pledged themselves to become missionaries to the heathen, if God is pleased to permit them to be, and have associated themselves, together with us, into a little band which is denominated by us, "The band of missionaries for foreign missions." They meet on Friday evenings in our room for a prayer meeting.

Eliza was a daughter of her generation and used the pious terminology then current. Even as the Jews divided the world into two parts, the Jew and the Gentile; and the Greeks in like manner spoke of the Greek and the Barbarian; so the devout Protestant of that generation classified the world's population into two groups, the Christian and the heathen. The latter term applied especially to all non-Christian peoples living overseas regardless of the degree of civilization to which they had attained or to the nature of their culture. The American Indians were included within the scope of foreign missions and were likewise cataloged as heathen. The Spaldings and their co-workers in Oregon introduced these terms into the thinking and the speech of the Nez Perces. Even to this day the non-Christian Nez Perces are often called "heathens" by the members of the Christian group and the term has been accepted without resentment.

In Eliza's letter of March 31, 1834, we find a statement regarding her motives for desiring to be a missionary to the heathen. She asks her sister this question: "What object can we engage in that will compare with the cause of missions?" And then Eliza answers her own inquiry:

> For this object I wish to exert my powers and spend my strength. The command of our Saviour, and the earnest desire of the heathen for the gospel, are sufficient to prompt us to cheerfully take our commission from the bleeding hand of the friend of sinners, and go to the heathen and bear testimony to them concerning that free salvation which He has in store for all those who will accept of Him on the terms the gospel proposes.

Henry and Eliza were taking the great commission to go into all the world and preach the gospel to every creature personally. It applied to them! Beneath the ecclesiastical clichés of that day which Eliza so freely used, we can discern a deep dedication of life and a profound sense of obligation. "When I reflect," she wrote to her sister, "upon the wretched condition of those benighted souls who are sitting in the gloom and shadow of death, I actually long to depart and be with them, to tell them the story of a Saviour's dying love." Writing from her home at Lapwai in Old Oregon in October 1836, Eliza returns to this theme:

> I trust the only object I had in view on coming to this heathen land was to labor for the temporal and spiritual good of those whose minds are shrouded in heathen darkness. I long to see these precious souls enlightened and interested in the blessings of that gospel which brings life and immortality to light.

CALLED TO OREGON

Spalding took only two years of theological training at Lane Theological Seminary, terminating his studies in the spring of 1835. According to Presbyterian standards, he was supposed to have taken three years' work beyond his college degree. Spalding may have felt it imperative to begin his life's work because of his age. Since he had decided to study for the ministry rather late, he was older than the average student. He had celebrated his thirty-first birthday the previous November.

Another consideration which may have entered into a change of plans was the fact that Eliza became pregnant in February of that year. Looking ahead to the fall, they realized that she would not be able to continue to supplement the family income. How would it then be possible for Henry to continue his studies and support a family?

For reasons not altogether known, Henry decided to apply for a government teaching position in the Choctaw tribe. Since there was some hope of securing this, he did not press his application for an appointment with the American Board of Commissioners for Foreign Missions. In the late spring of 1835, Henry and Eliza left Cincinnati to return to Eliza's home in the country between Holland Patent and Trenton, Oneida County, New York. This was Eliza's first visit to her parents for three years. While there Captain Hart presented his daughter and son-in-law with "a wagon, one horse & harness, $100 & some clothing." This was the famous wagon which was the first to break the Oregon Trail from the Rendezvous on Green River to Fort Boise. In July the Spaldings loaded their few possessions in their wagon and drove to Prattsburg, about one hundred and forty miles distant. No word had yet come from the government. Indeed, a distressing rumor had reached their ears to the effect that all teaching positions had been filled. So on August 7 Henry wrote to the American Board and, after telling of his efforts to get a government position as a teacher to some Indian tribe, applied for an appointment for himself and his wife to any Indian tribe "or on any other heathen ground." He reported that he expected soon to be ordained by the Presbytery of Bath.

Today it would be impossible for an applicant to receive any appointment from any mission board of our larger denominations on such short notice. Educational and ecclesiastical qualifications would have to be checked; a physical examination would be required; and psychological tests would be given. But then it was simpler. Spalding did enclose some letters of recommendation including one from the Reverend Artemas Bullard of Cincinnati. Bullard, in a letter dated August 14, 1835, paid tribute to Eliza. "His wife is very highly respected and beloved by a large circle of friends on Walnut Hills and in Cincinnati," he wrote. "She is one of the best women for a missionary's wife with whom I am acquainted."

Spalding was ordained on August 27, 1835. A few days later he received a letter from Secretary Greene, of the American Board, informing him of his appointment to the Boudinot station among the Osages in what is now western Missouri. Spalding accepted in a letter dated August 31 and explained: "It will be so late before we can start now that we cannot go by land, besides the circumstances of my family are such that it will not be safe to start after some 3 or 4 weeks delay, & it is thought best . . . to remain till March, then go by way of the Alleghany & Ohio." Here we find an indirect reference to the expected birth of a child. The rivers of the Mississippi Valley were the liquid highways of the West. Even though boat travel was exasperatingly slow by modern standards, it was much to be preferred to the tedious alternative of driving overland in a loaded wagon.

Eliza gave birth at Prattsburg to a stillborn baby girl on October 24, 1835. When Spalding began a diary in November, 1838, after his arrival at Lapwai, he first wrote a preface in which he gave a brief resumé of his early life, including the following:

> In Oct the Lord most righteously chastised us for our sins, in taking back the moment he was about to give us a little one. Mrs. S's sickness was protracted & severe but the Lord in infinite love restored her to health & in Dec met our dear friends in Trenton once more & spent a few weeks most happily & perhaps not altogether useless, previous to leaving in Feb.[7]

Sometime in December, after Whitman's return from the Rockies, Spalding heard about Whitman's search for associates to go with him and his bride, Narcissa Prentiss, over the Rockies to Oregon the next year. Such a report would have had only passing interest to Spalding as he and Eliza were already designated for the Osages. But when the suggestion was made that the Spaldings might be just the ones to go with the Whitmans, that was a different matter. The old love affair between Henry and Narcissa came up for discussion. Reference has already been made in a previous chapter of this book to the tactless remark that Spalding made publicly about not wanting to go into the same mission with Narcissa because he questioned her judgment. But when Whitman found it impossible to find anyone else to go and possibly after some urging on Whitman's part, Spalding consented to go to Oregon instead of to the Osages if the Board approved. This willingness Spalding stated in a letter he wrote to the Board on December 28, 1835.

Sometime during the winter of 1835-36, and again the chronology is confused, Narcissa's father, Judge Stephen Prentiss, had a talk with Spalding. Judge Prentiss was concerned regarding the advisability of his daughter being associated with Spalding in the same mission if there were any lingering jealousy or resentment on his part. Evidently Spalding assured the Judge that he harbored no such feelings towards Narcissa. No doubt Spalding pointed to his happy marriage with Eliza Hart. The evidence for such a conversation is found in a letter Narcissa wrote to her father from Waiilatpu on October 10, 1840, in which she said: "The man who came with us is one who never ought to have come. . . This pretended settlement with father, before we started, was only an excuse, and from all we have seen and heard, both during the journey and since we have been here, the same bitter feeling exists."

---

[7] The Whitmans also looked upon the loss of their little girl, Alice Clarissa, as a chastisement from the Lord for their sins.

There is no reason to believe that Secretary Greene, of the Board, had any suspicion of any complications existing between Spalding and the future Mrs. Whitman. In reply to Spalding's letter of December 28, Greene wrote on January 2, 1836, and said: "It does not seem to me desirable that yr designation should be changed to the Rocky Mountain Indians at this time unless you strongly desire it." And there the matter rested for the time being. Whitman continued looking elsewhere for associates and the Spaldings continued making their preparations to go to the Osages.

Sometime during the latter part of December, Henry and Eliza returned to the Hart home at Holland Patent to spend a few weeks before leaving for their mission station. Although we do not happen to know the religious convictions of Eliza's mother, we are told that Captain Hart was not a Christian. We have reason to believe that he was strongly opposed to the idea of his daughter going to the Indians as a missionary. If he had known that Henry and Eliza would be going to faraway Oregon rather than to Missouri, his opposition would surely have been more emphatic. Captain Hart died on February 29, 1846. A friend then wrote to Eliza: "I believe you are not to receive any property without you come here for it. This is very hard, but you know how much opposed he was to your remaining among the Indians." [8] Since Eliza never returned, it is assumed that she never received her part of the estate.

On Monday morning, February 1, 1836, the Spaldings left Holland Patent for Prattsburg. Captain Hart was to accompany them that far. In an affecting scene Eliza bade her mother, her sisters, and her brothers farewell. She was never to see any of them again except her younger brother Horace, who migrated to Oregon in 1846. On the day she started her journey, Eliza Spalding began her diary, evidently written only for herself, which follows.

[8] Drury, *Spalding*, 317.

Diary of Eliza Hart Spalding

In 1916 the oldest daughter of the Spaldings, Eliza Spalding Warren, published her mother's diary from February 1, 1836 to March 3, 1838, in her Memoirs of the West, the Spaldings.[1] *After March 30, 1838, Mrs. Spalding made very few references in her diary to contemporary activities but used it to record her religious meditations. The pertinent sections of this diary, the original of which is in the archives of Whitman College, follows with only minor changes in spelling and punctuation. See illustration on page 201.*

NEW YORK, February 1, 1836

This day I have taken a final leave of my dear parents' dwelling and all its inmates except dear father, who is to accompany us a few days on our journey. While I witnessed the emotions of grief on the part of my dear friends at parting with us, I was enabled in a great measure to suppress my own feelings, until after I had experienced the painful trail of separation. But I trust that it is the love of Christ which has constrained me to break away from the fond embrace of parents, brothers and sisters, and made me, not only willing, but anxious to spend and be spent in laboring to promote my Master's cause among the benighted Indians, who, though they have some idea of a Great Spirit, know nothing of His requirements, or designs respecting them. O blessed privilege to labor in the vineyard of my Saviour, and point the lost and perishing to Him, for He is the way, the truth, and the life.

PRATTSBURGH, STEUBEN CO., N.Y. Feb. 8, 1836

My affectionate and very kind father, who accompanied us as far as Prattsburgh, has left this morning to return home. Oh, what grief at parting, did his eyes which were suffused with tears, his trembling hand, and faltering voice as he bade me *farewell*, betray. . .

FEB. 18 [12], 1836 [2] I have been called to experience another pain-

---

[1] A section of Mrs. Spalding's diary, June 15-July 6 incl., was included in Elliott's *Coming of the White Women*, 1836, pp. 12-16.

[2] The Spaldings spent a week in Prattsburg before continuing their travels. In all probability Henry spoke in the Presbyterian church on Sunday, Feb. 7. There is evidence that he spoke the following Sunday at Howard, N.Y. where Whitman caught up with them on the afternoon of that day. The date of this entry in Eliza's diary should have been Feb. 12, and the date of the next entry, Feb. 14. Since

ful trial, parting with friends at Prattsburgh today. It is indeed trying to part with friends, with the expectation of not seeing them again in this world. But the privilege of laboring to promote my Master's cause among those who are destitute of a knowledge of His salvation, will more than compensate for all that I can sacrifice for this object.

HOWARD, N.Y.   FEB. 20 [14], 1836   To day we met with Dr. Whitman who has been laboring for some time to obtain associates to accompany him west of the Rocky Mountains to establish a mission among the Nez Perces Indians. Those dark minded heathen, having a few years since, learned something about the bible, are now very anxious to receive it and to have missionaries come and live among them.[3] Dr. W's object in seeing us was to ascertain if we were willing to engage in this expedition. He knew we were designated by the Board, under whose patronage we had put ourselves, to labor among the Osages. Yet in his correspondance with the Board, he learned that they were willing our designation should be changed, and we accompany him west of the Mountains, if we were willing. He had failed in every other attempt to obtain some one to go out with him in the capacity of a minister, and if he did not succeed in getting Mr. Spalding to engage in this expedition he should relinquish the idea of going out this season. We had but a short time to decide the question, whether to change our course or not — duty seemed to require it, and we are now with joyful hearts looking for our place of destination west of the Rocky Mountains.[4]

PITTSBURGH — MARCH 1st, 1836   We have at length after a tedious journey of two weeks by land carriage arrived at Pittsburgh, where we

---

wall calendars may have been nonexistent in those days, people often kept track of the days by the entries in their diaries or journals. A mistake made for one day was often carried through a series of entries. See subsequently in Mrs. Spalding's diary for entries beginning March 27. The correct date is indicated in the brackets.

[3] As a part of his argument to persuade the Spaldings to consent to a change of destination, Whitman reminded them of the Nez Perce "delegation" to St. Louis in 1831-32 to get the white man's Bible and Christian teachers. The publicity given through the religious press to this incident was the occasion for the sending by the Methodists of Jason Lee and his companions to Oregon in 1834. Also it was this account which first aroused Parker's interest in Oregon. No like delegation had ever come from China, Africa, or India asking for Christian missionaries. How could the Christian churches of the United States reject such an appeal? Whitman found this a potent argument in his plea to the Spaldings.

[4] In a letter to Greene dated Feb. 17, 1836, Spalding tells of Whitman's plea and of their willingness to go to Oregon. Spalding wrote: "He said all the other attempts to obtain a clergyman have failed and that if I refused, the Mission to the Rocky Mountains must be abandoned, at least for the present." The *Chicago Advance* of Dec. 1, 1870, published an interview by the editor with Spalding in which a dramatic description of the meeting in the Howard inn is given. "Taking a private room, they each prayed in turn, and then left Mrs. Spalding to herself. In about ten minutes she appeared with a beaming face, and said, 'I have made up my mind to go'." *Sen. Ex. Doc., no. 37, 41 Cong. 3 sess., p. 9.*

intend taking a steam boat for Cincinnati. It being now near the close of the week we shall remain here until the first of next week, that we may avoid traveling on the sabbath. We find here many warm hearted friends of the glorious cause in which we have embarked. The 3rd church in particular are doing much for the cause of missions. . .[5]

CINCINNATI MARCH 22, 1836[6] To day we leave Cincinnati in company with Dr. and Mrs. Whitman who are to be associated with us in laboring to erect the standard of the cross on heathen ground. We are to be accompanied as far as Council Bluffs by three missionaries who are designated to the Pawnees.[7] May God bless us in our intercourse with each other, and if permitted to enter upon the great work we have in view, may we find favor in the sight of the heathen, and our presence and labors amongst them be blest to their spiritual and everlasting good.

NEAR THE MOUTH OF THE OHIO MARCH 25, 1836

ON THE STEAM BOAT JUNIUS[8] The waters of the grand Ohio are rapidly bearing me away from all I hold dear in this life. Yet I am happy; the hope of spending the remnant of my days among the heathen, for the express purpose of pointing them "to the Lamb of God who taketh away the sins of the world," affords me much happiness. Surely, "the consolations of God are neither few nor small."

ON THE MISSISSIPPI MARCH 27 [26], 1836 On account of some detentions we have met with since we left Cincinnati we shall not get through to St. Louis before the sabbath but there is nothing in our circumstances that will render it necessary for us to remain on board this boat over the sabbath; shall, therefore, leave it this evening that we may spend the sabbath agreeable to the command of our God.

CHESTER, ILLINOIS, MARCH 28 [27], 1836

SABBATH EVE. We landed here last evening to avoid traveling on this precious, holy day, and it has been, indeed a sweet sabbath of

---

[5] Spalding preached in the Third Presbyterian Church of Pittsburgh on Sunday, February 28. While in the city, Spalding had opportunity to talk with the famous painter of Indians, George Catlin, who had been out on the western prairies in 1832. It was then that Catlin told Spalding that "he would not attempt to take a white female into that country for the whole continent of Am." When Henry told Eliza of this opinion she replied that she would trust in God "and go forward without fear." See Spalding's letter to Greene of March 2, 1836. Spalding added: "I hope we shall be able to take waggons."

[6] The Spaldings left Pittsburgh on the river steamer "Arabian" Monday morning, Feb. 29. Spalding had sold his horses at Pittsburgh but shipped the wagon. They arrived at Cincinnati on March 4, where they were joined by the Whitman party on March 17. In all probability this was the first time that Mrs. Whitman and Mrs. Spalding met. See Narcissa's comment about Eliza in her diary, April 7.

[7] Dr. and Mrs. Benedict Satterlee, and Miss Emeline Palmer who was on her way to be married to Samuel Allis.

[8] The mission party of nine, including the two Nez Perce youths whom Whitman had taken east with him in 1835, boarded the "Junius" at Cincinnati on Tuesday, March 22, hoping to get to St. Louis before Sunday.

rest to my soul. There is no church organized here, and but few who profess to love God. An elderly minister who has been laboring in this region for 18 years has occasionaly held meetings here in a private dwelling, and was expected to preach to them to day for the last time; but at his earnest request Mr. Spalding preached.[9] After the close the discourse, this venerable father in Israel earnestly and affectionately besought his people to improve the means of grace with which they were favored, pointing them to us, as heralds of the gospel to the heathen who were perishing for lack of its blessings which had been confered on them. In addressing us, he said, "18 years have I been laboring in this region, never before to day, has a brother in the ministry called on me to spend the sabbath; I have frequently heard of missionaries passing up the river, but I have not enjoyed the privilege of seeing them. Surely this is an Angel's visit." This has been indeed "a feast of fat things"[10] to us who are about leaving the borders of a civilized and christian land, and I have no doubt it has been to this dear father in Israel who has been laboring so long, single-handed and alone, in this region of moral darkness and death.

> How sweet a sabbath thus to spend
> In hope of one that ne'er shall end.

ON THE STEAM BOAT MAJESTIC.   MARCH 29 [28], 1836   We are now pleasantly situated on the Steamboat Majestic bound for St. Louis at which place we wish to land for a short time. The Lord is still prospering us on our journey, and the probability now is we shall arrive at Liberty in time to take the Fur Co. boat for Council Bluffs which is the only one that goes above the Garrison, 30 miles above Liberty.[11]

ON THE STEAM BOAT CHARITON AT THE LANDING AT ST. LOUIS. MARCH 31 [30], 1836

Arrived at this city last evening. Am not pleased with its appearance, particularly that part which is occupied by the French. The buildings are not splendid, many of them are uncouthly constructed, and it has the appearance of a city going to decay. While walking out this morning with Mr. Spalding, our attention was attracted by the chiming of the bells of the Cathedral and of multitudes flocking to it. Our curiosity was excited to call, but the unpleasant sensations we experienced on witnessing their heartless forms and ceremonies, induced us soon to leave, rejoicing that we had never been left to embrace such delusions.[12]

---

9 Mrs. Spalding, even in the intimacy of a diary written only for herself, always referred to her husband as "Mr. Spalding," never as "Henry."

10 A quotation from Isaiah 25:6.

11 The reference to the Garrison is to Fort Leavenworth. The "Majestic" arrived at St. Louis Tuesday evening, March 29.

12 The Spaldings shared with the Whitmans a strong anti-Catholic attitude. This was common among New England and midwest Protestants of that time.

APRIL 1, 1836 [13]   Left St. Louis this morning on board the Chariton for Liberty. The clerk is a Dea. in Mr. Wisner's church at St. Louis. He joins with us in our morning and evening exercises, which is held in the ladies cabin.[14] The Capt. is not a pious man, but appears favorably disposed. I have not noticed the scenery we have passed but very little, the weather has been unpleasant much of the time and I have contented myself in the cabin with my work and books. My mind is free from anxiety respecting the arduous journey we have in view. The promises of God are sufficient to calm and console the heart that is stayed on Him.

ON THE STEAMBOAT CHARITON   APRIL 7, 1836   The clerk met with us this evening to observe the monthly concert of prayer. It was a blessed season to us, who were on our way to the heathen, for we felt that we were the subject of many prayers. O may not the hopes of Christian friends respecting our usefulness among the heathen be disappointed. May not their prayers be bestowed on us in vain.

LIBERTY LANDING,[15] CLAY Co., Mo.   APRIL 8th, 1836   Arrived at this place yesterday and shall wait here the arrival of the Fur Co. Steam boat, which we expect will favor us with a passage to Council Bluffs. Thus far, journeying has proved beneficial to my health, and we all are now enjoying tolerable degree of health, except Mrs. Satterlee whose health is very feeble.

LIBERTY,   APRIL 14th, 1836   Still waiting the steam boat's arrival. It is now daily expected and we are very busy in making further

---

[13] Another minor error in a date. The steamer left St. Louis Thursday noon, March 31.

[14] Note the comment in Mrs. Whitman's diary for March 31 regarding how she and her husband, on their honeymoon, were enjoying the river scenery from the "top of the boat when the moon was shinning," at which time "Brother Spaulding called us to prayers."

[15] The missionary women were at Liberty from April 7 to about May 3. William H. Gray joined the party there on April 19. In his *Oregon*, Gray left his impressions of Mrs. Whitman and Mrs. Spalding, pp. 109 ff., as follows: "Mrs. Whitman . . . was a lady of refined feelings and commanding appearance. She had very light hair, light, fresh complexion, and light blue eyes. Her features were large, her form full and round. At the time she arrived in the country, in the prime of life, she was considered a fine, noble-looking woman, affable and free to converse with all she met." Regarding Mrs. Spalding, he wrote: "She was above the medium height, slender in form with coarse features, dark brown hair, blue eyes, rather dark complexion, coarse voice, of a serious turn of mind, and quick in understanding language. In fact she was remarkable in acquiring the Nez Perce language . . . She could paint indifferently in water-colors, and had been taught, while young, all the useful branches of domestic life; could spin, weave, and sew, etc.; could prepare an excellent meal at short notice; was generally sociable, but not forward in conversation with or in attentions to gentlemen. In this particular she was the opposite of Mrs. Whitman. With the native women, Mrs. Spalding always appeared easy and cheerful . . . She was considered by the Indian men as a brave, fearless woman, and was respected and esteemed by all."

arrangements for our journey. Mrs. S.'s health continues to decline, the symptoms of her disease appears somewhat alarming.

LIBERTY, APRIL 17th, 1836 Sabbath. Attended a prayer meeting in the village to day, which was got up a few months since by a number of pious females, who being deprived of the stated preaching of the gospel, felt the importance of social prayer. It was an interesting season, and we all seemed to enjoy it much. The sabbath here is regarded by the people generally as a day for amusement — the cause of religion has but few advocates.

LIBERTY, APRIL 23, 1836 This evening Mr. S. Allis, missionary among the Pawnees, and Miss Palmer of Ithica, who journeyed with us to this place, were united in the bonds of matrimony. Mr. Spalding has the pleasure of performing the ceremony. May they live long, and labor for the promotion of their Master's cause among the benighted Pawnees with whom they expect to spend their days.[16]

LIBERTY APRIL 27, 1836 To day Mr. S. and Mr. Gray with the two Nez Perces youths who came to the States with Dr. W. when he returned from the Mountains last year, and one young man to assist them, left Liberty for Council Bluffs. Doct. W. expects to join them in a few days, leaving the missionaries designated to the Pawnees, myself and Mrs. W. to take passage on the steamboat. It was necessary for the gentlemen to make this route by land on account of the waggons, horses and cattle purchased at this place.

LIBERTY, APRIL 28, 1836 Mrs. Satterlee's health is rapidly declining and we are fearful she will not survive many days. She has been informed that the probability is she must soon die. She said that she had not apprehended her case so dangerous, but had thought she should recover. She converses but little, is very stupid but when her sensibilities are aroused to a sense of her situation, she appears reconciled.

LIBERTY, MAY 1st, 1836 Sabbath. Today we have been called to perform the last act of kindness for our friend and sister (Mrs. Satterlee) that is requisite for the body. About 10:00 last night, after affectionately exhorting us to be faithful in our Master's service, she bade us farewel, assuring us that her hope and trust was in the Saviour, and soon without a groan, fell asleep (we trust) in the arms of Jesus. To day while preparing to follow her lifeless remains to the graveyard, to commit it to its mother earth, the Fur Co. Steam-boat which we expected would favor us with a passage to Council Bluffs, passed the landing without halting, refusing to admit any more cargo, or another passenger on board, leaving us to make other arrangements

16 Allis remained either as a missionary to the Pawnees or as a Government employee at the Bellevue Agency until 1851. Drury, *Spalding*, 364.

for our journey to C.B.[17] May we go to the right source for guidance
and direction in this and every other pursuit, that we may indeed
glorify God, our Saviour, in whose cause we hope we have embarked.

LIBERTY, MAY 3d. We have made arrangements to perform the
journey to C.B. by land. Have engaged a team to transport our baggage but we shall travel on horseback. An express is to be sent to
overtake Mr. S. and Mr. G. and have the waggons return and meet us.

FORT LEAVENWORTH [18] MAY 6, 1836 Arrived at this place yesterday and have been waiting here the arrival of the team which has our
goods. Intelligence has just reached us that the waggon is broken and
the teamster discouraged on account of the badness of the traveling.

FORT LEAVENWORTH, MAY 7, 1836 Saturday Have succeeded in
obtaining a team at this place to go on with our goods. We expect to
leave this place this evening and spend the morrow, it being the sabbath, at the Methodist mission station among the Kick-a-poos, 5 miles
from this place. We have been entertained here with that hospitality
which generally characterizes the people of the West.

KICK-A-POO MISSION, MAY 9, 1836 Spent the sabbath very agree-
ably with our friends and fellow laborers in the great work of converting the world at this station. Mr. Berryman and wife stationed here
under the patronage of the Methodist board, appear to be laboring
diligently and successfully for the good of this people. This morning
we leave this place and prosecute our journey through an uninhabited
country till we reach the Mission station among the Otoes.

OTOE MISSION STATION, MAY 19th, 1836 Arrived here today in
safety and good health except Mr. S. who has suffered much for nearly
a week in consequence of taking cold after taking calomel. Camping
out at night has not been so disagreeable and uncomfortable as I
anticipated. Traveling on horseback has appeared to benefit my health,
and I feel encouraged to hope, by the blessing of God that I shall be
enabled to endure the hardships of the long journey we have before

---

[17] The funeral service was scheduled for 3:00 p.m. on Sunday, May 1. Mr. and
Mrs. Allis, Dr. Satterlee, Mrs. Spalding, and Dr. and Mrs. Whitman were all expecting passage on this boat to Council Bluffs. The failure of the boat to stop gave
the suspicion that the American Fur Company was loath to give any encouragement to the missionaries to travel with the caravan. Naturally such a possibility
was most disconcerting to the Whitmans and Spaldings. However, in a letter Allis
wrote to Greene on July 14, 1836, he stated that there was a new captain on
board the vessel who evidently knew nothing about the previous arrangements to
take the missionaries to Council Bluffs.

[18] Writing to Greene from Fort Leavenworth, on May 5, Whitman reported: "I
have some fears with respect to Mrs. Spalding's ability to stand the journey . . .
Mrs. Whitman is very well and in good spirits." Whitman reported the death of
Mrs. Satterlee in this letter and had reason to fear a possible repetition of such
an occurrence.

us.[19] We expected to reach this place in time to leave Bell-view with the Am. Fur Co. under whose protection we expect to travel, as there is no safety in traveling in the Indian country except in large parties. But the Co. left that post 3 days since, and we are fearful if we go on we shall not overtake them, at least before they will pass the Pawnee villages — circumstances appear rather forbidding, and we feel somewhat disheartened.

MAY 22nd.   OTOE MISSION [20]   We have concluded to make an attempt to overtake the Fur Co. Shall leave this place to day with Br. Dunbar, a missionary among the Pawnees who is to accompany us till we meet with our expected guide. When we part with these dear Christian friends, we probably shall meet with no more in this world, unless other laborers come out to join us in our contemplated work.

MAY 24th.   ELK HORN RIVER   We reached this stream yesterday in time to cross, with nearly all our effects in a skin canoe. Our guide has arrived, and Br. D. leaves us this morning to return to the Otoe Mission where he is to spend a few weeks before going with his Indians on their summer hunt. Our guide is to remain with us till we overtake the Fur Co. We are pressing forward on our journey with all possible speed, in hopes of overtaking the Co. before they pass the Pawnee villages, on the Loup Fork.[21]

MAY 27   SOUTH SIDE OF THE LOUP FORK   Last night about 12 o'clock we came up with Mr. Fitz-patrick's camp.[22] Ourselves and animals

---

[19] Although a wagon had been taken along for the convenience and comfort of the women, it appears that Spalding was the first passenger. In a letter dated May 20, 1836, to Greene, he explained: "Two weeks last Monday I received in the breast a severe kick from a mule, the same day was thrown overboard into the Missouri R, and took cold. The pain increased every day till the Doct. came up, he bled and gave calomel . . . For two or three days I have been carried in a wagon." Mrs. Spalding in her diary makes several references to her riding on horseback, thus correcting the impression that is sometimes given to the effect that she always rode in the wagon.

[20] By this time the missionaries were so concerned about catching up with the fur company's caravan that they travelled on Sunday. While passing the Otoe Mission, where the Rev. Moses Merrill, a Baptist missionary, had entertained Whitman a year before, Spalding decided that he would have to leave most of his books. In his letter of May 20 to Greene, he listed some of the titles including all of his Hebrew, Greek, and Latin Bibles, dictionaries, and grammars. He asked Greene to replace some of the works he found it necessary to leave behind.

[21] Loup is the French word for wolf. This branch of the Platte River took its name from the Wolf branch of the Pawnee tribe.

[22] The mission party made a forced march of about sixty miles on Tuesday, May 24, to the Loup Fork in the vicinity of what is now Columbus, Neb. They arrived late at night. The march was particularly difficult for the cattle. By the time the missionaries had crossed the river the next day, the caravan was again in advance and another forced march was required to catch up. Although Mrs. Spalding here refers to arriving at Fitzpatrick's camp at midnight, Mrs. Whitman says that it was 1:00 o'clock on the morning of the 26th. This would explain how Mrs. Spalding, writing on the 27th, could refer to "Last night."

very much fatigued, having for four days past made forced marches in order to overtake the Co. as soon as possible. To day passed 2 Pawnee villages situated on the North Side of the Loup Fork, and are now camped for the night opposite the 3d. Multitudes of natives are crossing over to visit our camp. They inhabit a beautiful country. May they appreciate the kindness of those self-denying missionaries who are laboring to introduce among them the blessings of civilization and religion.

MAY 29th SABBATH MORNING This is the second sabbath that has dawned upon us since we left Otoe. But shall my pen record the manner in which we spent the last, and how we expect to spend this; and perhaps every sabbath during the remainder of this long, long journey we have before us. Oh, the blessed privilege of those who can every sabbath go to the house of God with the multitude who keep holy day, and do not feel themselves under the necessity of journeying on the Lord's holy Sabbath.[23]

JUNE 4th. PLAINS OF THE PLATTE [24] We have been traveling several days on the plains of the Platte. The region of country through which we have passed since we left the Missouri River, is a delightful country. No timber except on the water courses. The soil has the appearance of fertility. We have met with but few Indians. It appears that the natives who once roamed over these vast and delightful plains are fast fading away as is the Buffalo and other game which once in vast herds ranged throughout this country. We have seen a few Buffalo to day which is the first we have noticed.

JUNE 10th Still traveling along the Platte. The majestic sand Bluffs on either side assuming a great variety of appearances, and the extensive plains between the Bluffs and river, covered with beautiful flowers and roses, presents a delightful scenery to the eye of the traveler. I have been quite unwell for several days — and attribute my illness wholly to change of diet, which has been from necessity. Since we reached the Buffalo, our fare has been Buffalo meat. The provisions we brought from the settlement were only calculated to supply us till we could depend on Buffalo, consequently it is spent, and our sole dependance is Buffalo meat for our food through the remainder of our journey, which we do not expect to accomplish, if we are prospered, till some time in Sept. But I am resolved not to feel anxious about what awaits me, for my destiny is in the hands of Him who ruleth all things well.

---

[23] Here is but additional evidence to indicate how much the missionaries objected to Sunday travel. Somewhere in the writings of practically all of the missionaries of both the 1836 and 1838 parties are such references. This grim necessity of travelling on Sunday violated one of their most cherished religious convictions.

[24] Mrs. Whitman in her diary for this day refers to the fact that she, her husband, and the Spaldings were all riding in the wagon at this time.

JUNE 13th   Have reached the crossing place near Fort William,[25] and have camped for the night expecting to cross in the morning.

JUNE 14, 1836   Crossed this morning with all our effects in safety. Two canoes lashed together served for our conveyance. The stream at this place is very rapid. Yesterday while the Co. were crossing their effects, the wind was unfavorable, and in consequence of some mis-management on the part of the boatmen, several bales of goods were lost.

JUNE 15th   FORT WM   We are camped near the Fort, and shall probably remain here several days, as the Co. are to leave their wag-gons at this post and make arrangements to transport their goods the remainder of the journey on mules. It is very pleasant to fix my eyes once more upon a few buildings, several weeks have passed since we have seen a building.

JUNE 19, 1836   FORT WM   To day is the sabbath, and the first we have spent in quietness and rest, since the 8th of May. This morning an elderly man (an Englishman) came to our camp, wishing to obtain a testament. Said he had seen but one, for four years — had once in-dulged a hope that he was a Christian; but for several years had not enjoyed religious privileges — had been associated with ungodly men, neglected religious duties, and now feared he had no interest in the Saviour. I gave him a bible, which he received with great joy and thankfulness. Mr. S. in compliance with the request of the chief men of the expedition, met with the people under the shade of a few trees near our camp for religious services. A large assembly met, and were very attentive while Mr. S. made a few remarks upon the parable of the prodigal son.

FORT WM,   JUNE 21st   This day we are to leave this post, and have no resting place in view till we reach Rendezvous 400 miles distant. We are now 2,800 miles from my dear parent's dwelling, expecting in a few days to commence ascending the Rocky Mts. Only He who knows all things, knows whether this debilitated frame will survive the undertaking. His will, not mine, be done.[26]

JUNE 25   On the 22d we left the Platte.[27] Our route since that time

25 Or Fort Laramie, Wyoming, now a National Monument. Here the missionaries had to cross the North Platte River to the south bank. The caravan remained at the fort for eight days, leaving on June 21. The missionaries left their heavy wagon here and repacked their goods on animals. The average load was about 250 pounds.

26 Mrs. Spalding had some doubts as to whether or not she could survive the journey. Her whole system seemed to rebel against the exclusive diet of buffalo meat on which they were then living.

27 After leaving Fort Laramie, the Oregon Trail cut across the country in a northwesterly direction and met the Platte River again in the vicinity of what is now Glenrock, Wyoming, then west to what is now Casper, then southwest to the mouth of the Sweetwater. In order to follow up the Sweetwater to the summit of the Continental Divide, the caravan had to recross the North Platte to its west bank.

has been through a rugged barren region. To day we came to the Platte but do not find those beautiful plains we found before we came into the region of the Mts.

JUNE 26 Sabbath noon. Camped on the Platte and have the privilege of spending the remainder of this holy day in rest, but not in quiet, for the Co. are busy in making preparation to cross on the morrow. They are under the necessity of constructing a boat, as the river is not fordable.

JULY 4th Crossed a ridge of land today; called the divide, which separates the waters that flow into the Atlantic from those that flow into the Pacific, and camped for the night on the head waters of the Colorado.[28] A number of Nez Perces, who have been waiting our arrival at the Rendezvous several days, on hearing we were near came out to meet us, and have camped with us to night.[29] They appear to be

---

[28] As far as Mrs. Spalding's diary shows, this was just another day's travel. None of the contemporary writings of the missionaries makes mention of the great significance of this first crossing of the Rockies by white American women. In the article which appeared in the *Chicago Advance* for December 1, 1870, we find the following dramatic account:

"July 4th, they entered the South Pass. Mrs. Spalding fainted that morning, and thought she was about to die. As they laid her upon the ground, she said: 'Don't put me on that horse again. Leave me and save yourselves. Tell mother I am glad I came.'

"But the caravan stopped on the 'Divide,' and sent back for her, and she was borne on. She soon revived, and three hours afterward they saw the waters trickling towards the Pacific. And there — it was Independence Day, six years before Fremont, following in the footsteps of these women, gained the name of the 'Path-finder,' — they, alighting from their horses and kneeling on the other half of the continent, with the Bible in one hand and the American flag in the other, took possession of it as the home of American mothers, and of the Church of Christ." *Sen. Ex. Doc., no. 37, 41 Cong. 3 sess.,* p. 11.

A picture, representing this scene, appeared in O. W. Nixon, *Whitman's Ride through Savage Lands,* 1905, p. 56. The flag flies from a flagpole before the covered wagon as the mission party kneels in prayer. A different representation of the same incident is pictured in Eells, *Whitman,* p. 35. Here the artist pictures Spalding standing holding the United States flag on a shorter staff, with the two women, Whitman, and Gray kneeling.

Since the missionaries were accustomed to hold morning and evening devotions, it may be assumed that they had their usual worship service on the evening of July 4 when they camped at Pacific Springs on the west side of the Divide. And it is altogether probable that some mention was made in their prayers that evening of their arrival on the Pacific side of the Rockies. But some of the dramatic details of the prayer meeting described in the *Chciago Advance* are nothing more than the embellishments of a fertile imagination.

[29] Gray in his *Oregon,* pp. 118 ff., tells of a welcoming committee: ". . . some two hours before we reached camp, the whole caravan was alarmed by the arrival of some ten Indians and four or five white men, whose dress and appearance could scarcely be distinguished from that of the Indians. As they came in sight over the hills, they all gave a yell, such as hunters and Indians only can give; whiz, whiz, came their balls over our heads, and on they came. . ." The missionaries were warned that they were friends. One of this number was Kentuc

gratified to see us actually on our way to their country. Mr. Spalding, Doct. W. & Mr. G. are to have a talk with the chiefs this evening.

JULY 6.   Arrived at the Rendezvous this evening. Were met by a large party of Nez Perces, men, women, and children. The women were not satisfied short of saluting Mrs. W. and myself with a kiss. All appear happy to see us. If permitted to reach their country and locate among them, may our labors be blest to their temporal and spiritual good.

JULY 8   A few days rest does not yet appear to benefit my health.[30] My illness rather increases, but all is in the hands of my Saviour, who knows and will do what is for the best. I am happy to sink into His will, concerning what awaits me.

JULY 9   A trader of the H.B. Co. with a party of men has arrived and camped near. He has come to transact some business with the Am. Fur Co. and is to return in a few days to Walla Walla, — has kindly invited us to travel with his camp, promising to afford us all the assistance in his power. This seems a peculiar favor of providence, and quells our anxiety about a protracted and hazardous journey with the Indians who are to take another route and will be detained several weeks in order to take Buffalo.

JULY 12   My health is a little improved, and I have been able to write a few letters to my friends, which will be favoured by a gentlemen of the Am. Fur Co. We feel that we soon shall be situated, if we live, where opportunities for communicating with our friends will be few, but I hope it will be where we shall be useful in our Masters service.

JULY 13   Move about 10 miles to day, to join Mr. McLeod's camp, with whom we expect to travel the remainder of our journey.

JULY 18   Have commenced our journey again for Walla Walla in company with Mr. McLeod. The Nez Perces appear sadly disappointed because we do not accompany them. They say they fear we will not

who brought a letter from Parker for Whitman. Two others were Nez Perce chiefs — Tack-en-sua-tis or Rotten Belly and Ish-hol-hol-hoats-hoats, later better known as Lawyer. That evening these two Nez Perces "were honored with a place at the missionary board." Twenty-seven years later, or in 1863, Lawyer told Gray that that was "the time when his heart became one with the *Suapies* (Americans)." None of the Nez Perces was so enthusiastic in welcoming the missionaries as Tack-en-sua-tis. The first letters of both Henry and Eliza Spalding written from Lapwai bear frequent mention of him. However, after a year or so his friendliness seemed to cool.

'30 Gray, *Oregon*, 123. "Mrs. Spalding was quite feeble, and kept her tent most of the time." During these days at the Rendezvous when a number of the mountain men were regaling Mrs. Whitman with their stories of Indian fights and wild animals, Mrs. Spalding was showing attention to the natives. Gray wrote: "Mrs. Spalding, feeble as she was, seemed to be the favorite with the Indian women." Mrs. Spalding was also beginning to learn the Nez Perce language.

go to their country if we leave them. All appear very anxious to have us locate in their country, that they may be taught about God, and instructed in the habits of civilized life. One chief has concluded to go with us, notwithstanding it will deprive him of the privilege of securing a supply of meat for the winter.[31]

AUGUST 3d — FORT HALL Arrived at this place a little after noon, were invited to dine at the Fort, where we again had a taste of bread. Since we left Rendezvous, our diet has mostly been dry Buffalo meat, which though very miserable, I think has affected my health favorably. This Fort is situated on the south side of Snake River, was built by Capt. Wyath of Boston in 1834 — is exposed to the Black Foot, a savage tribe who glory in spilling the blood of the whites. Several men of this Fort have been killed by these savages. The blessings of the gospel would remedy this evil.

AUGUST 6 Yesterday my horse became unmanageable in consequence of stepping into a hornets nest. I was thrown, and notwithstanding my foot remained a moment in the stirrup, and my body dragged some distance, I received no serious injury.[32] I have suffered but little inconvenience in riding to day in consequence of being thrown from my horse yesterday. The hand of God has been conspicuous in preserving my life thus far, on this adventurous journey. Surely the Lord is my Shepherd, and I shall have nothing to fear, if I will but repose my whole trust in Him.

AUGUST 20, 1836 SNAKE FORT [Fort Boise] Reached this post yesterday — much fatigued — our route since we left Fort Wm. on the Platte, the 21st of June, has been rugged indeed, the country (except a little on the Snake R. about Ft. Hall) dreary, rough & barren. But notwithstanding I have often spoken of the fatigue & hardship I have experienced on this journey, I have experienced many, many mercies which ought to dissolve my heart in thankfulness & cause me to forget the inconveniences I endured on the journey, which by the blessing of God we hope in a few days more to accomplish.

To day is the Sabbath & we spend it in quiet of rest. In compliance with the request of the gentleman in charge of this establishment, Mr.

---

[31] Spalding to Greene, Sept. 20, 1836: "Tackensates is the name of the Nez Perce chief mentioned by Mr. Parker as having come three days to meet him and Doct. Whitman. He also gave us a horse at the rendezvous and said he would stick by us. He came with us to Wallawalla and we found him as good as his word . . . When at Fort Hall we told him he had better go with his people to the buffalo ground and furnish himself with meat for the winter. No, he said, he would trust to that; he wished to go with us. . . He is very strict in his observance of morning and evening prayers."

[32] In a postscript to Spalding's letter of Oct. 2, 1836, to the Porters, Mrs. Spalding wrote: "I was thrown from my horse twice, on our journey in consequence of his taking fright and becoming unmanageable, — but received no serious injury."

Spalding met with the people at the Fort for religious service — the audience was very attentive — have received many favors from the gentlemen of this Fort.[33]

AUGUST 30, 1836 Passed through the G[rand] Round to day — this is a large & very beautiful plain, — derived its name from its appearance, it is circular, surrounded by sloping mountains covered with Pines & Spruce — a beautiful river well timbered passes through it — the soil has the appearance of fertility & to the eye of the traveler who for many weeks has seen nothing by rugged & barren deserts, it presents a very grand appearance.

SEPT. 3d 1836 — FORT WALLA WALLA Reached this post to day. Mr. Pambran the clerk in charge of this establishment kindly received us into his dwelling as guests, for which may we feel true gratitude.

SEPT. 5 Have concluded to visit Vancouver — feel some what rested from the fatigues of the long journey we have in great mercy been permitted to close, for we do not consider the one we now expect to enter upon to morrow, connected with our journey across the Mountains.

SEPT. 14th, 1836 — FORT VANCOUVER Reached this place yesterday after a pleasant journey of 6 days from the time we left Fort Walla Walla (being detained 2 days by head winds) — met with the warmest expressions of friendship, & find ourselves in the midst of civilization, where the luxuries of life seem to abound. Saw many wretched natives along the river, who appeared destitute of the means of living comfortable in this life, & ignorant of the rich provision made for that which is to come.[34] May they soon be blest with the light of the Gospel of our Lord Jesus Christ & with the means for securing a more comfortable subsistance for this life.

SEPT. 22 — FORT VANCOUVER Yesterday Mr. Spalding, Doct. Whitman & Brother Gray left to explore the Cayuse & Nez Perces countries. Mrs. W. & myself remain here till they can select a location & return for us.

OCT. 29 — FORT VANCOUVER Mr. Spalding arrived here a few days since in the Co's Express boat, & we are now preparing to leave in a few days, to locate, we trust for life, in the Nez-Perces country. Doct.

---

33 The missionaries crossed the Snake River a short distance from Fort Boise (or Snake Fort) on Aug. 22. Gray, *Oregon*, 141, wrote: "Mrs. Spalding and Mrs. Whitman were ferried over on a bulrush raft, made by the Indians for crossing. The tops of the rushes were tied with grass ropes, and spread and so arranged that, by lying quite flat upon the rushes and sticks they were conveyed over in safety."

34 Gray, *op. cit.*, p. 146, tells of the excited curiosity shown by the natives along the Columbia River when they discovered that there were two white women in the boats. ". . . numbers of them followed our boats in their canoes to the Dalles, to look at these two strange beings who had nothing to carry but their own persons, and were dressed so differently from the men."

W. has fixed upon a location in the Cayous country, & brother Gray has decided to go to the Flatheads – thus it seems we are about to go to our respective fields, where heathen darkness reigns, single-handed & alone. May the unering hand of our covenant God be extended to guide, assist, & protect us, and bless us, and make us a blessing to the perishing heathen.

Nov. 3d – FORT VANCOUVER   We leave this place to day – have spent several weeks here very agreeable,[35] & I now find myself not only rested from the effects of our long journey across the Rocky Mountains, but in the enjoyment of good health. The agreeable society we have enjoyed, & the luxuries of life to which we have been treated, during our stay here, has made us feel quite at home, and almost to forget what we passed through on our journey to this region. Surely goodness and mercy has followed us all our days.

Nov. 14th, 1836 – FORT WALLA WALLA   Reached this post yesterday, after a protracted & tedious journey up the Columbia. The terrific rapids, whirlpools, &c, on this river, makes a journey up from Vancouver very undesirable to me. The protecting hand of our heavenly Father brought us safely through, & all our effects. May His mercies not be forgotten.

Nov. 22nd, 1836 – FORT WALLA WALLA   The Indians with our goods left here yesterday, for the Nez-Perces country, & we expect to leave to day, hoping soon to overtake them, though we have no fears as to the safety of our goods we have entrusted to their care.[36] They appear to be delighted with the idea of having us locate in their country, that they may be taught about God & the habits of civilized life.

Nov. 29 – NEZ-PERCES MISSION   Yesterday reached this desirable spot, where we expect to dwell the remnant of our earthly pilgrimage. As yet our dwelling is an Indian lodge, which must serve us sometime, for there is no preparation for building yet. Blessed be God that we have been spared to accomplish a long & tedious journey, with our lives & health & many blessings – and are now, we would humbly

---

[35] There is evidence that Eliza and Narcissa both took part in the activities of the school at the fort. Both of the women took time to purchase the necessary supplies for the homes they were about to establish in the upper Columbia River country.

[36] Spalding in a letter to Greene, dated Feb. 16, 1837, said that their effects were loaded on "21 horses." Allowing 250 pounds per horse, this meant that the total amount of the household goods with supplies amounted to about two and one-half tons. The Nez Perces were so happy to have the Spaldings settle in their midst that a party of 150 rode to Fort Walla Walla to escort them to Lapwai. Spalding wrote of his joy in coming to their journey's end: "On approaching this valley, my feelings were peculiar. Ten months had rolled away, rising every morning only to seek a new place to lay our heads at night. Now we were to camp for life."

hope, about to enter upon the glorious, blessed, but responsible work of laboring to introduce the blessings of that Gospel which brings life & immortality to light, among this benighted people, who have long felt that they were sitting in darkness & perishing for lack of knowledge. May we have heavenly wisdom & grace, to labor successfully for the promotion of our Master's cause in this dark portion of His vineyard.

THE NEZ PERCE MISSION HOUSE

The first letters that the Spaldings sent back to the Board and to their relatives and friends in the United States were dated from "The Nez Perce Mission House." Spalding had selected a site near a copious spring which flowed from the base of Thunder Mountain in Lapwai Valley about two and a-half miles up from the place where the creek empties into the Clearwater or Kooskoosky River. At this point the valley is about one-half mile wide between the foothills. The land was free of timber and proved to be very fertile.

Spalding was much more favored than Whitman in the type of Indians among whom he was to live. The Nez Perces were not only several times more numerous than the Cayuses, but they were also far more eager to learn from the white man. Since Whitman was twenty or more miles away from suitable timber for building, he was obliged to use adobes. Spalding, on the other hand, was near timber. Such logs as could not be found nearby could easily be rafted down the river. Until their own log cabin was erected, the Spaldings lived in an Indian lodge made out of buffalo skins. Gray, who went with the Spaldings to Lapwai to assist in building, remained about four weeks.

Under the leadership of Chief Tack-en-sua-tis, scores of the Nez Perce men offered to help. Indeed, there were not enough tools to supply all who volunteered. Some cut down pine trees of the desired size; others carried them to the location; others worked at the whip-saw cutting the boards; and still others under the direction of Spalding and Gray notched the ends of the logs and lifted them into place. One part of the house was completed by December 3 so that the Spaldings could move into it. In his letter to Greene of February 16, 1837, Spalding wrote:

We have now, through the astonishing favor of a kind Providence, a house 18 by 42 completed, with the exception of 2 doors, 2 windows, & a part of the under floor. 18 feet of one end is devoted to ourselves, with cellar, stove and 2 windows. The remaining 24, with chimney and 2 windows is a school room and place of worship. Posts grooved and filled with small timber split. Roof first timber closely laid, then a layer of grass, upon which is a thick layer of clay. All the timber and stone for the building was brought by the Indians, & much of the labor of filling and putting on the roof.

Until the place of worship was ready, we assembled for morning & evening prayers & worship on the Sabbath in the open air, & sometimes, before we closed the exercises, our bare heads would be covered with snow. We might as well hold back the Sun in his march through the heavens, as hold back the minds of this people from religious inquiries.

Spalding was fortunate in having the assistance of an interpreter who no doubt also helped them in learning the language. Eliza opened her school on January 27, and of this Spalding wrote:

Nothing but actual observation can give an idea of the indefatigable application of old and young, mothers with babes in their arms, Grand-parents & Grand-child. Having no books, Mrs. S. with her numerous other cares, is obliged to supply the deficiency with her pen, & print her own books, consequently she can spend but a short time each day in school. But her absence does not close the school. From morning till night they are assembled in clusters, with one teaching a number of others. Their progress is astonishing. . . Usually about 100 attend the school. . . They have learned a few verses & several tunes, which they sing very sweetly. . . Judging from the present, this people will probably acquire the English, before we do the Nez-Perces language, though we flatter ourselves, that we are making good progress.

From this it appears that the Spaldings began teaching English to the natives. Experience proved that this was not practicable, and before a year passed Spalding was at work reducing the Nez Perce tongue to writing.

Spalding in his letter to Greene commented further on the activities of his wife. "For the last 3 weeks Mrs. S. has assembled the girls twice a week for sewing. The attempt far surpassed our most sanguine expectations. Their work is really good." Eliza was also painting some simple pictures in water-color to illustrate Biblical passages. Of this Spalding wrote:

We have represented in paintings, several events recorded in the Scriptures, such as the passage through the Red Sea, the crucifixion of Christ, etc. These I explain first to my crier. I then go over with the subject to the people, the crier correcting my language & carrying out the history. . . If one is to leave camp for some distant part of the country, my crier and the paintings are sent for, and the whole night spent in going over with the subjects to prepare himself to instruct others.

As for food, the Indians were generous in supplying fresh game which supplemented some of the staple items as flour, beans, dried fruit, etc., which the Spaldings had brought from Fort Vancouver. The little herd of cattle driven from the States was divided. Spalding took five cows, a bull, and two calves. In his February 1837 letter, Spalding mentioned a calf three weeks old, so they had fresh milk. During the summer and fall of 1837, after the salmon began to come up the streams, the Indians brought all the fish that they could use. In a letter to Greene, written in September, Spalding mentioned having salted down forty large salmon in four kegs.

Spalding began his farming on a more extensive basis than Whitman in the spring of 1837. He journeyed to Fort Colville, a Hudson's Bay post on the upper Columbia River, in March 1837, leaving Mrs. Spalding alone at the time in an encampment of about fifteen hundred Indians. On this trip Spalding secured fifteen bushels of potatoes from Spokane Garry [37] for seed. Spalding returned home on April 3. In a letter to Eliza's parents dated May 1, Spalding wrote:

Eliza suffered no inconvenience from my absence, except an increase of labor, as the people continued to come for medicine & with questions of more or less importance to be settled, as when I am present.

That spring Spalding sowed two acres of peas and planted seven bushels of his potatoes. The balance of his stock he gave to the Indians to plant. He also planted an assortment of garden vegetables and set out a nursery of apple trees. A beginning had been made in animal husbandry, agriculture, and horticulture which, within a few years, was to make Lapwai the most successful of the four stations [38] which were finally established by the missionaries of the American Board in Oregon. Likewise, no other station had such a large school with so many on the average in attendance, and at no other place were there so many natives receiving Christian instruction.

MRS. SPALDING'S DIARY, JANUARY 1837 TO JULY 1840

JAN. 27, 1837   By the blessing of God we are now in a comfortable dwelling & in circumstances to devote a few hours daily to instructing the natives, who really appear eager to receive instruction. May we who have the privilege of being with this people in the capacity of teachers, be faithful & enabled to impart instruction to them which will be blest to the salvation of their precious souls.

[37] Spokane Garry was one of the Oregon Indians sent to the Red River school by the Hudson's Bay Company in 1825. For a time after his return, he was active in trying to Christianize and civilize his people. He introduced the cultivation of the potato among the Spokanes.

[38] Namely, Waiilatpu, Lapwai, Tshimakain, and Kamiah.

New York.
Feb 1 – 1836

This day I have taken a final leave of my dear
parents dwelling and all its inmates except dear
father who is to accompany us a few days on our
journey. While I witnessed the emotions of grief on the
part of my dear friends at parting with me, I was
enabled in a great measure to suppress my own
feelings, until after I had experienced the painful
trial of separation. But I trust that it is the love
of Christ which has constrained me to break away
from the fond embrace of parents, brothers and
sisters, and made me, not only willing, ~~I trust~~ but
anxious to spend and be spent in laboring to
promote my Masters cause among the benighted
Indians, who, though they have some idea of a Great
Spirit, know nothing of His requirements, or designs
respecting them. O blessed privilege to labor in the
vineyard of my Saviour, and point the lost and
perishing to Him, for He is the way the truth and
the life.

A PAGE FROM THE DIARY OF MRS. SPALDING
See text page 183.

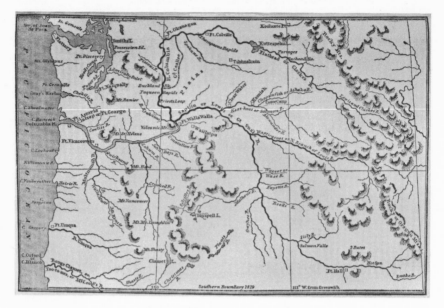

OREGON TERRITORY IN 1844

A map which appeared in the November 1844 issue of the *Missionary Herald,* and was republished in the July 1848 issue after news was received of the Whitman massacre. The mission stations of Waiilatpu, Clearwater, Tshimakain and Kamiah may be seen in the upper center.

TIMOTHY

One of the most faithful of the Nez Perces to the Spaldings, and a friend to the white men. Lived at Alpowa, on the trail between Lapwai and Waiilatpu.

MARCH 20, 1837 Our prospects of usefulness among the people appear very promising. They seem to manifest an increasing interest in instruction, particularly the story of the cross. I have prepared some paintings representing several important events recorded in scripture, these we find a great help in communicating instruction to ignorant minds, whose language, as yet, we speak very imperfectly. The children in particular are interested in learning to read, several are beginning to read in the testament. O may this people soon have the word of God in their own language to peruse, & embrace the truth to become a people, civilized, Christianized & saved.

JUNE 15th, 1837 We feel happy & satisfied with our situation & employment, though it removes us from almost all we hold dear on earth. The privilege of laboring to introduce the blessings of the Gospel of our adorable Redeemer among the destitute heathen will more than compensate for all we have laid aside for this blessed object.

We find this people anxious to receive instruction & to have their children educated. We have taken 8 native children into our family — as yet they appear promising. We hope to come into circumstances soon to do more to benefit the children for they are our hope of the nation. May the Lord help us to labor successfully for the promotion of his cause among this people & send us fellow laborers, & may this great harvest now ripe soon be gathered & saved in the kingdom of our Redeemer.

DEC. 3d, 1837 Through the astonishing mercy of God, I am now enjoying comfortable health. On the 15th of last month, I was made the joyful mother of a daughter.[39] My illness has not been severe, or protracted, & the little one is still spared to us & appears in good health — for these, & the nameless other mercies myself & husband have been made the recipient of, we would call upon our souls & all the powers within us to bless the Lord — & while we bless the Lord for mercies past, we would remember that we are to seek from Him all that we shall ever need. We would humbly pray God to remember us in relation to the little one he has in great mercy committed to our care & seek heavenly wisdom and grace to aid us in discharging the accountable duties of parents. Last sabbath, she with brother & sister Whitman's little daughter were given to God, in the covenant of baptism. O, may they indeed receive the blessings promised to Abraham's seed.

[39] She was named after her mother. She married A. J. Warren and died at Coeur d'Alene, Idaho, on June 21, 1919. In a letter to her parents dated April 21, 1838, Mrs. Spalding wrote: "Little Eliza is a great favorite with the natives, both old and young, and they are so determined to take her into their own arms, that they sometimes almost rend her from mine, and frequently when I am busy about my work, take her from the cradle and not unfrequently I have the mortification to pick a flea or a louse from her clothes. . ."

Doct. Whitman & wife left us yesterday, after a kind & agreeable visit of a few weeks. May the Lord go with them & bless them & their little one, and make them a blessing to the dying heathen among whom they dwell.

FEB. 20, 1838   Our dear babe is still spared to us, but is quite ill of a diarrhea. May we be enabled to do for her all that we should do, & feel an entire resignation to the will of our heavenly Father whatever it may be concerning her.

FEB. 22 – 1838   Little Eliza is very sick, her diarrhea has assumed an alarming appearance, & does not yield to any medecine we have yet administered. May she be spared, and "live before thee," O Lord, – but thy will, not ours be done.

FEB. 25th   O, the goodness of our heavenly Father, through His adorable mercy, dear Eliza appears to be recovering from her illness which we feared would soon terminate her earthly existance. To Him be the glory, and to Him would we feel to consecrate her anew, and ever feel she is His.

MARCH 10th, 1838   Eliza, now appears quite recovered from her late illness, for this mercy in particular we would now bless our God, and seek for blessings not only for the body, but for her immortal soul.

MARCH 19, 1838   I have lately received a note from Mrs. Whitman, in which she makes the inquiry "would it not be well for us mothers to devote a special season & unitedly present our infant charge before the mercy seat?" In reply, I have requested her to mention some hour that we should consecrate for this exercise. I will here insert a few extracts from the note I addressed her on this subject –

As our Heavenly Father has in great mercy, been pleased of late to add to our duties by committing to the care of each of us a tender offspring to train up for Him, I feel persuaded that it is not only our duty but a blessed privilege to unite in prayer for the early conversion of their precious & immortal souls. We may take encouragement from the word of God to associate for this purpose, for it assures us that united prayer is prevailing & more "that the promise is to us & to our children." The smallness of our number & our remote situation from each other seems to be a barrier in the way of our forming ourselves into an association [40] for the purpose of strengthning each others hands in the cause of infant instruction, yet we may unitedly observe a season for special prayer for divine assistance to enable us to discharge the duties that devolve upon us in relation to our infant charge. Our peculiar situation lays us under peculiarly responsible duties as

[40] Mrs. Spalding is referring to the Maternal Associations which were then rather common in church circles in the United States. Such an association was formed in Oregon after the arrival of the reinforcement of 1838. See a subsequent chapter on this subject.

mothers, & we shall need much grace and wisdom to fulfil the responsible duties that devolve upon us as Christian mothers, so that heathen mothers may see by our precept & example that the cares which relate to the bodies of their children are small, & that their chief & great concern should be to bring them up in the nurture & admonition of the Lord.

MARCH 28, 1838   I have received a note from Mrs. Whitman this evening in which she informs me that she has fixed upon the half past eight or nine o'clock in the morning of each day to be observed by us as a season of special and united prayer. If rightly improved they will be precious & profitable seasons. O for grace to improve this & every privilege, in such a manner that I shall glorify God in my body and spirit, which are his.

MARCH 29th, 1838   Resolved, to observe daily at nine in the morning, a season for reading some select portion of scripture & prayer, in unison with Mrs. Whitman, to seek divine assistance in discharging the responsible duties of mothers & for the early conversion of our children.

MARCH 29th, 1838.   Thursday morning   Read part of the 107th Psalm — selected the ninth verse for meditation ("For he satisfieth the longing soul & filleth the hungry soul with goodness".) It was cheering & encouraged me to implore the blessing of salvation for the little ones who are the special subjects of prayer at this hour.

MARCH 30th, 1838 [41]   Friday morning — Read part of the 45th Chap. of Isaiah — found a part of the nineteenth verse ("I said not unto the seed of Jacob, Seek me in vain,") peculiarly encouraging & interesting for this consecrated season.

A RECORD OF RELIGIOUS MEDITATIONS

Having made an agreement with Mrs. Whitman to observe the same time each day for their religious devotions, the nature of Mrs. Spalding's diary changes with the entry of March 29. Passing events receive only incidental mention. Rather, she makes reference to some passage from Scripture and then gives a short comment about it. She was faithful in making daily entries, such as are found in the notations for March 29 and 30 given above, until August 15. This part of her diary is not included in this volume.

Both Mrs. Whitman and Mrs. Spalding showed considerable devotion in their resolve to set apart an hour every morning when each had the care of a small child and was burdened with the many duties required in a pioneer home. On April 21, Eliza wrote: "Observed as usual the consecrated hour." So it was, day after day, for months. An

---

[41] This is the last entry of Mrs. Spalding's diary as published by Eliza Warren in *Memoirs of the West*.

analysis of the Scripture passages mentioned in these devotional exercises shows that she followed no systematic plan of Bible study. Evidently she turned from chapter to chapter as her fancy directed. In this section of her diary are found ninety-two references to the Old Testament, fifty-five of which are in the Psalms, and forty-seven in the New Testament.

At the request of the Whitmans, the Spaldings went to Waiilatpu in August. They left Lapwai on August 8 and arrived at Waiilatpu on the twelfth. Spalding, fearful of leaving a small flock of sheep [42] unattended at Lapwai drove them, together with several milch cows, the 120 miles to the Whitman station. During these days of travel Eliza made entries in her diary concerning religious meditations but did not refer to the journey itself.

A notable event took place at Waiilatpu on August 18 when the Spaldings, the Whitmans, and Joseph and Maria Maki, Hawaiians in Whitman's employ who were members of the mission church in Honolulu, organized the First Presbyterian Church of Oregon. This was the first Protestant church to be established on the Pacific Coast. The next day Spalding solemnized a marriage between Charles Compo, a former Roman Catholic, and his Indian wife after which service Compo was received into the church on confession of faith. Even such interesting events passed unrecorded in Mrs. Spalding's diary.

On August 21 William H. Gray suddenly appeared at Waiilatpu with his bride, Mary, and with the wonderful news that three more couples and a single man were following as a reinforcement to the Mission. They were the Reverend and Mrs. Cushing Eells, the Reverend and Mrs. Elkanah Walker, the Reverend and Mrs. A. B. Smith, and Cornelius Rogers. By the thirtieth, all had arrived. On September 1 the men met in business session and on the third the women got together and organized the Columbia Maternal Association with Mrs. Spalding as its first President.

On Tuesday, September 4, the Spaldings, the Grays, Charles Compo, James Conner (a former mountain man), some Nez Perces, the sheep, the cows, the pack animals and extra horses, started for Lapwai. They arrived at the mission station on Friday, the seventh. For several weeks Eliza found it impossible to record her times of devotion in her diary. The break comes from September 16 to the thirtieth. Then she wrote: "For two weeks past have been in circumstances unfavorable for recording the daily exercises I have observed, but they are registered in the Book of God's remembrance & will not be lost if they have been performed aright."

---

[42] The exact number is not known. According to a letter Spalding wrote on Feb. 18, 1842, he originally received five female and three male sheep sometime in the summer of 1838. Drury, *Spalding*, 186. This marked the beginning of Idaho's sheep industry.

On September 30, Mrs. Spalding resumed making her daily notations about her devotions. Many of the Bible passages selected reflect
her strong reliance on God's protecting care and directing providence.
She ceased making entries after September 19, 1839. This does not
mean that she thereafter failed to observe her daily devotions but
rather that she no longer felt the need to write out her meditations as
she had been doing. Her second child, a son named Henry Hart, was
born on November 24, 1839. With two little children to care for, Eliza
no doubt found it impossible to maintain her former schedule.

Dec. 20th 1840 [year should be 1839.]   The Lord has been pleased
to add to my duties & cares in the gift of a dear Son — born on the
24th ult. Though Eliza seemed to fill my heart, I find that another has
now an equal share of a mother's affection & solicitude. Only through
Jesus Christ strengthening me, shall I be enabled to educate these
precious lambs for Him who has committed them to my care.

April 12th /40 Sabbath. To day Mr. Spalding administered the
ordinance of baptism to our dear son, Henry Hart & a little son &
infant daughter of Mr. Conner & an infant son of Joseph. . .[43]

June [month should be July] 8th — 1840 [44]   Early this morning felt
that I was in deep waters where the floods overflowed me — & felt
impatient to be delivered from the trying straits in which my dear
husband & myself have long felt ourselves to be in, in our relations
with our brothers & sisters of this Mission. I greatly feared that the
unhappy state of things which seems now to exist amongst us, would
stand in the way of the salvation of the heathen, to whom we had been
sent as heralds of the gospel of our Lord Jesus Christ. I felt to desire &
pray that the few remaining sons of the Red Man might be given to
Jesus & that the Lord who is stronger than the strong man armed
would in infinite mercy appear for them.

I soon had the unspeakable happiness of feeling that Jesus was with
me in the deep waters, & that the design of my being kept there was
only to purify me from my sins — & my confidence that He would
glorify His great name in the salvation of many of these precious souls
about us, was greatly strengthened.

Lord, may I ever trust in thee — here am I, do with me as shall seem
good in thy sight.

[43] Spalding in his diary makes mention of these baptisms. See Drury, *Diaries of
Spalding and Smith,* 288. The infant son of Chief Joseph, later called Old Joseph,
was probably Young Joseph.

[44] The annual meeting of the Mission was held at Lapwai beginning on July 4.
Mrs. Spalding's error in noting the month as June is unexplainable. At this meeting
personality differences between Whitman and Spalding were so strained that
Whitman declared that either he or Spalding would have to leave the Mission. See
Drury, *Spalding,* 250. The old love affair between Henry and Narcissa came up
again for discussion. However, a spirit of brotherhood finally prevailed and a
reconciliation was effected.

JULY 28 — 1840 I have just been reading a sermon the title of which is, "Prayer for the children of missionaries" — It was delivered by a missionary, who appears to feel the importance of educating the children of missionaries for God, & the necessity of prayer, united prayer, to accompany the efforts made for this object. . .[45]

What missionary who has children, but will breathe the same desires in relation to his children, & for the same reasons?

Thus Mrs. Spalding's diary closes on this note of prayerful concern for the Christian education of her children.

[45] Mrs. Spalding copied off several hundred words of the sermon which are here omitted.

At Lapwai

THE COLUMBIA MATERNAL ASSOCIATION

The first woman's club to be established on the Pacific slope was the Columbia Maternal Association which was organized by the six women of the Oregon Mission of the American Board at Waiilatpu on Monday, September 3, 1838. It was modelled after similar Associations then common in Protestant church circles in the East.

While the men of the Mission were busy working out the details of an enlarged program, the women drew apart and organized their society. The first officers were: Mrs. Spalding, president; Mrs. Walker, vice-president; Mrs. Whitman, corresponding secretary; and Mrs. Gray, recording secretary. Mrs. Eells and Mrs. Smith were mere members. At the time of the organization, Mrs. Whitman and Mrs. Spalding were mothers. Mrs. Walker and Mrs. Gray were both pregnant, although Mrs. Gray was trying to keep this fact a secret.

The following preamble to the Constitution, which admirably sets forth the purposes of the Association, was adopted:

> Sensible of the evils that beset the young mind especially in a Heathen land, & confident that no arm but God's can secure our children or those commited to our care, from the dangers that surround them, to bring them early into the fold of Christ and fit them for usefulness here & glory hereafter, we the subscribers agree to form ourselves into an Association for the purpose of adopting such [methods] as are best calculated to assist us in the right performance of our Maternal duties.[1]

Never again after the initial gathering at Waiilatpu were all members of the Mission, including the women, able to be together at the same time. Only twice, February, 1839, and July, 1840, were all of the men able to assemble in the same place. Recognizing the difficulties of getting together because of their widely separated stations, the women agreed to meet in their respective stations "on the second & last wednesday in every month." The women also agreed to read suitable

---

[1] The original record book of the Columbia Maternal Association is in Coll. w. The June 1938 issue of the *Oregon Historical Quarterly* carried an article by the author on the history of this Association.

literature dealing with motherhood and the care of children at their meetings and to join in prayer for all of the mothers and children of the Association. Subscriptions were placed with the *Mother's Magazine*, the national journal of the movement.[2]

The record book of the Association carries the minutes of only one annual meeting, that held at Waiilatpu on September 3, 1839. This was at the time of a Mission meeting but the Walkers and the Eells were not able to attend. The minutes were kept in the handwriting of Mrs. Gray who added the names of the five wives of the independent missionaries and also those of Mrs. Jane McDonald and "Mrs. McKenlay", wives of Hudson's Bay officials. This brought the total membership to thirteen. The record book also listed the names and birthdays of twenty-five children, the last being that of Joseph McDonald, born March 14, 1846.[3] The book also recorded the deaths of several of the children beginning with that of Alice Clarissa Whitman on June 23, 1839.

The Federation of Women's Clubs for the State of Washington at their annual meeting held at Walla Walla, Washington, June 15-18, 1938, observed the centennial of the Columbia Maternal Association. At that time it was pointed out that the General Federation of Women's Clubs had been inspired by the story of the Columbia Maternal Association to create a committee on Religious Education in the home. One of the national leaders said: "I decided that if those women, under such difficulties, could bind themselves together to defend their children in matters of spiritual interests, we women today, facing other but equally difficult conditions in rearing children, could do as much without injury to our organization."[4] In a letter to the author dated June 22, 1938, Mrs. Ruth Karr McKee, a granddaughter of Elkanah and Mary Walker, wrote: "Thus an emphasis on spiritual instruction for little children in the home is brought into the program of the 2,000,000 clubwomen in America, through the reflected influence of that little group of women from a century ago."

THE SPALDING HOME ON THE CLEARWATER

The Spaldings had a distinguished visitor in April, 1838, when Jason Lee, head of the Methodist Mission in the Willamette Valley, called. Lee with several companions was on his way East to get reinforcements for his work. He visited the Whitmans at Waiilatpu from April 14-17 and then went to Lapwai where he remained until the twenty-

---

[2] Mrs. Whitman wrote a letter to the editor of the *Mother's Magazine* dated April 16, 1846, which appeared in vol. xiv, pp. 279 ff.

[3] Some of the entries of births and deaths were made by some other person than Mrs. Gray, who with her husband left the Mission in the fall of 1842.

[4] Drury, *Walker*, 265.

third. Sometime during the early days of 1839, Lee visited Portland, Maine, where he is reported to have "addressed an immense crowd in the Methodist Church." An interview with Lee appeared in the February 7 issue of the Portland *Christian Mirror* which contained the following:

> Mrs. Spalding was so oppressed with labor, that she could not have the society of even her own little daughter. The child was put in a rude kind of wagon in the morning to be drawn about by Indian children, while the mother was occupied with her domestic cares or the instruction of her Indian class, or in watching their garden and wheat field, or seeing that it was watched, lest the crop should be destroyed by the rapacity of brutes. She had been left without husband, or any white attendant or companion for two weeks in succession — her husband gone, perhaps to the coast or trading post or depot, to obtain seed, from the growth of which they might afterwards be sustained.

The wheels of the "rude kind of wagon," to which Lee refers may have been thin cross-sections of a log.

Within a year after the Spaldings had settled at the foot of Thunder Mountain in Lapwai Valley, they realized that a better location would have been on the bank of the Clearwater near the mouth of Lapwai Creek. The summer is often oppressively hot in that region, with the thermometer rising to 110°F or more. There would be more breeze and fewer mosquitoes along the river than in the narrow valley of the creek. Moreover, the river provided easy transportation when such was needed. So by the spring of 1838 Spalding had decided to build another cabin on the Clearwater.[1]

Whitman spent a week in June helping Spalding get the necessary timber down the river to the site. The natives were just as ready to assist as when the first house was erected. During the summer a cabin 32 x 22 feet, one and a-half stories high, with a fireplace at each end, was built. In a letter to Greene dated September 11, Spalding reported that he had used cedar shingles on the roof. This is the first mention of the use of shingles instead of a dirt roof in the history of the Mission. Short cedar logs are easily split and the cedar "shakes" make excellent shingles. Spalding divided his house into two large rooms, two bedrooms, and a "buttery" on the lower floor. Above were three small rooms and a storeroom. Henry and Eliza moved into their new house in September upon their return from the mission meeting at Waiilatpu, although the roof was not yet completed.

---

[1] The site was long known as Lapwai but when the government established a military post four miles up the creek about 1890, the name shifted to the new location. The old site then became known as Spalding. See illustration page 220.

The next four or five years were years of great growth in all phases of the missionary activity at Lapwai.[2] In a letter to Greene dated December 10, 1838, Spalding reported that with native help he had erected a house for the eight or ten native children that the Spaldings had taken into their home to educate. Later some of these young people proved to be valued assistants in the school. Spalding also reported the erection of a blacksmith shop, and a schoolhouse which measured 40 x 20 feet. The Indians were receptive to the Christian message and many cooperated in Spalding's endeavors to introduce the arts of civilization. Spalding's letters to the Board for these years overflow with enthusiasm as he describes one achievement after another.[3]

No Protestant missionary to Old Oregon was so successful in his efforts to civilize, to educate, and to Christianize the natives as was Spalding. And no missionary had a more enthusiastic and indefatigable assistant than Henry had in his wife Eliza. While Henry was teaching the men how to till the soil, and how to care for cattle, sheep, and hogs, Eliza was busy teaching the women how to spin, weave, knit, and sew. The versatile Henry managed to make a spinning wheel, in 1840, and then wrote for weaving equipment. A loom was in operation by August, 1841. This was the only loom in the Mission.

Both Henry and Eliza gave themselves without reserve to the work of the school.[4] A printing press arrived from the mission in Honolulu

---

[2] Spalding began a diary on November 26, 1838, which he kept with fair regularity until April 22, 1842. This was published in full in the author's *Diaries of Spalding and Smith*. This volume describes in more detail than can be given here the events at Lapwai during these years.

[3] No member of the Oregon Mission wrote so many long letters to the Board as did Spalding. Lengthy extracts from these letters were printed in the *Missionary Herald*, the official organ of the Board. Some of the selections published during 1837, according to A. B. Smith, painted a too optimistic picture and were, therefore, misleading. A summary of the number of column inches of the *Herald* devoted to the Oregon Mission gives the following for the years indicated: 1836—96 inches; 1837—234; 1838—148; 1839—48; 1840—193; 1841—31; 1842—9; 1843—113; 1844—44; 1845—21; 1846—6; and 1847—5. Beginning with 1841 when the editor discovered that there was dissension within the Mission, the amount of space given to Oregon was sharply curtailed until only the briefest mention was made in 1846 and 1847.

[4] In a letter dated Dec. 17, 1838, to Levi Chamberlain, a missionary of the A.B.C.F.M. in Honolulu, Spalding set forth his philosophy as follows: "My little experience in the work not with Indians only but with all men, convinces me that it is not the occasional, but the oft repeated & constant blow of the hammer that breaks the flinty rock. If a benighted people grown up in ignorance & superstition are to be evangelized, in my opinion, it can not be done while they are upon the wing, hearing a sermon only once in 3 or 12 months . . . Surely no one will think of attempting to introduce a system of education among a people who are in one place only a week at a time. No, I am fully convinced, if this people are to be permanently benefited by the gospel they must be settled. Efforts to civilize must go hand in hand with efforts to evangelize." The original letter is in

in April, 1839. From this press came primers, hymn books, and the Gospel of Matthew in Nez Perce. Eliza's letters bear frequent mention of her activities in copying lessons, helping to prepare material for the press, and finally in binding the printed product. With only the occasional and sometimes halfhearted assistance of the Grays or with the limited help of some of the independent missionaries or some passing immigrant, the Spaldings led in the gigantic task of changing the age-old living habits of a tribe of about five thousand people.

About one hundred families were cultivating land in the vicinity of the mission station at Lapwai during the spring and summer of 1839. In a letter to Greene dated April 1, 1840, Spalding reported that up to that time he had supplied "perhaps 750" hoes to the people. And on the twenty-second of that month he wrote: "Probably a hundred and fifty hoes are going from morning till evening." Henry and Eliza never lost sight of their ultimate goal, that of making Christians out of the natives. A settled community was basic to any systematic work in the school or for a continuous program of religious instruction. Civilization was but the necessary means by which evangelization could be effected.

All of this is background for the understanding of an illuminating letter that Eliza Spalding wrote to Mrs. A. T. Smith,[5] parts of which follow:

MRS. SPALDING'S LETTER OF FEBRUARY 14, 1842

MY DEAR SISTER . . . The Lord has blessed us this winter, with health and many opportunities for laboring amongst this people. Our meeting last fall with them continued nine days — was interesting and solemn — a great multitude were present — some few appeared serious and inquiring.[6] The Five Crows from Waiilatpu (who is a half-brother

the archives of the Hawaiian Mission Children's Society, Honolulu. Spalding once had his picture taken with a hoe in one hand and a Bible in the other to illustrate his philosophy of evangelization. See Drury, *Whitman*, 216.

[5] Mr. and Mrs. A. T. Smith, independent missionaries, arrived in Oregon in the fall of 1840 and spent that winter with the Spaldings. They remained until Aug. 25, 1841. Mrs. Spalding was writing to one who knew the Indians mentioned. The original letter is in the archives of Whitman College.

[6] Beginning in Oct. 1841, Spalding held protracted meetings for the Indians at Lapwai when, according to his estimates, about 2,000 were present. A number of the Indians expressed a desire to join the church but Whitman refused to permit them to become members until some differences between himself and Spalding were settled. See Drury, *Spalding*, pp. 274 ff. On May 14, 1843, when Whitman was absent on his eastern mission, Spalding received nine into the church including Levi, a brother of Timothy; Luke and his wife Eunice; Hezekiah or Fve Crows from the Cayuse tribe (only member of this tribe to join the Mission church); Asenath, wife of Joseph; Tamer, wife of Timothy; Olive, wife of Oliver; and Lyman, a Shoshone Indian "having been taken a slave when young," and his wife Lois. See Records of the Church, *Minutes of Synod of Washington*, 1936, p. 290.

of Joseph's) was present during the meeting and was particularly serious.[7] Joseph and Timothy [8] were very faithful with him and we humbly hope and trust their labors were not in vain. . . Near the close of the meeting, James became disaffected from some remarks of Timothy's which were well calculated to endanger the old man's craft.[9] He left in a few days for the Dalles. He has returned and now appears friendly.

Conner and Craig [10] have settled here. . . They appear kind and friendly. A good no. [number] of the people are spending the winter here. We have had a very quiet time with them thus far. Ellis was here during the meeting and remained several weeks, during which time he attended school, and was not only a scholar, but an assistant. He has never, before this, seemed favorably disposed. He now seems interested in what we are doing, and has resolved to go and do likewise, in some respects. He, with the Lawyer have concluded to settle at Kamiah this spring. We hope the Lawyer will receive a heifer calf for his services here this winter. He will if there are no objections on the part of the other members of the mission. Ellis has obtained a cow and two young cattle from W.W. He is also expecting Mr. McKinlay to furnish him with farming utensils and some mechanic tools, tin ware, etc.

He remarked that when he saw how comfortable we were in consequence of our own labors, he felt that he was very foolish to live in the manner he was living, since he was capable of laboring. He talks of taking some horses to the Willamette this spring to exchange for cattle, etc. He has the greatest number of horses, of any one amongst this people. We hope he may become a useful man. I paid a good deal of attention to him while he was in school,[11] and told him that it would

---

[7] See footnote 7 in section "The Tragedy at Waiilatpu."

[8] Joseph and Timothy were the first natives to be received into the church. They were baptized and received on confession of faith on November 17, 1839. Joseph later gave up his Christian profession, largely because of his loss of faith in the integrity of the white man, but Timothy remained as the most shining example of a native Christian. The original record book of the church is in the archives of the Presbyterian Historical Society, Philadelphia.

[9] James, sometimes Old James, was head of the band that lived in the Lapwai Valley before Spalding settled there. In this same letter Mrs. Spalding wrote of James: "Poor old man, his medicine business seems to be his delusion." James later gave Spalding a lot of trouble.

[10] James Conner, a former mountain man, was received in the Mission church with Timothy and Joseph. On Feb. 4, 1843, he was suspended "for the sin of Sabbath breaking, neglect of religious duties & fighting." He was also accused of polygamy, "sending a challenge to fight a duel, and vending liquor." See *Minutes of Synod of Washington*, 1936, p. 290. William Craig, another mountain man who had as his wife a daughter of Old James, took a homestead about eight miles up the valley from Lapwai. He also caused Spalding trouble.

[11] Ellis, who was then in his early thirties, had spent four years as a youth in the Episcopal mission school at Red River, (now Winnipeg, Canada). He had a good speaking knowledge of English. He was selected to be the first Head Chief of the Nez Perces in December, 1842, when Indian Agent Elijah White tried to

be well for him to have a school if he settled at Kamiah. The idea seemed to please him very much. The Lawyer has become deeply interested in learning to read. Himself and his two eldest children [12] are making good progress in learning to read.

A new school room now takes the place of the old one. It is 21 by 17 feet. The frame is of sawed timber, the covering is of boards matched. Three, 12 light windows, a writing desk extends across one side, a stove in the center and daily it is well filled with interesting learners. A class of adults have made it their business to attend school through the winter thus far. I will give their names as some of them are familiar to you. Joseph, Timothy, Luke, Lawyer, Stephen, Jason, Five Crows (Joseph's brother) [or] Hezekiah (the young man who attended the saw mill sometime, last spring), Lot, (Connor's father in law), Mary (Jacob's wife.)[13]

A few verses of scripture printed with the pen in a small book and given them, I think [has] done much to bring this class into school, and the daily addition of a few verses, I also think, has secured their regular attendance. Their books have cost me much labor, but when I see them and their progress, which is very encouraging, I feel more than compensated for all I do, and am constrained to say, it is a privilege! The form of their books, is a sheet of paper folded into eight leaves. They have now about 30 pages printed. About half of the class now print very well from a copy. . .

When the class of adults are about to commence reading, E[dwin] is generally seated by some one who needs attention. Sarah or Abigail by their father, Jane by her sister. This assists me very much. A class of boys which usually numbers between 20 and 30, are now under Edwin's care principally. Abigail, Ann and Matilda take charge of a class of girls, about the same no. of the boys. One class of small boys is under the care of Amos. A fine class of bright little girls are attended to by some of the large girls. . .

Delia [14] Jane and Sarah, with my assistance have made 24 yards of

introduce a system of laws among the Nez Perces. He died with several members of his family in the buffalo country early in 1848. See Mrs. Walker's diary, for April 6, 1848 (in vol. II of this work).

[12] Lawyer had two sons, James and Archie, to whom reference may here have been made. Archie Lawyer was ordained by the Presbyterian Church in 1881. Lawyer became Head Chief of the Nez Perces in 1848 and served as such until 1871. Contemporary references to him are usually as "The Lawyer" rather than as "Lawyer." See Drury, "I, The Lawyer," in New York Westerners, May, 1960.

[13] Here is the key to the success of Henry and Eliza Spalding as missionaries to the Nez Perces. They paid special attention to the chiefs and to the leaders of the tribe.

[14] Spalding, in the Record Book of the Mission church, makes note of the death of Delia, "wife of Edwin" in May, 1846. She died "of consumption." Spalding baptized her before her death and gave the following tribute: ". . . the most amiable Indian girl I was ever acquainted with, very regular in her Christian habits & character."

good substantial woolen cloth, it is some less than ¼ [of a yard] in width. Two thirds of the yarn was black, a little yellow, a little couloured with ink-powder and a little red baize picked to pieces and mixed with white wool make up the whole. They look to me much more comfortable and respectable in these dresses than in any others I have ever seen them wear. They have also knit themselves yellow stockings, which colour I should not fancy for my own use, yet admire to see them in theirs. . . Jacob's wife, Abigail Ann and Matilda have knit themselves leggins. . . Some appearances of civilization and improvement I think, we now really see. All Glory to God if any good has been accomplished through our instrumentality. I sometimes allow myself to feel, that perhaps God may be pleased to make use of the *weak things* to assist in building up His cause amongst this people. . .   E. H. SPALDING

MRS. SPALDING'S ILL HEALTH

Writing to his friend, A. T. Smith, on January 7, 1843, Spalding boasted that the enrollment of the school had risen to "two hundred and twenty-four in regular attendance, including all the principal chiefs and men in this vicinity." And on October 10 of that year, in a letter to Chamberlain in Honolulu, Spalding stated: "Last year about 140 families cultivated from ¼ of an acre to 5 acres each. . . This year I think the No has been increased 1/3. Last year one of the members of the church raised 175 bushels of peas, 100 buh of corn, some 400 of potatoes." [15] Seemingly the Nez Perces were making wonderful progress in their transition from the old ways to the new.

The enlarged enrollment in the school plus the many other increased demands upon her limited strength often resulted in Mrs. Spalding being physically exhausted. Following Whitman's departure for the East in October 1842, Spalding found it necessary to go to Waiilatpu. He left his wife alone with their two little children, Eliza and Henry Hart. While at Waiilatpu a messenger arrived with a letter from Eliza saying that she had suffered a miscarriage with a consequent severe hemorrhage. Spalding fainted before he had read the whole letter. He and an Indian companion left Waiilatpu at nine o'clock that evening and by daybreak had ridden sixty-five miles. They reached Lapwai before sundown and to Henry's great relief found Eliza not only still alive but resting comfortably. Spalding and the Indian established a record by riding the one hundred and twenty miles in nineteen hours.

After recovering from this illness, Eliza was able to resume her teaching for a time. Then some time in the late winter or early spring of 1843, she was taken ill with a severe cold which put her to bed for

---

[15] Original letter in the Spokane Public Library. The reference here is possibly to Timothy who was one of the most diligent in developing his farm.

a time. In a letter to old friends in Ohio, Eliza on July 29, 1843, gave many details about her home, her work at Lapwai, and her illness. The following extracts are taken from this letter.

The reaching of this people after the means of civilization, their desire to learn to read &c furnish much more work for us, than we should doubtless undertake to do, . . . We never get but two meals a day, & one of these are generally mush & milk — our correspondence with the civilized world is very limited, & long periods necessarily intervene between. Thus you see, our family cares are less than they might be, & our intercourse with friends less than we could wish, did it not rather intrude upon more important duties. . .

Our school house communicates with our dwelling house, which renders the difficulty of attending to my domestic affairs, & the school at the same time, much less, than it would be, were it otherwise. . .

I was obliged to leave the school on account of a severe illness, occasioned by taking cold which settled on my lungs & brought me very low with many hectic symptoms. The old chief . . . used to call every day to see how I was, & always expressed much regret that my place in school was vacant. He said he believed, that if I should die I should go to heaven, but he should weep to see my place in school & in the family, vacant. After I began to recover, he seemed to be much rejoiced, & told me, he believed I was spared in answer to their prayers, for said he, as the friends of Paul prayed for him when he was in prison, so have we prayed for you. . .

Another chief who is much interested in the school, & who rather excels in learning, called to see me one evening after it was thought I probably should not recover, & said he wished to express his feelings. This speech was most concerning what I had done in school, his gratitude for it & his grief in view of my being about to be taken away from them. Said he "could it be I would die in your stead that you might live to teach my people."

Other passages from the letters of Henry and Eliza could be quoted to show the large amount of time and energy the two were giving to their work, and also of the great affection that the natives had for Eliza.

During the summer of 1843, shortly after Eliza had written the letter mentioned above, she was stricken with scarlet fever. Dr. Whitman was then on his way back with the great immigration of 1843. There was no other doctor available. For nearly two weeks during the latter part of August, she hovered between life and death. Eliza was so certain that her end was at hand that she called her husband and children to her bedside and gave them farewell instructions. Spalding sent word to the Walkers and the Eells at Tshimakain to come and attend her funeral. However, Eliza began to recover. Then Henry and the two children became seriously ill with the same disease. Word was sent to Dr. Whitman to hasten to Lapwai. The messenger found Whitman in the Grande Ronde Valley. Turning the care of the immigrants over to faithful Stickus, Whitman hastened to Lapwai. He arrived there on September 25 and fortunately found all on the way to recovery.

These were some of the health hazards faced by the Spaldings in their lonely and isolated home on the bank of the Clearwater.

Two more children, both girls, arrived at the Lapwai home before the Spaldings were obliged to leave for the Willamette. They were Martha Jane, born March 20, 1845, and Amelia, born December 12, 1846.

THE PROTESTANT "LADDER"

One of the most unusual aids used by both Protestant and Roman Catholic missionaries in their endeavor to convert the natives of Old Oregon was a form of pictorial representation of biblical and Christian history called a "Ladder." The use of such a device may have arisen out of Spalding's use of pictures of biblical scenes which were painted by Eliza. From the very beginning of his work at Lapwai, Spalding used such aids. Gray remembered how Spalding once, wishing to emhasize the divine importance of work, had his wife paint a picture of Adam with a hoe in his hands and Eve with a spinning wheel.[1] Such pictures as those which showed the crucifixion made a deep impression upon the natives. Some of these water-colors passed into the hands of the Indians who cherished them with an almost superstitious awe.

In the late fall of 1838 the first two Roman Catholic missionaries arrived in Old Oregon. They were Abbé François Norbert Blanchet and Abbé Modeste Demers. They arrived by way of the Hudson's Bay Company's overland express from Montreal. During the spring or summer of 1839, Father Demers made two excursions to Forts Colville, Okanogan, and Walla Walla. It is quite possible that at these times he met some natives who had heard Spalding and who, perhaps, had obtained some of Mrs. Spalding's pictures.

Sometime during the summer of 1839, Fathers Demers and Blanchet[2] began using what came to be known as the "Catholic

---

[1] Gray, *Oregon,* 110.

[2] Opinions differ as to who first introduced the Catholic ladder. C. B. Bagley, *Early Catholic Missions in Old Oregon,* Seattle, 1932, vol. i, p. 77, referring to

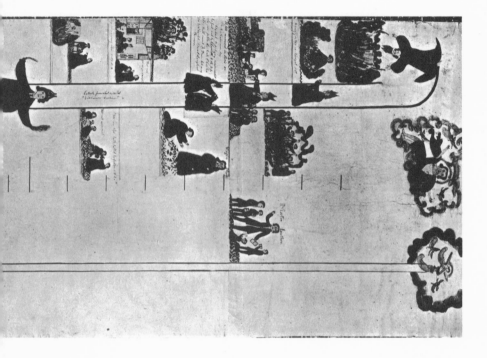

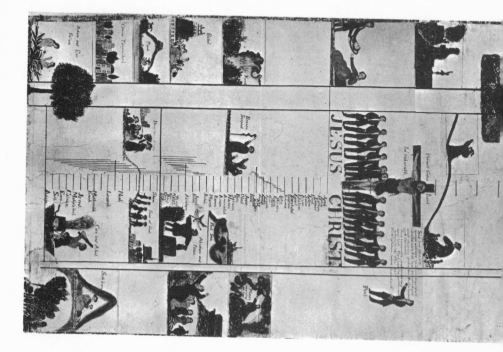

THE PROTESTANT LADDER
See text pages 218-225.

THE SPALDING CABIN AT LAPWAI

This home, built in 1838, is where the first white family in Idaho lived for nine years. From a painting by Rowena Lung Alcorn, 1936, made from photographs taken 1890-1900, and from other descriptive material. See text page 210. By permission of Caxton Printers, from Drury, *Henry Harmon Spalding*.

THE SPALDING MISSION HOUSE OF 1838
As it appeared about 1890.

Ladder," which the Cowlitz Indians called a "sahale stick" which meant "wood from above," or "wood from heaven." [3] This was at first a square or oblong board on which were marked forty short horizontal bars which represented the forty centuries before Christ. Then came thirty-three dots to indicate the years of his life, and then eighteen more bars and thirty-nine dots to bring the chronology down to 1839. Thus the priests were able to give the natives some idea of the passing of time. Father Demers is reported to have used a board 10 x 2½ feet. No doubt the word "ladder" was suggested by such a board with its horizontal lines representing centuries. From the primitive sahale stick came hand-drawn or printed ladders which included pictures, beside the bars, and points to indicate some event of Biblical or Christian history. Such scenes as the ark, Solomon's temple, and the crucifixion were typical. Finally in the Catholic ladder came representations of the departure of such "heretics" as Luther, Calvin, and Henry the Eighth, from the Catholic Church and their condemnation to hell.

Whitman in his letter of November 11, 1841, gives the following description of a "manuscript" ladder which was hanging in McLoughlin's room at Fort Vancouver. Whitman secured his information from two members of the United States Exploring Expedition which visited Oregon that year. He wrote:

> They can describe to you the picture of a tree in Chief Factor McLoughlin's room at Vancouver which represents all protestants as the withered ends of the several branches of Papacy falling off down into infernal society & flames as represented at the bottom. This gives a good idea of their manner of instruction to the Indians as drawn out in manuscript & given to them accompanied with oral instruction of a similar character. The possession of one of these manuscripts by an Indian binds him not to hear any more the instruction of Protestants so far as my observation can prove.

When the famous Jesuit missionary to Old Oregon, Father Pierre DeSmet, visited Fort Vancouver in the spring of 1842, he saw some of these ladders and was much impressed. He is reported to have said: "That plan will be adopted by the missions of the whole world." Following his visit to Oregon in 1842, Father DeSmet went to Paris at which time he may have had some ladders printed which he took back to Oregon when he returned in 1844. Blanchet was also in Europe in

---

Father Demers on his second mission to Cowlitz says: "The Catholic ladder was used here, for the first time, with great profit to all. . . ." The time was July, 1839. Carl Landerholm (Translator), *Notices & Voyages of the Famed Quebec Mission to the Pacific Northwest* . . . *1838-1847*, Oregon Historical Society, 1956, p. 40, states that Father Blanchet followed Father Demers at Cowlitz in Aug., 1839, and then introduced the ladder for the first time. Several of the extant copies of the Catholic ladder give Father Blanchet the credit of their origin.

[3] Landerholm, *op. cit.*, p. 61.

1844. It is possible that he too had some ladders printed. This we do know — there are a few Catholic printed ladders in existence with the following French title: "Echelle Catholique, Historique et Chronologique ou Maniere D'Expliquer de Catechisme aux Sauvages, Inventee dans l'Oregon en 1839, par M. Blanchet, Archeveque d'Oregon City." [4] These give no date of publication. The Oregon Historical Society has several Catholic ladders in its collection which is evidence that a number of "editions" were issued. The last one, bearing a United States copyright of 1859, measures five feet in length and two and a half feet in width. Several works dealing with the history of Roman Catholic missions in Oregon have reproductions of these ladders, most of which differ from each other. [5]

The manuscript ladders which were circulated before the printed copies were available often had individual differences. Spalding once claimed that he had a copy of a Catholic ladder which included his name along with that of Dr. Whitman's — no doubt in an uncomplimentary manner. [6] Catholic ladders were being circulated among the Cayuse Indians just prior to the massacre. Mrs. Victor in her *The Early Indian Wars of Oregon* tells of a meeting of Cayuses at the Catholic Mission on the Umatilla on December 19, 1847, at which time

> Edward Tiloukaikt arose, and displayed a "Catholic Ladder" stained with blood, and repeated what he asserted Dr. Whitman had said a short time before his death: "You see this blood! it is to show you that now because you have the priests among you, the country is going to be covered with blood. You will have nothing but blood!" [7]

---

[4] On June 14, 1938, the author called on Father Cornelius Byrne, Desmet Mission, Desmet, Idaho, shortly before the main building burned, and secured from him a broadside, 21¾" x 22", giving a Catholic ladder with the French inscription here given. This item is now in Yale University library. Oregon Historical Society in Portland has a similar copy.

[5] Some of the books which have pictures of Catholic ladders are: Charles D. Schreibeis, *Pioneer Education in the Pacific Northwest*, Metropolitan Press, Portland, ca. 1938, p. 65 gives picture of 1839 sahale stick, and on p. 66 shows ladder of 1842. The Oregon Historical Society owns a set of *Rapports sur les Missions du Diocese de Quebec*, 1839-42. The report for 1843 contains a reproduction of the ladder designed by Bishop Blanchet. Landerholm's work, *op. cit.*, includes a fold-out of a Catholic ladder reproduced from the original in Bancroft Library. Bagley, *op. cit.*, vol. II, p. 119, has a picture of another ladder. Oregon Historical Society has at least four Catholic ladders. A replica of a Catholic ladder painted on a split log has been erected at the St. Francis Xavier mission, just off highway 99 on the banks of the Cowlitz River in Washington.

[6] Spalding to Mrs. F. F. Victor, from Lapwai Agency, June 29, 1865. Original in Coll. w.

[7] *Op. cit.*, p. 115. The implication of this quotation as used by Mrs. Victor is not clear. Did Dr. Whitman smear the ladder with blood as an object lesson to the Indians?

The Protestant missionaries were quick to notice the effectiveness of this form of visual education. By picturing the Roman Catholic Church as departing from the true apostolic faith, and by showing the Pope falling down into hell instead of the heretics, a Roman Catholic ladder could be changed into a Protestant ladder. Rev. A. F. Waller, one of the Methodist missionaries in the Willamette Valley, was accused by Bishop Blanchet of doing that very thing. "Protestant ministers stop at nothing in sowing tares in the field," wrote the Bishop. "They have fabricated an imitation of our historic ladder, and have not hesitated to place a mark on it at the sixteenth century to indicate the rise of their religion." [8]

The most effective device used by any of the Protestant missionaries, however, to counteract the influence of the Catholic ladder, was a ladder painted by Mrs. Spalding. Just how many of these were circulated is not known. Spalding in his letter to Mrs. Victor, referred to above, mentions having one and states that she made "perhaps 500 like ones for the interested Indians." The figure is too high to be believed. Only one of the ladders painted by Mrs. Spalding is known to be extant and that is the one now in the Oregon Historical Society's museum in Portland.[9] Spalding has given a good description of the ladder in his letter to Greene dated February 12, 1846, from which the following is taken:

> Two meetings on the sabbath where I exhibited the Protestant Chart, which by the way I will here describe & the cause of it. The Catholics in this country have had printed (I suppose in the states) a vast No. of small charts on which the Road to Heaven is exhibited & from which Luther is represented as branching off in a road that leads to hell. These as also brass medals representing Christ on the cross are scattered profusely among the Indians of the Mountains & among as many of this people & Kayuse & the people of Chimakain, as they can induce by the assurance of Heaven, promise of wordly gain, threats &c., to accept them. They tell the people that Luther laid down his black gown & cross together & went off in the Road to hell after a wife & never returned & that all American preachers, *i.e.*, all Protestants are on the same road to destruction.[10]

To meet this attack I have planed & Mrs. S. has drawn & painted a chart about 6 feet long & 2 wide containing two ways, one nar-

---

[8] Landerholm, *Notices & Voyages*, 45.

[9] A reproduction first appeared in *Oregon Historical Quarterly*, Sept. 1936, with text by Nellie B. Pipes. The central portion of Mrs. Spalding's painting appears in *Westward on the Oregon Trail*, American Heritage Junior Library, 1962.

[10] Spalding to Greene, Feb. 3, 1847: "Great Nos. of what is called the 'Catholic Ladder' are distributed among the tribes among whom our stations are located. Upon this chart Protestants are represented as leaving the road to Heaven & are in one to Hell."

row & one broad. After representing briefly some of the important events of the world before the christian era & the crucifixion of Christ, I come to Paul, whom I represent as pointing to one who has turned off from the narrow way where he has left his wife & children & with black gown & a cross in his hand is just entering the Broad Road.

A few of Paul's prophecies concerning the man of sin are translated & printed as proceeding from his mouth such as he shall forbid to marry etc. After he has left his wife & entered the Broad Road, he is represented as the Pope with a sword in one hand & torch or fagot in the other, a king kissing one foot & a bishop the other. Further up he is represented with 5 children by his side & again as receiving the bleeding head of Admiral Coligny who was beheaded at the great slaughter of St. Bartholomew & has his head sent by Charles ix to the Pope who ordered public thanks to be given to Charles & a jubalee to be proclaimed throughout France,

Boniface ix & Benedict xiii are represented as contending with deadly weapons. Tetzel receiving a sum of money from a young man whose father has escaped hell all but one of his feet, is represented. A Nunnery is drawn from which a young priest has come out & is paying 18s to get the sin of Fornication pardoned according to "Taxa camarae Apostolicae" of the Chancery court of Rome.

The lifeless body of a father killed by his own son for money, is represented with the mother & sisters weeping on the bleeding corpse, & at a little distance the murderer before a priest receiving pardon for 10s 6d according to the same book. Some of those burnt in queen Mary's reign are drawn, the Burning of Bibles in the N of N.Y. State is drawn. Luther is represented as leaving the Broad road and returning to the narrow way. The end of the Man of Sin is represented by his falling back into hell at the approach of the Lord Jesus Christ who is coming in the clouds of heaven with his holy angels. . .

Monday morning proceeded on my journey. . . About 9 oclock came to a village of some 40 lodges, alighted, wrang a bell although most of the people were already around me, unrolled the Chart & talked about 2 hours. Rode hard the rest of the day to reach another village . . . & I explained the Chart to them as long as brush could be found for a fire light.

The ladder was painted on heavy paper which was fastened at the top to a roller. Mrs. Spalding used bright colors as green, red, blue, brown, yellow, and black. The apostles and Saint Paul were pictured as being clad in the conventional garb of a Protestant clergyman of her day, modeled perhaps after her husband's best Sunday suit. To give variety Eliza painted the apostles with either green coats and brown trousers or brown coats and green trousers. A generous amount of red was used to suggest the flow of blood from the gory heads of the victims of the massacre of Saint Bartholomew as well as the flames of hell leaping up to welcome the Pope himself. No explanation is at hand to account for Spalding's reference to the burning of Bibles in the northern part of New York State.

The injection of such bitter religious rivalries in the work of evangelizing the Oregon natives, on the part of both the Roman Catholic and the Protestant missionaries, was unfortunate. A discussion of the differences in doctrine and practice existing between the two great branches of Christendom was entirely foreign to the thinking of an Oregon Indian. Some of the Indians were quick to capitalize on these rivalries to their own advantage.

THE LAST FOUR YEARS AT LAPWAI

The last four years that the Spaldings spent at Lapwai, 1843-47, were difficult and increasingly discouraging. The peak of their success came in 1842 and 1843 when the school room was crowded; when girls were working at the spinning wheels and the loom; when both the sawmill and the grist mill were in operation; when nearly one hundred and fifty families were cultivating the soil; and when hundreds, and on special occasions up to two thousand, attended religious meetings. But by the spring of 1847 all had changed. The schoolroom was empty, the spinning wheels and loom were silent; both mills were still; enthusiasm for farming had diminished; and only a few attended the worship services. The Spaldings were so discouraged in the spring of 1847 that they even considered leaving Lapwai and moving to the Willamette.[1]

The basic reason for this complete reversal of conditions and prospects at Lapwai was the rise of a lawless and rowdy element within the tribe. There were many reasons for this. To begin with, these were transition years for the Nez Perces. The annual immigrations of white people started with the few who entered in 1842. The first Indian

[1] Spalding in his letter to A. T. Smith, Feb. 22, 1847, (original in Spokane Public Library) refers to the arrival at Lapwai of Horace Hart, brother of Eliza, in the fall of 1846. Horace was advised to stake a claim in the Willamette Valley. Spalding wrote: "I would like he would get a claim in the vicinity of good, pious neighbors, and the reach of a school and church as I think Mrs. Spalding and our children would live with him for the benefit of the children. In which case, I should hope to spend a good part of each year itinerating among this people, while they might allow me to remain in the country. It's quite possible that we shall be sent out of the country very soon, in which case, I shall need a claim myself. . ." The Spaldings' concern for the welfare and education of their four children was an important factor in this consideration of the advisability of leaving Lapwai.

agent for Oregon had been appointed, Dr. Elijah White. In the fall of that year, Dr. White visited the upper Columbia River country, met with the native chiefs, and induced them to accept a code of eleven laws — but they were white man's laws based upon his conception of justice. Spalding quickly printed this code on his press at Lapwai. A head chief for all of the Nez Perces, Ellis of Kamiah, was selected to enforce the laws. However, instead of stabilizing the tribe the introduction of the laws seems to have weakened the authority of the sub-chiefs.

Mrs. Spalding, in a letter to her parents dated April 5, 1844, commented on the deteriorating situation as follows:

> The prospects of the poor Indians in this region, never seemed to us, so dark, as they do at present. . . They have it is true, laws, and a principal chief whose business it is to punish evil doers, and who doubtless would, had he power to enforce the laws. But he has no power, but persuasion, and this avails nothing with those whose hearts are fully set to do evil.[2]

Joel Palmer, a member of the 1845 immigration, visited Lapwai in April, 1846, in order to buy horses. After paying high tribute to the accomplishments of the Spaldings, in the book which he subsequently published under the title *Journal of Travels*, Palmer wrote: "It is impossible for one family to counteract all the influences of bad and designing men, of whom there are not a few in the country. They need assistance." [3]

The reference to "bad and designing men" probably referred to such characters as Tom Hill, Old James, and William Craig. Even as Whitman had his Joe Lewis, so Spalding also had a half-breed in his midst, Tom Hill. Of him Spalding wrote as follows in his letter to Greene of January 24, 1846:

> Tom Hill, a most blasphemous debassed infidel half breed Deleware,[4] who has been some years in the Mts spreading his poison, returned this fall with this people from Buffalo. He pretends to know all about the origin of the white man's religion & the design of Missionaries. Tells them that Americans drove his people from one country to another, till but few are left.

Of course there was much truth in Tom Hill's account of how the white man had treated the Indians in the East. Spalding claimed that

---

[2] Original letter in Presbyterian Historical Society, Philadelphia.

[3] *Op. cit.*, pp. 233 ff.

[4] Spalding, in a letter to Greene, Feb. 3, 1847, seemingly referring to Tom Hill, calls him "a Shawnee Indian of the basest infidel principles, who has been some 7 years among the Nez Perces. He is an enemy to all religion."

Tom Hill had "so ingratiated himself into the feelings of the Nez Perce Indians, that he has succeeded in persuading about one hundred lodges to acknowledge him as their chief." [5]

Old James, the medicine man, became more and more hostile. He began to make demands upon Spalding for payment for wood and water rights, and for the use of the land. "They are told," Spalding wrote, "that people in the civilized world purchase their land & water privileges. This touches a chord that vibrates through every part of an Indian's soul — that insatiable desire for property." [6] Spalding learned that Craig was one of the ringleaders of the opposition. On January 24, 1846, Spalding wrote: "His house is a resort for gamblers, & the disaffected. . . He is the man who told the Indians to destroy the mill-dam a few years since. . . Last year he surveyed his claim taking in all my premises, mills, & buildings & sent it to the Willamette to have it recorded. . ." [7] Craig told the Indians that they did not have to obey the laws that Agent White had instituted.

Conditions went from bad to worse in 1846 and 1847. Spalding was repeatedly threatened with physical violence and several times man-handled. In his letter of January 24, he wrote: "I have had a gun cocked & presented to my head for 15 or 20 minutes. . ." He told of how his wife had been insulted.

> At one time probably 500 people were collected threatening to go to my house tie & whip my wife & for no other reason than because she had sent to the chief of the place requesting him to send away two of his men who had just presented themselves before the school naked & painted with the most horrible figures, & continued their indecent jestures till Mrs. S. was obliged to leave the house. Simply because she had protested against such conduct & had requested protection, she was now the only guilty person in the matter & consequently the only one to be punished.

Many acts of vandalism took place during these years. The mill race was filled with dirt; fences were torn down; windows were broken; the machinery at the grist mill was dismantled and parts thrown into the water; and some things were stolen. On August 3, 1847, Spalding reported a distressing incident to Greene:

> A few minutes before your letter arrived one of my oxen came up in great agony, both ears cut off close to the head & his tail off. Soon after another came up with his tail & one ear off. It was done by an Indian . . . who is brother-in-law to Craig. . .

---

[5] Palmer, *Journal of Travels*, 235.

[6] Drury, *Spalding*, pp. 322 ff. gives more details of Spalding's difficulties during these years.

[7] Craig's effort to file a claim on the Lapwai mission property was unsuccessful.

Spalding in his letter of February 3, 1847, to Greene, tells how a band of rowdies disrupted the school:

> They collected daily, with or without horses, painted with every horrible figure, stood around the windows & doors, took advantage of every door that might be opened to slide in & steal, threw stones at the house, windows &c. entered the school room holding in one hand the rope of their horse & in the other some hideous object with a view to create confusion in order to induce me to say or do something to restore order which would give them an excuse to use their whips or cords on my person, spitting in at the windows & doors, in various ways insulting myself & my wife. . .
>
> Not an individual raised a finger to restore order. In fact there were but two individuals of any influence in the school, & they were persecuted for their attachment to the school. Two years before when an individual great or small without or within, showed any disposition to disturb the school, he was immediately taken in hand by the chiefs who carefully kept the strictest order.

A few weeks later, or on April 2, Spalding reported a more favorable development. Some chiefs had called to express their regrets over the disturbing incidents. "The visit is most encouraging," wrote Spalding, "I have not for a long time witnessed such apparently genuine friendship. They say the Infidel party are too strong for them to manage." The school was closed because of the intimidations and threats of the opposition. However, Spalding continued his worship services. In his report to Greene of February 3, 1847, he wrote:

> But a mere fraction now remain attendants on the Sabbath worship & these are camped 5 miles distant from which place a horse is sent every Sabbath morn for me to ride up. The No. thus far this winter has averaged 108. . . I know not there has been a conversion for the last two years, but one has been received into the church since I last wrote. The sabbath which was once very strictly observed, is now generally desecrated. Family worship which a few years since was very generally observed is now abandoned by nearly all except the members of the church.[8]

Whitman's intercession with the Board in behalf of Spalding was successful. The order issued in the spring of 1842 calling for the return of the Spaldings and the closing of the Waiilatpu and Lapwai stations was rescinded. After Whitman's return, a better feeling existed within

---

[8] According to the Record Book of the First Presbyterian Church of Oregon, twenty Nez Perces and one Cayuse joined the church during the Mission period. Spalding used this same book to record the names of those who were baptized and who joined the church at the time of the great revival which began in the fall of 1871. At that time Spalding and his associate, Rev. Henry T. Cowley, baptized about 1,000 Nez Perces and Spokanes.

the Mission. We read no more about internal bickerings and divisions. When Secretary Greene learned of the serious illness of both Eliza and Henry when they had scarlet fever in the summer of 1843, he wrote a letter of sympathy. The Spaldings received the letter the first part of October, 1845. Henry replied on the seventeenth, saying: "Tho' your expressions of sympathy did not reach us till two years after the affliction, they were, nevertheless, comforting."

The long period of time needed for communication with the East was one of the trials of the Oregon missionaries. This delay of two or more years to get a reply to a letter sent from Oregon to the States, or sent from the States to Oregon, seemed to have discouraged the relatives and friends of both the Whitmans and the Spaldings from writing. Once in a letter to Eliza's parents, Henry pled: "And why will you not write us at elast twice a year? Imagine yourselves in our situation & I am sure you will not fail to grant us this favor." [9]

In one of Spalding's last letters to Greene, written from Lapwai and dated August 3, 1847, acknowledging a letter from Greene dated November, 1846, he wrote:

I most heartily thank you for this letter on account of the good advice & the christian sympathy expressed for Mrs. S. in her lonely situation. Perhaps she is among a very [few] of your missionaries who would consent to remain in this lonely situation not only excluded from female society except as she visits one of the stations once in 2 or 3 years, or some one of the sisters come this way once in several years; but often left entirely alone when duty calls me away from home for days & weeks. The dangers to which she has been exposed three or four times during my absence, has made me very unwilling to leave without some white person to remain with her.

In this same letter Spalding tells of an incident which took place during one of his absences. Some Indians called on Mrs. Spalding demanding payment for some corn which they claimed had been damaged by some of the Spalding's cattle. Mrs. Spalding refused to pay or to be intimidated. Spalding wrote: "They talked about killing her & her child & burning the house over their dead bodies. She told them to proceed to do what they pleased, she should give no property & shut the door in their faces. . ." [10] Because of such incidents, the Nez Perces long remembered Mrs. Spalding's courage.

---

[9] Letter of Spalding to Captain Hart, April 22, 1840. Original in Presbyterian Historical Society.

[10] When this incident took place, Spalding with the two older children, Eliza and Henry, was on a trip to the Willamette. Mrs. Spalding was home with her little girl Martha Jane, then a little over a year old. Before Spalding left, he made arrangements for an immigrant of the previous year, Newton Gilbert, to stay at Lapwai during his absence.

Joel Palmer, in his *Journal of Travels,* mentioned the fact that the Spaldings received no salary. He wrote: "In this lonely situation they have spent the best part of their days, among the wild savages, and for no compensation but a scanty subsistance." When the American Board sent out its missionaries to Oregon, there was no agreement about any salary. The missionaries seemingly were content to go only with the guarantee of travel and living expenses. Of course nothing was said about furloughs, educational benefits for children, or a retirement plan. Once on the field, the missionaries by their own labors became largely self-supporting. In 1840 the full cost of sustaining its thirteen missionaries in Oregon was about three thousand dollars. The previous year Spalding's total expense account amounted to about two hundred twenty-five dollars.[11] In all fairness it should be stated that the missionaries often received barrels of clothing and other supplies from their relatives and from interested churches in the East.

Spalding was able to increase the holdings of the Lapwai Mission by the natural increase of his flocks and herds and also by his industry in making hoes from old iron in his blacksmith shop and trading four hoes for a horse. For a time the demand for hoes was so great that some of the Indians offered "a horse for a hoe." [12]

When the Spaldings were obliged to leave Lapwai in the closing days of December, 1847, they were able to take only a limited amount of their household goods and other necessities with them. In the inventory which Spalding later compiled for the American Board for a claim to the government for compensation, Spalding listed property which totaled $10,048.11.[13] This included eleven buildings, one hundred one head of cattle (with two-year old steers valued at twelve dollars each), thirty-nine horses, thirty-one hogs, two wagons, 1 carriage, 1 cart, and 1 horse cart. He listed a small orchard with four bearing peach trees, 1 pear, and fifty-six apple trees of which six were bearing. Left behind in the house were 1 feather bed, two rocking chairs, four settees, and two spinning wheels. Although this was about one-third of the value placed on the goods lost at Waiilatpu, it should be remembered that many more people were involved at the Whitman station. No value was placed on the goods and livestock the Spaldings were able to take with them. On the whole, however, the extent of the material development of the Lapwai station during the eleven years the Spaldings lived there reflects great credit to the industry and frugality of both Henry and Eliza.

---

[11] More details regarding the cost of the Lapwai mission may be found in Drury, *Spalding.*

[12] Drury, *Spalding,* pp. 218 ff.

[13] There is no evidence that the American Board ever received any compensation from the government for the losses claimed. Appendix II of Drury, *Diaries of Spalding and Smith,* contains the full inventory of the Lapwai Mission.

Added to all of the other complications mentioned above which contributed to unrest among the natives, the winter of 1846-47 struck with great severity in the Nez Perce country. The thermometer dipped once to 30° below zero, according to Spalding's estimate. The Nez Perces, who had no shelters to protect their animals and no barns in which to store fodder, lost about one-half of their cattle and many of their horses.

At the time of the Whitman massacre, Eliza was at Lapwai with her three youngest children, a young woman by the name of Mary Johnson, her brother Horace Hart, and a hired man by the name of Jackson who had gone to Waiilatpu with Spalding the previous week and had returned with the pack animals. On Saturday, December 4, W. D. Canfield arrived with the dreadful news of the massacre. He was one of the immigrants who was at Waiilatpu at the time the tragedy began but managed to escape. Although he had never been over the trail before, he knew the general direction and had walked the one hundred and twenty miles in about five days. Mrs. Spalding immediately called for two of the most trusted chiefs, Timothy and Eagle (undoubtedly the same as Jason, one of the members of the church), and sent them to Waiilatpu to see if they could get Eliza and to learn more of what had happened. The next day a friendly Indian arrived with news that Spalding had escaped. Later Timothy and Eagle returned saying that the Cayuses had refused to release Eliza.

Sunday came. Craig invited Mrs. Spalding and the children to retire to his home eight miles up the valley but Mrs. Spalding refused to move on the Sabbath day. This strict observance of the Sabbath in such an hour of crisis was another incident long remembered by the Nez Perces. On Monday the move was made. Just as they left, some discontented members of the Nez Perce tribe, from Joseph's lodge, rode up to the Spalding home and engaged in some looting. For the most part, however, the Nez Perces at Lapwai rallied at once to the protection of Mrs. Spalding.

Spalding, after some harrowing experiences on his way back on foot to Lapwai, was reunited with his family on Tuesday, December 7. When Ogden reached Fort Walla Walla on December 19 and began negotiations which resulted in the release of the captives held at Waiilatpu, he sent word to Spalding for him and his family to join the others at the Fort. The Spaldings with an escort of about fifty friendly Nez Perces, many of whom regretted their departure, arrived at Fort Walla Walla on January 1. There the parents were reunited with their daughter, Eliza. Timothy was broken-hearted over their departure. He is reported to have said to Mrs. Spalding: "Now my beloved teacher you are passing over my country for the last time. You are leaving us forever and my people, oh my people will see no more light. We shall meet no more in the schoolroom & my child, oh my children will live only in a night that will have no morning." [14]

Upon their arrival in the Willamette Valley, the Spaldings were received into the home of their friends, Mr. and Mrs. A. T. Smith. In the summer or early fall of 1848 they moved to the banks of the Calapooya, a tributary of the Willamette near the present town of Brownsville. There Spalding settled on a claim. Matilda Sager was received into the Spalding home.

Eliza was in feeble health at the time of their departure from the upper Columbia country. From the following quotation in a letter of hers to her sister Lorena, dated August 5, 1850, we may suspect that Eliza had tuberculosis. She wrote: "I have suffered very much with sickness since we left the Nez Perce country. I think this climate is very unfavorable for diseased lungs & I cannot but feel that I shall not long survive our dear departed ones." [15] Doctors were few and their fees were high. Spalding once paid one hundred dollars to a physician who traveled from Salem to Brownsville to attend his wife.

Eliza Hart Spalding died on January 7, 1851, in her forty-fourth year. She was buried in the cemetery on a little hill to the east of Brownsville. Henry erected a tombstone over her grave with a two hundred-word inscription. Included in his encomium was the following: [16]

> In 1836 Mrs. S. & Mrs. Narcissa Whitman accompanied their husbands across the Rocky Mountains to commence a mission among the Indians of Oregon. They were the first white females that ever crossed those Mts.

Henry Harmon Spalding died at Lapwai on August 3, 1874, and was buried in the cemetery adjoining the old mission site. In September,

---

14 From Spalding manuscript, Whitman College.
15 Original letter in Presbyterian Historical Society.
16 The full text of the inscription is as follows:

SACRED TO THE MEMORY OF
MRS. ELIZA HART SPALDING
Who died January 7th 1851, aged 48 years 4 months and 27 days

Born in Berlin Connt. Educated at Clinton N.Y. and Hudson Ohio: Married to Revd. H. H. Spalding A.D. 1833, and in 1835, with him entered the missionary service under the care of the A.B.C.F.M. In 1836, Mrs. S. & Mrs. Narcissa Whitman accompanied their husbands across the Rocky Mountains to commence a mission among the Indians of Oregon. They were the first white females that ever crossed those Mts. They continued to be devoted laborers in the mission until Nov. 27th, 1847, when Dr. & Mrs. Whitman and 12 others were cruelly massacred by the Cayuse Indians. Mrs. Spalding was respected and esteemed by all, and no one had greater or better influence over the Indians. She loved the work and hoped to the last that the mission

1913, the remains of Mrs. Spalding were moved from Brownsville, Oregon, to be laid beside those of her husband. In the summer of 1925 the Presbyterian Synod of Washington dedicated a suitable marble monument to the memory of these two pioneer Oregon missionaries, over the double grave.

---

would be resumed, but the shock of the massacre and the trial and suffering occasioned by those sad events, laid the foundation for the sickness, which finally caused her death.

She always felt that the Jesuit missionaries were the leading cause of the massacre.

She died in peace trusting in her Saviour, "Rest sweet dust, till Jesus bid thee rise."

A later generation of Presbyterians, apologetic over the anti-Roman Catholic attitude which Spalding advertised in this inscription, buried the tombstone either at the time the remains of Mrs. Spalding were removed to Lapwai or at the time the present monument over the two graves was dedicated. The transcription here given was taken from a photograph of the original stone given to the author, about 1935, by Mrs. F. C. Koehler of Spokane, Wash. The picture is now in the archives of the Eastern Washington State Historical Society, Spokane.

Mrs. William Henry Gray

Mary Augusta Dix Gray

William Henry Gray went to Oregon as a mechanic or lay assistant with the Whitman-Spalding party of 1836. At the time he was engaged to a young lady whose name is not known. Being impressed with the enthusiastic reception given by the natives to the missionaries, Gray decided to return in 1837 for reinforcements. He was, no doubt, also eager to be married and to take his bride to Oregon. Always resourceful, Gray conceived the idea of driving a band of horses over the mountains and across the plains to the Missouri frontier and selling them. He secured the services of at least four natives to go with him. Gray with his companions left the Rendezvous in the summer of 1837 in advance of the returning caravan, contrary to the advice of experienced mountain men. True to predictions, they were ambushed by the Sioux at what is now Ash Hollow, Nebraska, on August 7. Gray's Indian companions were killed, his horses stolen, and he barely escaped with his life. A bullet passed through his hat leaving two holes and a minor scalp wound as mute testimony of his narrow brush with death. He received a second wound on the right temple.

As soon as opportunity afforded upon his return East, Gray called upon the young lady to whom he was engaged. According to the account given by Gray to William Mowry, who included it in his *Marcus Whitman*,[1] the mother of his betrothed made inquiry about the two bullet holes in the hat he was wearing. Gray then told of how the Sioux had ambushed his party at Ash Hollow. At once the mother of the young lady emphatically declared that no daughter of hers would ever undertake the dangerous overland journey to Oregon. So the engagement was abruptly terminated.

Gray spent several months during the winter of 1837-38 at the College of Physicians and Surgeons, Fairfield, Massachusetts, and thereafter appropriated the title of "Doctor" until he and the reinforcement of 1838 arrived at Waiilatpu. Dr. Whitman quickly corrected the use of the title.[2] During these months, Gray was carrying on corre-

---

[1] *Op. cit.*, p. 86.

[2] Whitman to Greene, Oct. 22, 1839, after he had noticed Gray's name listed in the *Missionary Herald* as "Doctor Gray." Whitman wrote: "I cannot conceive how you have been so much imposed upon to report him as a Physician. What can a man learn in sixteen weeks of public lectures (which is barely all he can

spondence with the American Board regarding a reinforcement to return with him to Oregon the next year. Following the decision of the Prudential Committee of the Board to send Elkanah Walker and his bride to Oregon, Gray wrote to Walker from Fairfield on December 18, and inquired as to whether or not Walker had found "Mrs. Walker." He then added: "Mrs. G. is yet to be found." [3] Mowry tells us that "One after another, the eligible young ladies in the vicinity were recommended to him. None of them, however, attracted the favorable attention of the young missionary." [4]

Early in February, 1838, Gray was a guest in the home of Samuel Parker in Ithaca. Even as Parker had told Marcus Whitman about Miss Narcissa Prentiss, so he told Gray about Miss Mary Augusta Dix.

Mary was one of the seven daughters of Mr. and Mrs. John Dix. She was born at Ballston Springs, New York, on January 2, 1810. After making their home for a time at Champlain, New York, the Dix family moved to Ithaca where they attended the Dutch Reformed Church. The whole family was musically inclined and it is reported that it was not unusual on Sunday to see the mother and her seven daughters, all dressed in white, in the church choir loft.[5] Mary had joined the Congregational Church of Canton, Onondaga County, New York, before she became a member of the church in Ithaca.[6]

Records concerning Mary's early life and education are scanty. She is reported to have attended a school at Seneca Falls, New York. Judging from her extant letters, Mary must have had a scholastic training comparable to that of the other women of the Oregon Mission.

No one could have lived in Ithaca in those days without having heard of Samuel Parker. After an absence of over two years and two months, Parker returned to his home in Ithaca on May 17, 1837. He was by that time a world traveler. He had gone out to the Missouri frontier in 1834; he had crossed the Rockies and explored the Pacific Northwest in 1835; he had visited the Sandwich Islands and had rounded Cape Horn in 1836-37; and he had written a book. His *Journal of an Exploring Tour beyond the Rocky Mountains* was published in 1838.[7] There can be no doubt but that Mary Dix knew about Samuel Parker. She also knew something about Oregon before she met her future husband.

---

boast) to entitle him to that distinction?" It is difficult to see how Gray had this many weeks of actual classroom instruction at the college since he did not get back to his home until Oct. 1837, and he was in Ithaca the first part of the following February. This period includes the holidays.

[3] Original letter in Coll. Wn.

[4] Mowry, *Whitman*, 87.

[5] Douthit, *Souvenir of Western Women*, 38.

[6] See notation made by Spalding in Records of the First Presbyterian Church of Oregon regarding her previous church membership.

[7] Parker's book became the first popular travel book on Oregon, going through five American editions, and one each for England and Germany.

According to a family tradition, William and Mary first met at a church social held in Ithaca on Wednesday evening, February 14.[8] William probably had learned from Parker more about Mary than she happened to know about him. Indeed, he might have been a complete stranger to her when he drew her apart from the company and told in glowing terms the prospect of a missionary's life in Oregon. Tradition says that he proposed marriage that evening. It was all so sudden, Mary wanted time to think it over. By this time Gray was as anxious to be married and be on his way to Oregon, as Whitman had been two years earlier. Of course, there was a big difference. Whitman was engaged and by February 14, 1838, Gray was not.

William followed up his proposal by a letter which he wrote to Mary the next day. In terms totally lacking in sentiment, William magnified the greatness of the missionary's calling. The crucial question was, would she be willing to devote her life to the great object of taking the saving Gospel to "6,277,000 natives on our own continent." Time was getting so short for Gray that he could not afford a repetition of the previous refusal. He wanted a wife to go back to Oregon with him. He was convinced that Mary was just the person, and to convince her he wrote the following letter. It was a challenge to faith rather than a declaration of love. The misspellings found in the letter reflect William's lack of a good basic education.

FEBRUARY 15th, 1838

MY DEAR FRIEND: With your permission I will drop a line to you hoping that it will aide you in the conclusions to which you are about to come in reference to the proposition already made you.

First let me say that it is no ordinary undertaking upon which you are about to enter. thousands will immediately feel your influence and tens of thousands must in time, and unnumbered souls may bless the hour in which you did decide to devote your life to the Salvation of 6,277,000 natives on our own continent, yet you must remember that to do good to the natives requires a firme and unshaken fixed purpos in your owne heart that whatever others may think or do *my duty* must and shall with devine assistance be performed.

Whatever connection may be formed let it only be that the gospel may be given to the ends of the Earth. Second. — Do not flatter yourself with the idea of entering upon a work and field that can be cultivated without personal example and effort on your part nor that there is no trial that awaits you when you reach it or before, — you wil remember that human nature is one and

[8] These dates are on the basis of recently discovered evidence and correct the statement given in Drury, *Spalding*, 193, that they first met on February 19.

the same the world over — and where the restraints of the Gospel has never been felt and acknowledged — many things you may expect to meet and see that will appear revolting, yet you will remember that it is to reform and render more happy the beings for who good you may be permitted to devote your life.

When trials and difficulties arise then you must — remember the promis of Him who bled for us — and gave his life a ransom for a lost and guilty world — never my dear friend let your heart be fixed on any Earthly object — and then you may expect never to be disapointed. Our acquaintance is short — our personal feelings — cannot now be strong — and here let me again repeat, let your confidence be placed alone on our Redeemer and I have no hesitation in believing that he will — I have the authority of his word to say that I know he will overrule all things for the good of them that love him.

In case you accompany me you must do it from your own choice and because you love the cause of our Redeemer and love to labour for the good of the benighted Natives.

On my part so far as I have the controll of my own powers nothing shall be wanting to render you usefull in the field to which you go — our object is and must be to do good — while we live.

Time will not permit me to say more at present. I must hasten to return to this place and then to my field, if possible we must leave by the 21st. to reach Independence to prepare in season for our departure to our field. I remain my dear friend yours truly in the Gospel of our Redeemer [9]   WM. HENRY GRAY.

The appeal must have struck a responsive chord in Mary's heart because five days later, or on February 20, Mary gave her consent. This we know from a postscript, dated the twenty-first, that Gray added to a letter Parker was sending to Walker regarding the outfit a person should take when going overland to Oregon. Gray announced: "I have not known till yesterday that I was to have a companion go out with me." The wedding took place in the Dutch Reformed Church of Ithaca on Sunday evening, February 25. Mowry gives the following account:

> The bride usually sang in the choir, but on this occasion she sat in the front pew with Mr. Gray. The house was filled to overflowing. At the close of the service the minister came down from the pulpit, the couple arose, and the marriage ceremony proceeded by which Mr. William H. Gray and Miss Mary Augusta Dix, daughter of John Dix, Esq., of Champlain, New York, were made man and wife.[10]

[9] Original owned by Miss Mary A. Gray of Portland, Oregon, a granddaughter of William and Mary. It is here published with permission for the first time.
[10] Mowry, *Whitman*, 88.

Up to this time nothing had been said to the American Board about Gray taking a wife with him to Oregon. The very fact that he got married seems to imply that of course the Board would accept her as one of their missionaries. Mary's pastor, the Reverend John C. F. Hoes, hastened to write to the Board to recommend his parishioner. He commented:

A word in reference to their engagement and marriage. Many of our pious people think they were very premature. Tis true their acquaintance had been short — of but two or three weeks continuance — but Mr. Gray came well recommended to the Rev. Samuel Parker, thru' whom he became acquainted with Miss Dix.

Regarding Mary, Hoes wrote:

I would say she is a highly consistent member of my church; a devoted teacher in the S.[unday] School. . . She is a woman of good and well disciplined mind — has devoted considerable time to teaching . . . is prepared in an eminent degree for usefulness. . . Their outfit has been almost entirely procured by the cheerful liberality of the ladies of my church in conjunction with those of the Presbyterian church in this place.[11]

We can imagine that the announcement of the sudden engagement and of the forthcoming marriage on so short notice caused considerable comment among the members of the women's societies in the two churches. Sewing bees were hastily called and a missionary woman's outfit quickly assembled. In addition, according to Hoes, some seventy dollars was also contributed.

The couple left Ithaca on Monday, February 26, for Oregon. Characteristic of Gray's impulsiveness, they hurried on ahead of the other three couples who were to go with them across the country. It was not until April 15 that the Walkers, the Eells, and the Smiths caught up with the Grays at Liberty, Missouri.[12]

Shortly before Mrs. Gray's death in 1881, her eldest daughter, Caroline (Mrs. Jacob Kamm of Portland) visited her mother at which time she asked: "Mother, I have often wondered how you, with your education and surroundings, the refinements of life that you were accustomed to, and your own personal habits, could possibly have made up your mind to marry a man to whom you were a total stranger, so short a time from your first meeting with him, and going with him on such a terrible journey, thousands of miles from civilization, into an unknown wilderness, across two chains of mountains, and exposed to countless dangers — Mother, how did you ever do it?"

---

[11] Original in Coll. A.

[12] Since vol. II of this work will contain the overland diaries of Mrs. Walker and Mrs. Eells, details of the overland journey of the Grays in 1838 will be given there.

After a few moments' pause, the mother replied with great earnestness: "Carrie, I dared not refuse! Ever since the day when I gave myself to Jesus, it had been my daily prayer, 'Lord, what wilt thou have me to do?' And when the question, 'Will you go to Oregon as one of a little band of self-denying missionaries and teach these poor Indians of their Saviour?' was suddenly proposed to me, I felt that it was the call of the Lord and I could not do otherwise." [13]

So far as is known, Mary Gray did not keep a diary of her overland travel or of the first part of her life in the Oregon Mission. The Coe Collection of Yale University Library has seventeen of her letters which were directed to Mrs. Walker or to other women of the Mission. From this collection the following two letters have been selected to show something of Mrs. Gray's personality. The first was written on the "Steam Boat Belle of Missouri" on April 4, 1838. The Grays were then on their way to St. Louis. The letter was postmarked St. Charles, on April 6, and was addressed to Mrs. Walker at St. Louis. The three couples following the Grays arrived in that city on the ninth, and had to leave for Independence late the afternoon of the same day. Hence they had but little time to make the purchases Mrs. Gray requested. The letter follows:

LETTERS OF APRIL 4 AND SEPTEMBER 29, 1838

Dear Sisters We are happy in learning by a line received from Doct. Weed that you all arrived at Cincinnati in good health and spirits, and are hastening to join us at Independence. We have indeed been almost impatient to commence our acquaintance with those whom we not only expect to be our companions in privations and dangers, but sharers with us in the blessed privilege of teaching the benighted heathen the knowledge of a Saviour and the habits of civilized and refined society. Be of good courage my sisters and may the Lord strengthen and sustain you.

My husband has a very lame arm today, occasioned by vaccination [14] — is quite unwell and therefore wishes me to say to you that he has neglected or forgotten to purchase any spices to take with us on our journey across the mountains, and if you think it necessary, wishes you to procure some at St. Louis — he thinks it will be well to have a small quantity of nutmeg, cinnamon, and cloves — and he also wishes you (your husbands I mean) to buy about 40 lbs of crackers which he likewise forgot. Do not fail of bringing the crackers — try and procure such as will keep a good while.

The Steam Boat is running as fast as she can and if you have ever

---

[13] *T.O.P.A.*, 1897, p. 92.

[14] This is the only reference to vaccination found in any of the writings of the missionaries.

attempted to write on a boat in full motion, I need make no other excuse for sending you such an ill looking note.

Affectionately your Sister in Christ   Mary Augusta Gray
p.s. My husband says it will be necessary for you to hasten on as fast as possible, as the Company expect to leave by the middle of this month — think you will do well to take the first Boat that comes up the river after you reach St. Louis. You will be obliged to travel one Sabbath, start when you will.

Yours,
                           M. A. Gray

The second letter selected was written from the Spalding station at Lapwai shortly after their arrival on September 7, 1838. Spalding was still in process of building his new home and Mrs. Gray refers to the discomfort experienced because the house was not enclosed. Shining through the descriptions of raw pioneer life is Mary's idealism of being a missionary to the "benighted heathen." It was this high sense of duty which gave these men and women the strength and determination to carry on regardless of physical privations.

Clear Water   Sept 29, 1838

Dear Sisters   I embrace with pleasure this opportunity for answering your kind letters of the 13th. The —ing is so cold that it is almost impossible to keep warm in our open house and now my fingers are nearly stiff with cold; still I will try to write at least one letter. We are yet in an unsettled condition as respects our house, but the sound of the saw, the plane and the hammer, and the cheerful voices of the workmen lead us to hope that a few days will find us comfortably settled in our new home. They are going to commence the chimney in the kitchen today — this done we shall have our room with a large buttery, clothes closet, and chamber stairs finished. We expect to have two bed rooms off the front room, and 3 or 4 rooms besides closets up stairs.

We assemble the children every day for instruction, and I find it a pleasure to teach them notwithstanding my ignorance of the language. I have learned a few words so that I get along very well when Mrs. S. cannot attend the school. We labor under great disadvantage for want of a school house, but we hope this evil will soon be remedied by the erection of a building that will answer the double purpose of school house and house of worship. The Sabbath is a busy day with us. There is always some one present ready to receive instruction. I have an interesting scholar in Muatisp,[15] the deaf & dumb boy whom I give lessons on the slates. I spend some time every day in teaching the children to sing, — they learn the tunes very soon but find it difficult

---

[15] Or Mastaps. Spalding in his letter to Greene of Feb. 12, 1846, writes of "Mr. Craig & our Deaf & Dumb man assisted us."

to remember English words. We have taken a little boy on trial whom we think of giving the name of Lyman Beecher, also have in view a little girl 4 or 5 years old whom we think of taking as Hannah Moore, when our house is in a situation to enlarge our family. I feel greater anxiety to do something for this people as I see more and more of their degredation.

Much has been done for them considering the short time that has elapsed since they saw the first germs of civilization, and first heard the joyful sound of salvation by Jesus Christ, but notwithstanding they are in some measure enlightened. We know that the knowledge they possess will only enhance their misery, unless the Holy Spirit set (sic) home the truth with power upon their hearts. How important then that we pray much for the blessing of God upon our labours.

We shall be happy to join your [prayer fellowship] on Friday afternoon, circumstances would not permit of it last week, but we hope to be able to in future. We have observed the M[aternal] Association but in order to do this we were last Wednesday obliged to resort to a grave to find a place sufficiently retired from public gaze, — hope it was not an unprofitable season. I trust you will be greatly blessed in your meetings, and in all your endeavours to do good. . .

I think Sister Spalding would enjoy pretty good health if she did not labour so hard. I endeavour to assist her what I can but we are obliged to labour under a great inconvenience at present. It will be better soon. . . Remember me in love to all, with a kiss for little Alice. Husband joins in compliments to yourselves & husbands.

Affectionately yours,
                                                        M. A. GRAY

Four Unhappy Years

The high idealism with which Mary Gray entered upon her duties as a member of the Mission gradually diminished before the abrasive effects of personality conflicts and her husband's feelings of frustration. Friction developed during the winter of 1838-39 between Mrs. Whitman and Mrs. Gray because the latter thought that Mrs. Whitman had spread abroad the news of Mrs. Gray's pregnancy. In a letter to Mrs. Walker dated "Clear Water, February 23, 1839," Mrs. Gray wrote:

> The second day after our arrival at W.[aiilatpu] Mrs. Whitman in conversation with me commenced questioning me relative to my situation. I evaded her first question but she continued her questions until I could no longer evade them without hurting her with rudeness. This I was unwilling to do, & supposing I might place come confidence in her, told her some circumstances but she drew her own conclusions. I told her I wished her to keep her views to herself — for I felt uncertain — she said she must tell her husband — to this I made no reply, for I supposed it would be of no avail, but thought he as a physician would feel it out of place to publish such things — but I found that my favors were soon spread abroad, and how could it come but through Mrs. W.?

The men of the Mission gathered at Lapwai on February 22, 1839, to consider some items of business. On that day Spalding wrote in his diary:

> Mrs. Whitman & Mrs. Gray do not suceed in settling their difficulties. Mr. Gray in all probability was the first person that made known the fact in this country that his wife was pregnant, but wishes to make himself & wife think that Mrs. Whitman pumped the secret out of Mrs. Gray & then communicated it to Mrs. Spalding & she to me, whereas Mr. Gray communicated the fact to me long before. A very little matter indeed to cause such a difficulty.

One month later or on March 20, 1839, Mrs. Gray gave birth to a son at Lapwai. They called him John Henry Dix.

A far more serious problem than the tiff that arose between the women was Gray's consuming desire to have a station of his own. Upon the arrival of the reinforcement of 1838 at Waiilatpu, none of the three other couples wanted to live with the Grays. The criticism centered not on Mary, who seems to have been generally liked, but on her husband. Therefore, in the reorganization of the Mission, the Grays were sent to live with the Spaldings at Lapwai. At the Mission meeting held at Lapwai in February 1839, when all of the men were present, it was voted to have Gray take charge of the secular affairs at Lapwai in order to permit Spalding to spend more time itinerating. This was in line with Gray's status as a lay assistant. At the September Mission meeting, also held at Lapwai, Gray requested permission to explore for a new station. There was some opposition, especially from Spalding, but a reluctant permission was granted.

The Grays left Lapwai on September 11 for a tour of exploration and were absent until October 18. Even before Gray left, Spalding found it necessary to resume the responsibilities of taking care of the secular affairs of his station. According to a letter Mrs. Gray wrote to Mrs. Walker and Mrs. Eells on October 23, they found two sites that appealed to them. The first was "not far below Okannagon Fort," and the second "is near the mouth of the Yankamaw,[1] a short day from W.W." After making their explorations, the Grays called on Dr. Whitman who, evidently, vetoed any idea that the Grays had of starting a new station that fall. "How trying," wrote Mrs. Gray to her sisters at Tshimakain, ". . . when we wish to be located and commence our Missionary labours we must be treated in this manner. But I trust Dr. W's word is not law in this Mission." And Mrs. Gray added: "I do sincerely hope your husbands will favour our settling at one of the above named places." However, both Walker and Eells joined with Whitman and Spalding in opposing the opening of a new location at that time.

The Grays returned to Lapwai in an unhappy mood. William brooded over what he considered to be his inferior status in the Mission and decided that he would leave the Mission if he could find suitable employment elsewhere. Although nothing has been discovered in contemporary writings about his intentions, subsequent evidence shows that Gray had decided to apply to the Hudson's Bay Company for work.[2] He left Lapwai on October 21. Spalding, in his diary, made note of the fact that Gray was going to Vancouver but did not indicate the reason. Judging by an entry in Mrs. Walker's diary for November

[1] Or Yakima. The mouth of the Yakima River is a little below the present city of Richland, Wash. The missionaries also referred to it as Shimnap.

[2] Marshall, *Acquisition of Oregon*, vol. II, p. 82, quotes testimony of Gray given in a trial held in Aug. and Sept., 1869. When Gray was asked if he had applied for a position in the school at Vancouver for his wife, he replied in the affirmative. He was also asked: "Did you at the same time seek employment at Vancouver?" His answer: "My impression is that I did."

6, Gray was seeking the support of Walker and Eells. Mrs. Walker wrote: "Recd. letters from Mr. Gray who is in a big trouble."

Shortly after arriving at Fort Walla Walla, Gray wrote back to Mary and requested her to join him at the Fort. In her letter to Mrs. Walker written from Walla Walla on December 3, Mrs. Gray explained: ". . . husband hoped when he requested me to come to this place, that the Mission would consent to our going to the Yankama [Yakima] & felt it important for me to be here as soon as possible on account of the cold weather." An example of the amazing boldness and fortitude so characteristic of the women of the Mission is to be found in the story of Mrs. Gray's one hundred and twenty-mile trip from Lapwai to Walla Walla. She left Lapwai on November 11 carrying her eight-month-old baby and with no escort except some trusted Nez Perces. According to an entry in Spalding's diary, it began snowing the second day after she left. Spalding had some misgivings about the advisability of a lone white woman attempting such a journey with no escort except some friendly Indians. On the day she left he wrote in his diary: "God in great mercy grant her a comfortable journey. It would be better if her husband were here with her to pitch the tent & make everything comfortable nights. Jacob & his two boys & the five cows go with her. Also takes the babe. Poor little boy, I fear he will suffer."

Gray left for Fort Vancouver on October 31. It is quite possible that he wanted his wife and child at Fort Walla Walla in case he was successful in finding employment at Vancouver. However, he was not successful and in great disappointment was obliged to return to Walla Walla. It is possible that Gray's subsequent ill-will to the Company may be traced back to this failure to find work. There was no other course open but to return to Lapwai. This they did, arriving there on December 28, 1839.

Gray was in a most unhappy mood when he and his family resumed their residence at Lapwai. There was nothing to do but to wait until the next meeting of the Mission, which was scheduled for July, 1840, and then ask for a clarification of his status. In the meantime strained relationships existed between Gray and Spalding. Brooding over his troubles, Gray wrote critical letters about Spalding to the Board on March 20 and April 15, 1840. He blamed Spalding for assuming too much authority and for ignoring the orders of the Mission. It was Spalding's misfortune to have had Gray living at Lapwai at that particular time.

When the Mission meeting was held in July, Gray's case came up for review and permission was finally granted to him to open a new station at Shimnap, at the mouth of the Yakima River. The Grays then moved to Waiilatpu to make the necessary preparations. Because of a number of unforeseen developments, nothing was done during the following year to commence the new work at Shimnap. All of this is background for the diary that Mary Gray began keeping in May, 1840. This she kept, at first with almost daily entries and then only with occasional notations, until September 21, 1842.

Mrs. Gray's diary is important for the new light it throws upon the everyday life of the women. She talks about her sewing, the problem of having servants whose language you can not speak, the children, and other little details of running a frontier home in the wilderness. The "H" in her Diary probably stands for "Husband," rather than for "Henry." This diary has never before been published.[3] She writes at first at Lapwai, then while at Waiilatpu.

MRS. GRAY'S DIARY, MAY TO AUGUST 1840

MAY 1840

SABBATH MAY 10th. I have spent the day in reading writing meditation & prayer. Little son appears quite well to day. A good many Indians have come from different directions to day to attend worship. Oh that the truth may be dispensed to them in its purity & prove a blessing to their souls. I am a good deal afflicted with tooth-ache today.

MON. 11th. I have spent most of the day in sewing & baking. Husband returned from Walla Walla this afternoon.[1] He left the packs, and the Hawaian & his wife as he supposed a short distance behind. The packs came up at sundown said the woman had fallen from her horse, & they had stopped. H. sent a boat for them. They got here about 10 o'clock. She does not appear to be much hurt. H. brought me a box of figs [2] presented by Mr. Ermatinger.

TUES. 12th. We rose late this morning — up late last night — unpacking goods. All appear to feel the effect of yesterdays ride but are able to go to work. Jacob & Hannah, our man & woman appear very well. Little son can speak a number of words.

WED. 13th. Sent a letter to Mrs. Smith this morning & some figs. Give some to Mrs. Spalding & a piece of fresh pork Mrs. W. sent me. Mr. Spalding & family left this morning for a short journey — expect to return tomorrow — do not know their object in going.[3] No children

---

[3] The transcription here used of Mrs. Gray's diary was made by one of her descendants in Aug., 1951.

[1] Gray had left Lapwai on May 5 for Fort Walla Walla to get some supplies which had arrived there. He escorted back with him a Christian Hawaiian couple, Jacoba and Hannana. Mary does not always spell the names the same. For the sake of consistency, the spelling is given as Jacob and Hannah.

[2] Possibly a box of dried figs from the gardens of Fort Vancouver. In a letter to Mrs. Walker dated Feb. 15, 1840, Mrs. Gray writes of Ermatinger: "He is the same lively talkative man he used to be."

[3] See Spalding's diary for this date. Drury, *Diaries of Spalding and Smith*, 290. He and his family had a two-day outing to Lake Waha. It seems strange that we of this generation, 120 years later, know more of the details of this incident in the affairs of the Lapwai station than did Mrs. Gray, a participant at the time.

have come to be taught today. Hannah making herself a skirt — I went out this evening and assisted H. in the garden.

THURS. 14th. I have spent all the time I could spare from my family today in the garden. Leave little son with Hannah — feel very much fatigued to night. Mr. Sp. & family returned this afternoon.

FRID. 15th. I have to day been learning Hannah to wash. She is unaccustomed to my way & gets along very slow — has been all day washing calicoes & flannels & I have assisted her some too. This afternoon the Ind. arrived from Mr. Smiths who carried up his goods — Brought letters. One for H. 1 for me. Mrs. S. sent some flowers [4] & seeds. sent back some cocoa — spent a short time in the garden.

SAT. 16th. Have been baking, sewing &c. to day. Hannah has ironed & made butter. Little son rather unwell this afternoon.

SABBATH 17th. Jacob & Hannah attended native worship with me this morning — Text Matth 7th. 9, 10 & 11. Husband has been reading — Hunters S. Biography — character, & History of Joseph. He paints in lively colours the errors in Josephs education. the danger of parental fondness carried to excess &c. &c. May we be profited by this days privileges & be better prepared to discharge our duty to our beloved child.

MON. 18th. I have to day with the assistance of H. planted my flower bed. Left little son with Hannah, also seeing to the dinner. When I returned I found the water had all boiled out of the kettle & the meat badly burned. Little son seems to be daily increasing in activity both of mind & body.

TUES. 19th. This morning copied 3 letters for H. to Messrs. Walker & Eells & Doct. Whitman — wrote Mrs. Eells. They are not yet sent — spent remainder of the day sewing & attending to my family.

WEDNES. 20th. I have been a good deal tried to day with the slow movements of Hannah. I had a large washing to do & have been obliged to do nearly half of it myself besides the cooking & other housework. Almost sick to night — Ellis [5] arrived today. says Mr. Griffin [6] is still on this side of the Mt. not able to cross on account of snow. The Indian does not go to Tshimakain with the letters. H. concludes not to send — thinks of writing to the gentlemen of the H. B. Co. respecting the school at Nasqualla.[7] We feel that we cannot do much

---

[4] Mrs. Smith was then at Kamiah. This is one of the few references to flowers in the writings of the missionary women.

[5] Ellis, of Kamiah, who was to be made the first head chief of the Nez Perces in the late fall of 1842.

[6] Rev. and Mrs. J. S. Griffin had arrived in Oregon as independent missionaries in the fall of 1839. In the spring of 1840, the Griffins endeavored to start a mission at Fort Boise but were not successful. They returned to Lapwai in the summer of 1840 and later moved to the Willamette Valley.

[7] Gray was still hoping to be able to get a position in the Hudson's Bay Company. At this date the Mission had not reconsidered its former action regarding the opening of a new station.

connected with this mission while it remains in the situation it now is. I trust the Lord prepares the way before us & directs us to some place where we can labour effectually for the upbuilding of his cause — a little rain this afternoon.

THURS. 21st. Very pleasant to day & very warm. I have been engaged in sewing — gave Hannah one of my dresses she has been enlarging it — This afternoon paid the molasses, vinegar & darning needles borrowed of Mrs. Spalding.

FRID. 22nd. Hannah has washed for herself to day & done some of my ironing. I have been baking, sewing & making a set of bed curtains — No meeting this afternoon — Mr. S. in the room till supper time — After supper they went to the garden. I feel to pray for the prosperity of Christ's Kingdom here if we do not meet together — O: that we might all see eye to eye and go forward harmoniously in the work of the Lord. But it is not so — dissentions & discords reign among us. . . Commenced writing to Mrs. Whitman to day.

SAT. 23rd. A little rain this morning — H. has been moving the little sawmill frame for the purpose of making us a house — could raise a few Indians to assist him but with the assistance of oxen & horses he got it moved in good season — no time to write to day — occupied with family duties.

SABBATH 24th. I have been most of the day listening to H. who has been reading Hunters Sacred Biography. . .

27th WEDNES. We observed the meeting of the Maternal Association this afternoon in Mrs. Spaldings room. No one present but Mrs. S. & myself & Hannah. She prayed in the Hawaian language. The natives are mostly absent. The 11th Chap. of Eccl. was read, also a piece from the Mothers Magazine showing the importance of educating our children exclusively for the Service of God — the impossibility of training them for God & the world.

28th THURS. This morning finished a letter to Mrs. Whitman & one to Mrs. Eells — sent them by Mastaps to Walla Walla. Feel a good deal tried with our present situation on account of our dear babe. He is so much exposed to danger from the nearness of the water [8] and has so many temptations to mischief & disobedience, that I feel that Divine aid alone can preserve his body from death, & his disposition from serious injury. O that God would give us wisdom, patience, meekness & every needed grace, to direct & assist in the training of this beloved child for Himself.

JUNE 1840

THURS. 4th JUNE. I have been much affected to day in view of the

---

[8] Mrs. Gray had reason to fear. Alice Clarissa Whitman was drowned in the stream near her home on June 23, 1839. After the Grays left Lapwai, Leverett, the little son of the independent missionaries, Mr. and Mrs. P. B. Littlejohn, was drowned in the mill race at Lapwai on Mar. 29, 1843.

distinguishing mercy of God towards us Who in the midst of sickness & death is granting unto us life & health. There is a great deal of sickness among the natives. There are but very few residing about us, they being absent to obtain roots & fish, but the sick are brought here from various quarters to receive medical aid. Two were brought this afternoon from up Snake River extremely low — a girl who had been sick 4 weeks, & a boy 3 weeks. The boy seemed much distressed & nearly exhausted when he arrived. H. administered medicine [9] & gave directions respecting his drink, food, etc. but his friends disregarded his directions & went to feeding him in large quantities. He lived but a few hours after arrival — was probably dying before he left the boat.

SABBATH 7th. The girl is still living but probably will not recover. She has many very bad symptoms. I have spent a good deal of time for 2 or 3 days past in waiting upon her & other sick folk. Other sick ones are better. Husband & self are much fatigued & nearly sick — feel unfit for reading, meditation or any other employment.

MON. 8th. Today letters arrived from Waiilatpu. A meeting of the Mission is to be held at this place the first of July next. I feel anxious as to the result of the meeting, as it probably will decide not only as to our future course, but the fate of the mission. The sick about us appear better, have a little more hopes of the sick girls recovery.

WEDNES [June] 10th. This afternoon we observed our Maternal meeting — read a part of the 19th Chap. of Matt. commencing with the 13th verse & Dr. Scotts comments upon it — also a very interesting letter from Mrs. Dr. Reed, London in the Mothers Magazine — feel to commend our Dear babe to the watchful care of our Covenant keeping God, praying that he would give wisdom to direct us in all things concerning him.

FRID. 12th. Yesterday we moved into our new house,[10] yet unfinished — feel much easier about our little Son — have been meditating on what would be his condition should one or both of us be taken from him in this heathen land, but the promises of God are sure, & I will leave him, my husband, self & all things in his gracious hands.

SABBATH 14th. Felt quite unwell this morning. After the people had gone to meeting husband bled me. After meeting several persons came into our house. Sampson son came in at the window.[11] Those

---

[9] All of the missionaries gave out simple remedies. Because of Gray's short course at the Medical College, he probably knew more about medicine than any other person in the Mission except Dr. Whitman.

[10] Spalding in a letter to Greene dated April 1, 1840, reported that a sawmill had begun operation at Lapwai on that day. In the inventory of the Lapwai station, made after the Whitman massacre, Spalding listed a "wood" house, *i.e.*, a sawed lumber house, in contrast to a log building, 20 x 20. This may have been the house to which Mrs. Gray here refers.

[11] Here is a good example of the insolence which some of the more rowdy elements of the natives displayed to the missionaries. Spalding had a Nez Perce whom he called Samson working for him.

who were in reproved him. H. told him it was good to go out & come in at the door. He was very insolent and talked very bad to the Indians who reproved him. H. told him it was sabbath, not to talk so, he continued, & H. asked him several times to go out doors, he refused & H. took hold of him to put him out. I entreated him not to. Before he got him out his father came in   caught hold of husbands shirt & tore off 5 of the buttons, two from his pantaloons. H. disengaged himself & attempted to explain matters. Soon an old chief came in & reproved Sampson sharply. He soon made off with himself. His son remained as long as he pleased & then went out at the window. H. & I with our little son returned to our room as soon as we could & resumed our reading, which had been interrupted by their coming in.

Tues. 30th. My time for several days past has been occupied in taking care of the sick & in making preparations for the annual meeting. We are expecting some of the brethren tomorrow.

JULY 1840

Thurs. 9th. Today the meeting closed. All the brethren were present.[12] None of the ladies except Mrs. Whitman. Mrs. Eells & Smith were detained on account of ill health — Mrs. Walker, by her family. She wrote a letter, directed to all the sisters, giving some account of their progress in the Maternal cause. We had a meeting but could do no business as only Mrs. Spalding, Whitman & myself were present.

The Mission have voted to have H. commence a station at Shimnap. Most if not all approve of his accepting the invitation to open a School at Nasqually for the children of the gentlemen of the H. B. Co.[13] He thinks now of putting up a house & preparing for one of the new Missionaries whom we are expecting & then going to Nasqually.

Mon. 13th. This afternoon H. started for W. W. & Shimnap, in co. with Dr. W. & wife & Mr. Rogers to see what arrangements he can make about building at Shimnap &c. Left Huelo[14] & Hannah to take care of me & little son.

Tues. 14th. This morning Kisme Timini brought back the mule which H. took — badly injured — took it to Mr. Spalding to be taken care of.

Wednes. 15th. Jacob is at work in the garden. Mr. Sp. came this morning & borrowed two spades. Conner came to day & said the crows were eating up the corn — wanted to get 20 load of ammunition & Mr. Grays Rifle & bullet moulds. Said he would settle with Mr. Gray for ammunition. I let him have them.

---

12 The sessions began on July 4 and continued to July 9. The tensions with which the meetings began were dissolved by confessions of error and an evident desire to settle difficulties.

13 Here is evidence that by this time Gray had discussed with his brethren the possibility of taking a position with the H.B.C.

14 Unidentified.

THURS. 16th. The young Kayuse who has spent some years at the Willamet arrived last night from Grand Round, Says Mr. Griffin was to be at Dr. Whitmans last night. A Kaw Indian was killed a few days since at G. R. by his own people for his bad conduct. Jacob & Hannah have been all day washing.

SAT. 18th. H. arrived this afternoon very unexpectedly. The Doct. & Mr. R. thought not best to go to Shimnap at present — advise him to wait till the expected associates arrive. Dr. W. seemed to think it best that we should leave the mission & take charge of the school for the children of the H. B. Co.

MON. 27th. Observe to day as a day of fasting & prayer in reference to what it is our duty to do respecting going to Shimnap or taking charge of the H. B. Co.s School. O that the Lord may direct us. We feel desirous to know & do our duty & pray to be directed to that field where we shall be the means of saving the most souls & doing most to promote the glory of God in helping to build up the Redeemer's kingdom.

AUGUST 1840

WEDNES. AUG. 12th. To day Mrs. Spalding & self observed the M. Association. Read a part of the Sermon of Mr. Perkins, Missionary in Persia, on the Subject of Prayer for the children of Missionaries. It is encouraging to think that any are waking up to this subject. Truly these children need the prayers of Christians & so do their parents. . .

SABBATH 16th. Have recently been much impressed with the situation of this people, with their degradation & darkness & the want of Spirituality & Zeal for God among us his professed followers — attended Native worship. . .

On September 7, following the July, 1840, Mission meeting, the Grays left Lapwai for Waiilatpu. A series of events caused the postponement of any effort to move to Shimnap before the annual meeting of the Mission held at Waiilatpu in June, 1841. Again the Mission reversed itself and directed Gray to give up the idea of starting a new station. He was to stay at Waiilatpu and help Whitman. Gray was the victim of the oscillating policy of the Mission. In 1839 he was given the right to explore; in 1840, he was given permission to move; and in 1841, he was told to stay at Waiilatpu.

The Grays lived at Waiilatpu for two years, or until they left for the Willamette Valley in the early fall of 1842. During their last year's residence, Gray erected a 32 x 40 house which was sometimes called the Gray, or the emigrant, house. Two more children were born to the Grays at Waiilatpu. They were Caroline, born October 16, 1840, and Sophia, March 12, 1842.

MRS. GRAY'S DIARY, JANUARY 1841 TO SEPTEMBER 1842

JANUARY 1841

SABBATH JAN. 3rd. Several important events have transpired since I last wrote.

On the 7th of Sept. last we left Lapwai with a view to commence a station at Samnap. After a dangerous passage down S. river we reached the Columbia in safety. Here we learned that Dr. W. who was to go with Husband to select a building spot had gone to Samnap [Shimnap]. H. immediately procured a horse and went up. They found that the site they intended to select had been all overflown & most of the tillable land in that vicinity. Dr. W. advised not to settle then proposed that we go to his house and spend the winter or at least a little season. We accordingly came and have remained here since. On the 16th Oct. God in great mercy gave unto us another babe, a lovely little daughter, whom we call Caroline Augusta. Thus are our responsibilities increased, as is also our debt of gratitude to God the Author of all our mercies.

At the date just named letters were received at this station, stating that Mr. Smith was warned by the Indians to leave Kamiah in one day & requesting Dr. W. or H. or both to come up immediately. Dr. W. & Mr. Black[1] went. H. could not leave me. Mrs. A. T. Smith nursed me & Mrs. W[hitman] who was sick at the same time. Mr. [A. B.] Smith concludes to spend the winter at K[amiah] as the Indians promised that he should not again be molested.

Mr. S.[2] has written to the Board to be dismissed from this Mission. Our prospects at present look dark as a mission. The Lord only knows what is in reserve for us. O that he could make use of us to glorify his Great Name in the conversion of the Heathen.

Yesterday was my 31st birthday. How unprofitable have been the years of my past life. May I henceforth live more to the Glory of God. I would renewedly dedicate myself, and all that I have & am to the Services of my Precious Redeemer.

FEBRUARY 1841

FRID. 12th. . . Mrs. W[hitman] Mrs. L[3] [ittlejohn] and myself

---

[1] Unidentified. Dr. Whitman was called away from Waiilatpu at the time the Gray baby was expected because of a crisis in Kamiah where the lives of the A. B. Smiths had been threatened. At the time of childbirth, Mrs. Gray was attended by her husband and Mrs. A. T. Smith, wife of one of the independent missionaries who had arrived at Waiilatpu that fall.

[2] By this time Asa B. Smith and his wife Sarah, at Kamiah, were so disheartened that they had decided to retire from the Mission.

[3] Mr. and Mrs. P. B. Littlejohn, independent missionaries, arrived at Waiilatpu in the fall of 1840 and spent the following winter there. Narcissa had known Mrs. Littlejohn as Adeline Sadler, back in New York State. Of all the missionary women, she is the only one that Narcissa ever referred to in her letters by her first name.

met this afternoon for prayer — felt the Lord to be present with us. O that we may do nothing to grieve His tender Spirit — meeting this evening. O that my dear Husband may this evening be melted down at the foot of the cross & awake & do our first works, & may we instead of being hindrances to each other, be helpers of each others joy in Christ & be coworkers together with Him, in building up his kingdom.

Sab. 14th. I feel to thank the Lord that I can gain any nearness of access to the mercy seat. . .

JUNE 1841

June 13th Sabbath. To day we gave away our little Caroline Augusta to God in baptism Baptised by Mr. Eells — blessed privilege.[4] May we educate her for his service & glory.

APRIL 1842

8th Friday. My large family & the wants of a comfortable dwelling [5] together with my numerous cares & duties, which required all my time & strength, is the reason why my journal has been neglected for so long a time. Many important events have occurred since my last date, but as they are recorded in Husbands business journal it is unnecessary to add them here. I will however mention that God has greatly increased our responsibility & laid us under renewed obligations to himself, by giving us another immortal being to train for his glory. She was born on the 12th of March 1842. May God give us grace to do our duty to her, faithfully.

MAY 1842

6th Friday. My mind has been much exercised of late, with regard to brother John & sister Caroline, who were in an unconverted state the last news we received from home. I have written a letter to brother John expressing some of my feelings for him & urging him to the duty of living for God. Sent the letter to N.Y. to cross the Mts. with Mr. Rouan [?] I hope he will receive it kindly. Sent one also to Bro & Sis Godley On the 16th April we received information of the death of my beloved father. While we mourn our loss, we mourn not as those with out hope. Blessed be God for all his goodness. He died the 8th of April of inflamation on the lungs.

15th Sabbath. We have had to day, the inestimable privilege of dedicating our little daughter to God in baptism.[6] We have named her

---

[4] The Mission meeting of June, 1841, held at Waiilatpu opened on June 9 and continued to June 14. On Sunday, June 13, the communion service was held and several children were baptized including Leverett Littlejohn, Helen Mar Meek, and Caroline Gray.

[5] The Grays had moved into their new house in Nov., 1841.

[6] The annual Meeting of 1842 was held at Waiilatpu in May. All were present but Mrs. Spalding. A baptismal service was held on Sunday, May 15, when several children were baptized including Marcus Whitman Walker, Mary Sophia Gray, and one or more of the halfbreed children in the Whitman home.

Mary Sophia. (Mr. Eells officiated.) O for grace to perform our covenant vows & may she & our other children early become subjects of renewing grace. I have to day finished a letter to Mother. . .

JUNE 1842

26th SABBATH. Have been reading to day the memoirs of Mrs. Sarah L. Smith formerly Miss Huntington, Norwich, Conn. She appears to have been a woman of ardent piety & active zeal, with an enlightened understanding & elevated mind & glowing imagination, & a very affectionate heart.

I feel greatly condemned for my coldness & inactivity in the service of my blessed Master & am resolved try & live nearer to him in future. I have been much inclined to complain of the want of an opportunity to do much good but fear the reason may be, that I have not been faithful in that which is least. O that I may be content to move in whatever sphere God sees fit to place me. I want humility.

27th MON. Mrs. McKinley [7] who has been at the Drs. for a month past & was confined a fortnight since with a little daughter, started for home this morning in company with her husband. She is in an interesting state of mind & seems to be inquiring the way to Zion. Her husband also appears thoughtful — have been conversing with Mrs. W[hitman] about its being our duty to pray especially for them. Two Indian women, the wives of one man called this morning with some berries to trade for dresses for their children. They seem very anxious to clothe them. I let them have one dress and a pattern for another which I cut. These women are sisters. Polygamy is very common among this people & one man often marries sisters. It reminds of Jacob with his *tender eyed Leah* & *beloved Rachel.* O how much human misery has been, & still is experienced from this cause.

29th WED. Observed our Maternal meeting this afternoon. Mrs. Whitman & Hannah present. We feel that we greatly need the guidance of the Holy Spirit to aid us in training up our beloved offspring for Himself.

JULY 1842

1st FRIDAY. Observed the female concert of prayer for this Mission & the cause of Christ generally in this country this afternoon. . .

3rd SABBATH. The day I spent mostly in reading meditation & prayer. Have noted in my plan book some passages to be remembered from the Mothers Magazine. I esteem this a work of intrinsic merit. . .

4th MON. Our nations Jubilee — We observed the monthly concert this afternoon.

7th THURS. Sent a letter to Mrs. Barclay to day.[8] Spoke to her of the importance of preparing for another world.

---

[7] The native wife of Archibald McKinlay, then in charge of Fort Walla Walla.

[8] Wife of Dr. F. Barclay at Fort Vancouver.

9th SAT. This morning Mr. Walker arrived from Tshimakain & brought me a letter from Mrs. Walker & one from Mrs. Eells for Mrs. Whitman & self. All well at that station. H. received a letter from Mr. McKinley stating that Mr. Demerse a R. C. Priest was about to commence a Mission station at Alexandria, in New Caledonia & Mr. De Smitt [9] one among the Ponderays in the F. Head. language. He, Mr. De Smitt, expects to establish a Station at Okanagan next year. The man of sin is spreading himself far & wide in this land, & all the faith & zeal & energy which the Christian can put forth, will be called into action, in order to stop him in his course of error & sin. O let us be up & doing!

15th WEDNESDAY. Mr. Walker left about noon for home, & Mr. Sp[alding] soon after. I sent letters to Mrs. Walker, Eells & Spalding. My time very much occupied, so that I have but little time to devote to my children or to my own heart. Little Mary requires as much of my time as can be spared from other duties.

We observed our Maternal Meeting this afternoon. . .

We are glad to learn by Mr. W[alker] that some of the gentlemen of the H. H. B. Co. are becoming more attentive to the subject of religion. Mr. Douglas is said to have erected a family altar in his house. Mr. Alexander formerly very profane, is reported to be studying his Bible & Mr. Mc D. to be seriously inclined.

17th FRIDAY. We have had a good meeting this afternoon.

19th SABBATH. . . This afternoon had a Meeting. H read a sermon from The Fountain of Life Text. . .

22nd FRI. This morning H. started for Walla Walla. He is almost sick from the fatigue of harvesting. I sent by him Letters to Mrs. Munger, Mrs. Clark, Mrs. A. T. Smith & Mrs. McKinley. . . The Indians are returning from Willamette with cattle. We observed our Friday concert. Mrs. W. is very unwell to day.

23rd SAT. . . Husband & Dr. W. returned this afternoon.

24th SABBATH. I had an interesting season of prayer this morning — have prayed that God would show us whether it be our duty to leave this mission or remain in it. H. feels that it is our duty to leave. O that we may not be left to act from false impressions & wrong views of duty. . . This afternoon had a meeting — Dr. W. read the discourse. . .

25th MON. Have been a good deal tried with Hannah to day. I told her to night that if she remained here she must do as I told her. She has disobeyed me two or three times today & has been very lazy. I told her I did not wish her to be all day doing the work in the kitchen, that there was but little to do now & it was good to do it quick that she might have a good deal of time to read & sew.

[9] Father Pierre Jean De Smet, the pioneer Jesuit missionary to Oregon. Mrs. Gray's reference to the Pope as "The man of sin" was characteristic of the attitude of all of the missionaries of the American Board in Oregon.

Husband has written to be dismissed from the services of the Board [10] — [erased]

26th Tues.   This morning Hannah came out dressed in her nicest gown which was entirely clean, to go to washing. I told her it was good for her to wear her dirty dress till she was most done washing & then take it off & wash it. She was highly offended & after some saucy talk & some conversation with Jacob she brought her two best dresses & laid them in my room. Previous to her talk with Jacob I gave her the 12 of Rom & 3 of Col. to read. After reading them and talking with J. she brought in the dresses & her testament pointing to the 8th of Rom. Mr. Gray told Jacob to come in & we had a long talk. Jacob seemed satisfied but Hannah went to bed & laid all day, said she was weak probably owing to her rage in the morning. Near night she went out & washed her dirty dress. I have made cheese & baked & taken care of my family — feel very much fatigued to night.

27th Wed.   Hannah put on the dress she washed last night, probably wet, & went to washing. I assisted about washing & did the house work. This afternoon had our Maternal meeting — children quite interested in repeating & singing their hymns & answering questions upon them. Hannah refused to attend the meeting. Indians report that Americans are near, with sheep & cows — sold a little coat to Suia's wife for some berries. The Indians teaze very much for clothes for their children.

29th Frid.   Husband seems nearly sick — is very much tried with the state of the Mission. He has this week written to the Board to have his relations transferred to some other Mission, or to be dismissed.

Hannah continues stubborn disobedient & selfwilled. She now pretends she cannot understand any thing unless I talk Indian. This I have never been in the habit of doing & do not wish to — meeting at Mrs. Whitmans.

30th Sat.   Hannah has done some better to day. Mr. Thompson, Banks & Mart arrived this morning from New Mexico.[11] They are very anxious to settle here & the Indians are quite as anxious to have them. Husband & Dr. W. do not feel at liberty to encourage them. Poor creatures, they know not that they are inviting in, those who will, doubtless, eventually drive them from their lands. O that they would turn unto the Lord & arise from their degradation & sin, that they may be saved & their name may not be blotted out.

31st Sabbath.   Have spent most of the day in reading when not

---

[10] Gray had resolved to resign from the Mission before he learned of the fateful order of the Board, dated Feb. 25, 1842, which called for the return to the States of the Spalding, Smith, and Gray families.

[11] Unidentified would-be settlers.

occupied with my children — meeting at Dr. W.s — H. read one of Martins sermons.[12]

AUGUST 1842

2nd TUES. Monthly concert not attended last evening because Dr. W. was absent & did not return in season. I feel a great desire to do something for the spiritual benefit of this people, & what shall I do? I can not converse with them intelligently on religious subjects because I am not sufficiently acquainted with their language, & my other duties especially to my children seem to forbid my studying the language. But I can pray for them & O that I may have a lively sense of their situation that I may bear them continually in my prayers to the Mercy Seat.

I have been teaching a woman to braid straw this afternoon. She has done well.

3rd WED. Hannah has shown to day that she can be industrious & do her work quick. She has been washing, & did up the work after breakfast which it sometimes takes her half a day to do. She has spoken a little English to day. Husband has hired Mart a man from the Mts. to work for the Mission. He has a young Indian wife. I have been learning her to braid to day.

5th FRID. This afternoon our attention was arrested by the cry which the Indian women make over their dead. We, Mrs. W[hitman] self & children, went to the lodge & found that a very old man had just breathed his last, & his daughter was wailing over him. Soon the other women united with her & the cry became general. It was truly a doleful sound, & reminded me of the wailings of the pit. O how my heart did pity as I looked upon them. Death must ever appear to them dark & shrouded with gloom, until they open their hearts to receive the glorious light of the Gospel of Jesus Christ, who is, the resurrection & the life. . . We returned & united our prayers in behalf of this people & the cause of Christ generally in this region.

6th SAT. The old man was buried this morning — very few people here. They are off drying Salmon & berries for the winter.

7th SABBATH. Have spent most of the day in reading — read the origin & progress of Universalism, a doctrine calculated more than any other to deaden the energies of the church so far as it has influence. . .

8th MON. This morning Mrs. Banks & Mrs. Tompson called on us. They are native women of the Snake tribe & speak a little English. The former was a slave, & was bought by her husband for $200.00

---

[12] Henry Martyn, 1781-1812, was a famous Anglican missionary to India. Not having an ordained minister at Waiilatpu, those living there often read a sermon as a part of their Sunday worship service.

dollars. They appear much more intelligent than our native women; probably bacause they have lived with white men. We gave them a good many squashes, cucumbers, etc. when they went home; Mrs. Tompson, materials to make some moccasins for us.

Caroline is learning to talk very fast. John H. improves some in reading. Mary is healthy & Grows very fast.

10th WED. Yesterday the Indian woman came & sewed her bonnet — has made it too small. . .

Observed our Maternal Meeting this afternoon — had reading the scriptures & prayer, & singing with the children — questioned them on the hymns they sung. We then dismissed the children & read some remarks to parents from Cotton Mathers "Way of doing Good".

14th SABBATH. Husband is very unwell to day. Took medicine this afternoon. The Dr., Jacob & Munger are also unwell. No man at the meeting but Dr. W. I have read to day the funeral sermon of Dr. Griffin of Newark by Dr. Spring of New York. . . I have also been much interested in reading an account of the Nestorian Christians by Mr. Perkins their Missionary.

19th FRIDAY. Have been trying to write some letters home this week, but have been too much disturbed by Indians &c. to accomplish much — have had an Indian woman sewing for me for two days past. She has made a pair of leather pants for H. & done some other sewing.

This evening Dr. W. & H. received a letter from Mr. W[alker] & E[ells] giving it as their opinion that it was not best for Mr. Sp[alding] & Dr. W. to change places.[13] Husband is exceedingly tried with their decision, for he thinks Mr. Sp[alding] will never change his course while he remains at Lapwai. He, Mr. Sp[alding] has given cattle to Craig to dispose of for half the profits, which were promised to Mr. Rogers by the Mission. He says he must leave the Mission if it will support Mr. Sp[alding] in his present course. Dr. W. has gone to T[shimakain] to see Mr. W. & E. on the subject.

Mr. Tompson returned to day with Craig. Mr. T. was thrown from a horse & badly injured. We observed our meeting this afternoon.

20th SAT. Wrote a note to Mrs. McK this morning & copied a letter for H. to Mr. W[alker] & Eells. Mr. Craig & Newbanks,[14] came down this morning also Mrs. Newbank & Mrs. Tompson with her children. They all took dinner with us. Mrs. Tompson brought the moccasins she had been making for me, four pair of which were wrought with beads, contrary to my request. I gave her a dress pattern as she wished for pay. Gave them melons & cucumbers to take home.

---

13 Gray had introduced a motion at the annual meeting of the Mission, held in June, 1842, which called for Spalding and Whitman to exchange stations. This would have placed Whitman, as the Mission doctor, in a more central location. The motion passed but in July, when both Walker and Spalding were at Waiilatpu, they and Whitman felt such an exchange would be unwise. Eells concurred.

14 Unidentified.

21st. SABBATH. Attended native worship this morning. H. spoke to the Natives from the 12th chap. of Acts. This afternoon he read a sermon from H. Martin. Two of Mr. McK's. men were present also Craig, Newbanks & wife etc. Gave Craig some tracts. We have been deeply interested to day in reading an account of the Annual meeting of the A.B.C.F.M. held at Philadelphia in Sept. 1841. They are distressed for want of funds. When will the churches come up to this work as they should?

22nd MON. I have been busy to day in arranging husbands wardrobe, so that he may be ready to go below, if he thinks it duty when the Dr. gets back. To night after the children went to bed, John Henry said to me, come here Mama, I want you to sit down here & talk to me about Jesus Christ. I sat down & talked with him awhile he seemed quite attentive to what I said & wanted me to talk longer.

23rd TUES. Have been busy sewing to day.

24th WED. Have done housework to day & assisted about washing a good many Indians about. H. had 21 in the cornfield today. It is very difficult to keep them from stealing.

25th THURS. Have been sewing most of the day for H.

26th FRID. This morning Hannah churned & went to taking up the butter in little handfuls & working it in her hands. She must do it quick or it would be oily. She went on a while as before holding it a long time in her hands. I then told her she must not do so; she would spoil the butter. She put it away & said she would make no more. She has ironed a little & washed her dress. She will not wear any dress I have given her because I told her it was not good to put on her best dress to wash in when it was clean.

This afternoon Mrs. W[hitman] told me that Hannah was talking about us to Mungo & the Indians & every body she saw, she says I am all the time scolding at her — says I am not a Christian. I get mad & tell lies. Thus she goes on, poor woman! She is certainly to be pitied as well as blamed for her course.

I have ever meant to treat her kindly & have always avoided scolding at her. No matter how pleasantly I speak to her if it is to tell her how to do her work she calls it scolding. She is not to be told like a child.

I feel as though I could not have my mind tormented by her freiks [?] any longer. We shall probably make arrangements to have them leave as soon as possible. Mrs. W[hitman] says she does not want her. She thinks we have treated them, Jc. & Han., too well & now they are paying us for it.

27th SAT. I have not called upon Hannah to do any thing to day. She has spent most of the day in her room. I have finished the ironing & baked. We heard to night that Jacob was going below.

28th SABBATH. This has been a day of rest for the body, but I find it difficult to draw off my mind entirely from the trials & cares of the past week. I feel some relief in casting myself upon the Lord who alone is able to sustain & direct me — attended native worship to day. Husband spoke to them, gave them the history of Joseph. English worship at our house. H. read the 2nd sermon in John Flavels Fountain of Life. . .

29th Mon. Hannah got breakfast & washed the dishes, swept the kitchen & went into her room & has spent most of the day there. I do not ask her to do anything. I have been very busy baking, starching & ironing &c. Dr. W. returned this afternoon. H. thinks he shall go to Willamette soon.

30th Tues. Hannah has been washing up all her clothes to day. She & Jacob both seem to be making preparations to be off. They say nothing to us about it. Husband expects to start for Willamette to morrow.

31st Wed. Last evening Jacob told H. that he was going home. H. talked with him some, told him he had better wait till he returns from Willamette. J. said Hannah wanted to go home. H. asked him what he would say to Mr. Emerson [?] & Bingham.[15] He began to tell over some of Hannah's pretended grievances. H. then told him how sadly she misrepresented things. This morning H. had a very plain talk with Hannah & told her that she MUST behave herself better. I have asked her to assist me some to day.

I have been busy all day in preparing H. to go below. He has not gone to day because the horses did not come in season. John H. was quite sick this morning — is better tonight. We gave him a billious pill this morning.

SEPTEMBER 1842

1st Thurs. John H. is still complaining — gave him salts this morning. H. started for Willamette about nine o'clock this morning. He had another talk with Jacob & Hannah. They appear better to day. I have had some fears about being left alone with them.

2nd Friday. Have been instructing an Indian woman about making some clothes for a little boy. Have had three women sewing carpet rags a part of the day. Hannah is doing nice. Jacob hunting his horse.

3rd Sat. The Indian woman came again this morning to sew on the boys clothes. I have been to work on my carpet what time I could get. Hannah ironing — Jacob off for horses I believe.

4th Sabbath. I have spent most of the day in reading Baxters Life & his "Saints Rest." This afternoon attended meeting at the Drs. He read two sermons from Flavels, Fountain of Life. . .

5th Mon. Jacob spent the day again yesterday in hunting his horse — did not get back till in the night. I had an Indian woman to

---

15 American Board Missions in Hawaii.

work on my carpet to day. John H. is quite unwell. I keep him on light diet.

6th Tues. I have had same woman to sew again to day. I have been colouring Hannah baking. The woman told me that they had bad worship at the Catholic lodge. She said she was going to attend our worship hereafter. John H. appears better.

7th Wed. There is a report that a company from across the Mts. are near here. Feather cap [16] arrives to day from Grand Round with his family. He appears as thoughtless as ever.

Hannah has been washing to day. She had a native woman to assist her. I have made catsup, cut tomatoes for drying &c. &c. Little ones all seem to be well now.

8th Thurs. Have had Simons wife to sew for me again today. Have almost finished two dresses for Caroline. We have heard nothing from Husband since he left W. W. He wrote Dr. W. from there.

9th Frid. Dr. White [17] arrived here from the states about 10 o'clock this morning. He brought 2 letters for husband. Dr. White is appointed by the USA government as Indian agent for Oregon, & he has come out in that capacity with a company of 115 individuals, most of them settlers. A Mr. Lancaster & wife turned back after being out a few days, having lost their little daughter, & Mrs. L. being very sick. They had one individual drowned & another accidentally shot. This evening I was happily surprised by receiving a letter from husband. Jacob has had a fit of the Ague to day — is quite sick.

Soon after the arrival of Dr. White, Squire Crocker & Alex. McKay arrived & some more to night. There are several encamped near here. The remainder are far back, probably some days.

10th Sat. To day Mr. Geiger [18] & several others called. Mrs. Perry and the widow Callihan stay all night. Squire Crocker & Mr. McKay eat & lodge here. Dr. White & Mr. Burns have eaten several meals here. Mr. Perry eat supper here. Mrs. Whitman & Mrs. McKinley &c. arrived from W. Walla to night.

11th Sabbath. Many of the travelers attended native worship. We had English service about two o'clock. Dr. Whitman read a sermon from Flavels "Fountain of Life" & made some stirring remarks.

---

[16] Feathercap, another name for Tamsucky, one of the Cayuse subchiefs. In all probability he was the one who tried to enter Mrs. Whitman's bedroom on the night of Oct. 6, 1842, shortly after Dr. Whitman left for the East.

[17] Dr. Elijah White, the first Indian agent to be appointed for the Indians west of the Rockies. He was formerly a member of the Methodist Mission in Oregon. Strange to say Mrs. Gray makes no mention in her diary of the fateful order of the Board which was carried to Oregon by Dr. White.

[18] William Geiger, of Angelica, N.Y., one of the 1843 immigrants. Later he was employed by Whitman. Other names mentioned by Mrs. Gray in this entry are not identified.

Dr. White made some remarks also. I have very little time to myself to day on account of company.

12th   MON.   Squire Crocker & McKay left to day & several others, Messrs. McKinley, McDonald & Hule, arrived this morning. I took dinner with them at the Drs. They left this evening. Mrs. Mc. stays with me. Came this eve.

13th   TUES.   Dr. White, Mr. Guyger left this morning (today). I sent 3 letters to H., one from self including a copy of 2 from Mr. Green — one for the Mission & one for Dr. W. A letter from Mr. Jackson & one from — I have been cutting a dress for Mrs. McK to day. Letters from Mr. Littlejohn & Ermatinger for H. arrived to night.

14th   WEDNES.   Mrs. McK has been preparing tomatoes for jelly. I have been baking &c. to day. This afternoon several more individuals arrived from the States. Mr. & Miss Brown stay at the Drs. tonight. Jacob & Hannah still sick — able to do nothing at all. I have to wait on them some.

15th   THURS.   Mrs. & Miss Brown called this morning — got some cucumber & tomato seeds. Mrs. McK & self have been washing & making jelly. Hannah walking about some — does nothing yet. Jacob had a slight shake to day. He has his potatoes dug & put in the cellar today.

16th   FRID.   Awoke this morning & found the cellar filling with water. The Dr. is having the drain fixed to day.[19]

I have had one Indian woman mending shoes & another working on the carpet. Hannah had a chill to day.

17th   SAT.   Mr. McKinley came for his family this morning. He took dinner here. They returned this afternoon. Several more Americans arrived this afternoon. The Indians say the Dr. is bad. He sends away the Americans.

18th   SABBATH.   . .Meeting at the Drs. this afternoon. Dr. W. read a sermon from Cecil   Subject Lot's fleeing from Sodom — several — several Americans present.

19th   MON.   The first news that greeted my ears this morning was that Cupup Cupup's son had hung himself.[20] He was about 12 or 14 years of age. He got angry with his father which was the cause of his hanging himself. O how my heart bleeds when I look at this poor degraded people wilfully closing their eyes against the light, & plunging headlong to destruction. Indians about the house last night at the buttery window.

---

[19] The irrigation ditch which flowed by the Gray house had evidently been blocked and had overflowed.

[20] This is one of the few references discovered by the author to any of the natives committing suicide during the mission period. See index of vol. II of this work for a similar reference in Mrs. Walker's diary.

Mr. Smith & family, Mr. Lovejoy [21] & several other Americans arrived today. Mr. S. said they were starving — wanted to buy food. As the Dr. was gone I sold him some flour — took one dollar for. He said he would pay the remainder another time.[22] Gave him some butter & cheese.

20th Tues. Mr. Smith called this morning & left another dollar for the things he got yesterday. . .

21st Wed. Caroline was sick all last night. I was up several times with her. Gave her salts & a soap injection. Husband returned this morning — brought several letters from the Islands. One for me from Mrs. Smith & one from Mrs. Barclay. He has engaged to build & superintend the Oregon Institute. We shall leave for Willamette as soon as possible. Mr. Lovejoy takes tea with us & spends the night.

---

[21] Mr. Smith is unidentified. He was, no doubt, one of the immigrants. A. L. Lovejoy is the one who accompanied Dr. Whitman on his famous ride in the fall of 1842, as far as Sante Fe.

[22] Here is the first reference to the sale of produce to the incoming immigrants at the Whitman station. Some of the immigrants later accused Whitman of charging exhorbitant prices, but they were unacquainted with costs in Oregon.

In the Willamette Valley

The Prudential Committee of the American Board, having before it about sixty thousand words of complaint, largely concerning Spalding, written by Smith, Gray, and Rogers, adopted the following resolution on February 23, 1842:

> Resolved, that the Rev. Henry S. Spalding be recalled, with instructions to return by the first direct and suitable opportunity; that Mr. William H. Gray be advised to return home, and also the Rev. Asa B. Smith, on account of the illness of his wife; that Dr. Marcus Whitman and Mr. Cornelius Rogers be designated to the northern branch of the mission; and that the two last named be authorized to dispose of the mission property in the southern branch of the mission.

This was the fateful order which Dr. Elijah White delivered to Dr. Marcus Whitman at Waiilatpu on September 9, 1842.

But conditions had changed greatly since the letters of complaint, dated in 1840 and 1841, had been written. At the time the order arrived, Gray and his wife had already made known their plans to leave the Mission. The Smiths and Rogers had already severed their connections. Spalding and Whitman had composed their differences. The beginning of the annual Oregon immigration emphasized the importance of the strategic location of Waiilatpu. Of the three stations, that at Tshimakain was the poorest from the agricultural point of view. To have the Spaldings leave and to close Lapwai and Waiilatpu would be disastrous to any further usefulness of the Mission.

Whitman called a special meeting at Waiilatpu, beginning September 26. The first item of business was the acceptance of Gray's resignation. Strange to say both Eells and Spalding voted against accepting it. Gray and Whitman were in favor. Walker, as Moderator, cast the deciding vote for the resignation. Out of this meeting also came permission for Whitman to go East to intercede with the Board for Spalding and for the two southern stations — but that is another story.

Thus William's six years service and Mary's four years with the Oregon Mission of the American Board came to an end. After moving to the Willamette, they lived for two years at Salem where Gray served as General Superintendent of the Oregon Institute, a Methodist school which later evolved into Willamette University. The Gray family then moved to Oregon City, where they stayed for two years, and then in 1846 they settled on a farm at Clatsop Plains south of Astoria. There they remained, except for a brief residence in 1860-1 at Okanogan, for the rest of their lives.

Gray took an active part in political, community, and church affairs. He and his wife were charter members of the First Presbyterian Church of Clatsop Plains, organized on September 19, 1846. This boasts the distinction of being the oldest Presbyterian church for white people to be organized on the Pacific Coast. In 1870 Gray published his *History of Oregon* which, although highly biased, remains an important work on the early history of that area.

After moving to the Willamette Valley, Mary Gray gave birth to six more children, one girl and five boys. Altogether she had nine children, seven of whom reached adulthood. She had the largest family of any one of the six women of the Oregon Mission. Mrs. Walker had eight. When the news of the discovery of gold in California reached Oregon, Gray was one who hurried off to seek his fortune in the gold fields of the Sierras. He left his wife and seven little children, the oldest of whom was only ten, in their farm home on Clatsop Plains. Just what success he had as a gold miner is not known. While in California, Gray became acquainted with the Reverend Albert Williams, pastor of the pioneer First Presbyterian Church of San Francisco. When the Gray's eighth child, a son, was born on June 28, 1850, he was named Albert Williams.

One of Mrs. Gray's extant letters comes from this period. Writing from Clatsop Plains on August 9, 1849, to Mrs. Walker at Oregon City, she speaks of her work making butter and cheese. She wrote:

> You inquire how I get along with our large dairy. Mr. Gray disposed of two-thirds of it previous to his leaving, the remainder I take care of with the childrens help. It keeps me very busy, but I am blessed with good health & so are the children. We miss Mr. G. very much and are quite anxious for his return. I shall look for him in six or eight weeks unless he writes to the contrary.

Thus we see the indefatigable Mary at work, taking care of a large family of children, making butter and cheese for the family and for sale, and running a dairy.

Following the completion of the transcontinental railroad in 1869, the Grays went back to their old homes in the East. That was in 1870. They then had to go by sea from Portland to San Francisco before being able to take the railroad. After crossing the Continental Divide, the line of the Union Pacific followed rather closely the old Oregon Trail. What memories of their epic-making journey of 1838 on horseback must have surged through their minds as they viewed the passing scenery of what is now Wyoming and Nebraska, from the car windows.

Mary Gray died at her home at Clatsop Plains on December 8, 1881, in her seventy-second year. Myron Eells remembers her as being "a lovely woman." [1] William lived until November 4, 1889, when at the age of seventy-nine, he died.

---

[1] Eells, *Whitman*, 320-21.

Mrs. Asa Bowen Smith

Sarah Gilbert White Smith

The youngest of the six women who made the transcontinental journey in 1836 and 1838, was Sarah Gilbert White, the wife of Asa Bowen Smith. She was only twenty-five when she went to Oregon. She is the only one of the six who is not known to have kept a diary. Source material about Mrs. Smith is scanty. Only three of her letters are known to be extant [1] and a copy of a fourth. We see Sarah largely reflected in the writings of her husband and of her associates.

Sarah Gilbert, the daughter of Deacon and Mrs. Alfred White of West Brookfield, Massachusetts, was born on September 14, 1813. We know very little about her early life and education. Since an older sister by four years was sent out as a missionary to Singapore by the American Board in 1834, we may safely assume that Sarah's parents were deeply interested in foreign missionary work. Just when or under what circumstances Asa Bowen Smith came into Sarah's life and proposed marriage is not known. After becoming engaged, the two talked about the possibility of going to Siam as missionaries under the American Board. In the meantime Sarah's sister, Adeline, had married Ira Tracy, also a missionary of the same Board, at Singapore. They were eager to have Sarah and Asa go to nearby Siam. The two sisters could then see each other occasionally.

Following the return of William H. Gray from Oregon in the fall of 1837, the Board reconsidered the application of Smith to go to Siam. Sometime during the latter part of February or the first part of March, 1838, Greene wrote to Smith and asked whether or not he and his fiancée would consider going overland to Oregon with the Gray party. Asa hastened to consult with Sarah. Writing to Greene on March 10, he said: "I arrived here yesterday & have proposed the subject of going to the Indians beyond the Rocky Mountains & find that so far as respect the field of labor, Miss White & the whole family are much pleased." Only one question seems to have been raised and that was whether or not Sarah could stand the difficult overland travel. Here we find the first hint of Sarah's delicate health. "The only objection in the minds of any," wrote Smith, "is the hardship of the journey." And again, "We hope that Miss White may be able to bear the journey & that it will

---

[1] These three letters, dated June, Dec. 18, and Dec. 22, 1839, are given in full in Drury, *Diaries of Spalding and Smith*, pp. 99, and 117 ff. This volume gives in detail the story of the two years the Smiths spent at Kamiah.

result favorably in respect to her health." Smith wrote that there would no question whatever if they could go to Oregon by sea. However, he added: "As I must write something this morning, I will say that probably we shall go."

None of the other three couples of the reinforcement of 1838 was put under such pressure for an immediate decision. By March 10, when Smith replied to the Board, the Grays had been married for about two weeks and were well on their way. Both the Walkers and the Eells had been married on March 5 and were saying their farewells and journeying towards New York City. If Asa and Sarah were to join the reinforcement, they had to act quickly. On March 12, Smith wrote to the Board giving word that they were willing to go, although he added: ". . . we feel that it is a great undertaking to make so long a journey on horseback." Asa and Sarah were married on Thursday, March 15, and arrived in New York on Monday, the nineteenth. They were unable to get to New York in time for the special meeting held for the outgoing missionaries in the Brick Presbyterian Church on Sunday evening, when the instructions were given.

Asa and Sarah are the only ones of any of the thirteen members of the Oregon Mission who had their portraits painted before going to Oregon. Miniatures of each had evidently been made before their marriage. These were first reproduced in the *Missionary Album* published in Honolulu in 1937. The picture of Sarah shows her to be an attractive brunette. When Mrs. Walker first met her on Monday, March 19, she made the following comment in her diary: "She is a little dear."

The mission party left the frontier on April 23 and then the trials of the overland journey really began. Only two tents could be taken for the four newly-wedded couples. The Grays and the Eells had one; the Walkers and the Smiths had the other. Mrs. Walker's diary, which was written only for herself, reveals as does no other document the little points of friction which inevitably arose because of the hardships and sheer physical exhaustion attendant upon horseback travel. By May 3, Mary noted: "Our company do nothing but jaw all the time. I never saw such a cross company before."

The Walkers and the Smiths hung a sheet across the middle of the tent they occupied to give a semblance of privacy. However, sheets are not sound-proof. On Sunday, June 10th, Mrs. Walker wrote:

> Thus far I have been enabled to keep my temper on all occasions though my feelings have been tried exceedingly by some of the company. The uneasy, fretful disposition of Mrs. Smith, together with her persistent whispering are very unpleasant to me. Her husband is much of a hog at table as I have seen.

When the mission party camped at the Rendezvous on the Popo Agie River, the Smiths left the tent and built for themselves a separate shelter. On June 26, when they were still at the Rendezvous, Mrs.

Walker wrote in reference to Mrs. Smith: "She has seemed to cry half the time." When we recall Smith's sharp criticism of the Board's action in sending the reinforcement of 1838 to Oregon by the overland route, we have reason to believe that both Asa and Sarah often regretted their decision to accompany the party. But once on their way, there was no turning back. Sarah could only give vent to her frustrations in tears.

The crowded conditions at Waiilatpu following the arrival of the reinforcement, when four couples and three children had to crowd into the Whitman house, created fresh tensions. On October 3, Mary noted: "Mrs. W[hitman] has said and done many things that do not suit Mrs. S[mith] to-day." It is rather significant that when one room of the new house was completed early in December, the Smiths were the ones who moved into it.

In the following March the Walkers and the Eells left for Tshimakain, near Spokane Falls. The Smiths and the Whitmans were alone at Waiilatpu. Smith was busy studying the Nez Perce language with Lawyer as his teacher. In the first part of February, 1839, Smith and Walker went to Lapwai to help Spalding and Rogers build a grist mill. While the four men were together, Smith made known his desire to move to Kamiah. He was so emphatic in his statements that he said "he would leave the Mission rather than be connected with Dr. Whitman." The situation precipitated by Smith was so critical that Whitman and Eells were summoned so that a Mission meeting could be held to settle the matter. The two men arrived on Friday, February 22. The meeting lasted for three days, not counting Sunday. This shows the seriousness of the problem.

Several alternatives were debated. Smith's proposal to open a new station at Kamiah, sixty miles from Lapwai, was rejected. Then the suggestion was made that the Whitmans open a new and a more central station and let the Smiths take over Waiilatpu. This plan was tentatively accepted although it was not pleasing either to the Smiths or to the Whitmans. By April 20, Smith in a letter to Walker was able to report: "The Dr. expects to remain here himself & expects that I shall leave in the autumn. . . He says much about my going to the upper country of the Nez Perces." [2] Thus by this time Whitman was in favor of Smith moving to Kamiah.

THE SMITHS MOVE TO KAMIAH

Although the Mission meeting held in February had vetoed Smith's plan to move to Kamiah, no prohibition was laid down against the idea of his spending a short time there to study the language. So some time during the closing days of April or the first part of May, Asa and Sarah Smith moved to Kamiah in the very heart of the Nez Perce

[2] Original in Coll. c.

country. There a rude shelter was erected in which the Smiths camped out during the summer of 1839. In a letter written to Mrs. Walker sometime in June, 1839, Sarah gives the following description of their cabin: "We are very pleasantly situated this summer in a little grove of pines, & in a little cedar house of three rooms, kitchen, buttery, and bed room. The whole costs about one weeks labor, no floors or windows. But very comfortable & pleasant for us." [3]

However, in Sarah's letter to Mary Walker of December 22, 1839, she referred to the cabin as "a mere shed," [4] and Asa, writing on January 17, 1840, to Levi Chamberlain in Honolulu, reported: "I spent the summer here in a mere hovel studying the language." [5] Spalding visited the Smiths at Kamiah in July, 1839, and noted in his diary under date of the ninth: "He is living in a very open house without floor or windows, much to the injury I think of Mrs. Smith's health. His food, pudding & milk, is quite too simple I think." The Smiths did have a fresh milch cow with them.

When the Mission met in business session at Lapwai September 2-5, 1839, permission was officially granted for the Smiths to open a new station at Kamiah. All of their goods were moved that month and by November 11 another and a much better cabin had been erected. On December 22, 1839, Sarah wrote her third letter to Mrs. Walker, in which she enclosed a drawing of her house.[6] This measured 14½ by 28 feet and was divided into three rooms, a bedroom, buttery, and kitchen. Each of the two larger rooms had one small window. Nearby was the original cabin erected the previous summer. The two buildings were on the north bank of the Clearwater, about four miles downstream from the present First Presbyterian Church (Indian) of Kamiah. Although Smith was faithful in conducting religious services for the natives on Sunday and in giving instruction during the week days, no effort was made to open a school. During the spring and summer of 1840, from one hundred to two hundred and seventy-five natives were fairly regular in their attendance upon these meetings. Most of Smith's time was spent in language study and on agriculture.

MRS. SMITH'S ILL HEALTH

Beginning with his letter of August 22, 1839, Smith made repeated references to his wife's ill health in his letters to the Board. In this letter of August 22, he wrote: "Mrs. Smith who has been feeble this season in consequence evidently of an affection of the liver." In his letter of the following February 4, he referred to her trouble as being a "spinal affection." And on August 31, 1840, he wrote: "Our situation

---

[3] Drury, *op. cit.*, p. 99.

[4] *Ibid.*, p. 118.

[5] Original in Hawaiian Missionary Children's Society.

[6] The drawing is given in Drury, *op. cit.*, p. 113.

has been the more trying on account of Mrs. Smith's health. The case has become critical & gives me no little anxiety. The hardships & exposures she has passed through have been too great for her constitution to bear up under."

Smith's letters to the Board for this period also show an increasing tendency to criticize the Nez Perces for their selfishness. In all probability this attitude became known to the natives and may have contributed to the incident which occurred on October 13. On that day two of the principal natives "in the most absolute terms & in the most insolent manner" ordered the Smiths to leave Kamiah at once. They had no one to turn to except a Hawaiian by the name of Jack, who then was working for Smith and living in the older cabin. Smith wrote in his diary: "Mrs. S. was very much frightened at their rage & ran out to call Jack." After pleading for time to get ready to go, the two rowdies left.

Smith wrote at once to Spalding and Whitman, begging them to hasten to Kamiah. Gray copied off Smith's letter on October 16 and sent it to Greene, together with a copy of a letter Mrs. Smith had written to Mrs. Whitman and Mrs. Gray, which had been enclosed with her husband's letter. Mrs. Smith's letter follows:

> DEAR SISTERS — I did not anticipate when I commenced this that I should have to tell you what has this day transpired. We have again in the most absolute manner been ordered to leave this place immediately even tomorrow. Never did I see such a day as this. Never did I before feel that our lives were in danger. *But I feel so now.* The talk was in the house and though Mr. Smith was calm, he was as white as a piece of cloth. The Indians became so insolent and so warm with anger that I thought it time to call Jack.
>
> I with difficulty got him within the house. One of them held the door to prevent his coming in. But Mr. S. opened the door himself & let him in. I fear to stay another day as we were ordered to leave tomorrow. I do not know what they will do with us if we do not. Mr. S. is forbidden to speak to the people again. We hope that some one will come to our help as soon as possible. We shall send to Mr. Spalding to come up tomorrow.
>
> Yours in great haste.   S. G. SMITH.
>
> P.S.   Feel extremely tired to night, excitement has over come me.

The Smiths spent a sleepless night. Jack slept in their kitchen. The next day the men returned and again demanded that the Smiths leave but this time they were less belligerent. Spalding arrived on the fifteenth and reported that he too had had trouble with rowdies at his station. The saner and better elements within the tribe began to assert themselves so that the trouble died down. Already discouraged over the missionary outlook among the Nez Perces and with a sick wife on his hands, Smith was quite ready to leave. Whitman also went to

Kamiah arriving on October 22. He and Spalding talked with the natives and after securing promises of good conduct advised the Smiths to remain for the time being.

Realizing the lonely situation in which the Smiths were placed, Spalding and Whitman made arrangements for the Reverend and Mrs. Harvey Clark to spend the winter of 1840-41 with them at Kamiah. The Clarks were independent missionaries who arrived at Waiilatpu in the fall of 1840. Smith in his letter to Greene, of October 21, 1840, questioned the advisability of remaining through the winter when his wife's health was so feeble. He wrote: "Her spinal difficulty remains & this causes such a nervous state of the system that it seems highly important for her future safety to be in a more quiet situation & where she may enjoy more society." With the assurance of the Clarks spending the winter with them, the Smiths consented to remain.

On February 22, 1841,[7] Smith wrote again to Greene and said:

> What we shall do I know not at present. One thing is very certain. Our situation here is extremely unfavorable to Mrs. S's health. Last season she suffered much for want of society Being feeble & able to do but little, her mind is left to prey upon itself, her spirits sink, & she often feels that our lonely situation is more than she is able to endure. Her health has been rather better during the winter, but is now beginning to sink again, & the prospect is that she will be no better than she was last summer. The spinal difficulty remains.

The Clarks left Kamiah about March 1 and again the Smiths were left alone. On April 29, Smith reported to Greene: "Soon after I wrote her health began to decline more rapidly so that by the first of March she was completely prostrated & from that time to the present she has been confined almost entirely to her bed." There was nothing to do but to leave.

Mrs. Smith was too ill to ride on horseback, so she was taken down the river in a canoe. They arrived at Lapwai on April 21. Spalding noted in his diary that she was "not able to sit up much," but he added, "I am fully persuaded that this is not the principal reason of Mr. Smith's leaving the Mission."

Evidently Walker wrote to Smith trying to persuade him not to leave the Mission. Smith replied from Fort Walla Walla on May 3. "Imagine yourself," he wrote, "in my situation with your wife prostrate with a chronic disease, with little or no hope of recovery . . . [having] the necessity of having the care of everything in the house . . . to mend your own clothes, of making your own butter, baking

---

[7] The letter given in Drury, *op. cit.*, p. 188, written by Smith to Walker and dated Feb. 22, 1840, should have been dated 1841. The manuscript shows 1840 but internal evidence, as the reference to Harvey Clark who did not arrive until the fall of 1840, shows that the time was 1841.

& perhaps washing & making your bed, sweeping & of doing the almost numberless & nameless things which are necessary to be done in keeping house. . . In such a situation, I ask, would you feel it your duty to remain in this country?"

No portages were necessary in the four hundred-mile trip from Kamiah to Fort Walla Walla, but from Walla Walla to Fort Vancouver three portages were made, each from one-half to a mile-and-a-quarter in length. At these places Mrs. Smith was carried in a hammock suspended from a pole carried by two men. They arrived at Vancouver the last part of May. After considerable delay, they were able to get passages on a ship bound for Honolulu on or about December 21. The ship took thirty-five days to make the passage. They arrived on January 25, 1842.

NEARLY FOUR YEARS IN HAWAII

After their arrival in Hawaii, Sarah's health began to improve. Smith requested a transfer from the Oregon to the Hawaiian Mission, which was granted. The Smiths remained in the Islands until October 15, 1845, when they sailed for the States going via Hong Kong and Cape Town. For some of the time they were in this Mission, they were stationed at Waialua on the island of Oahu,[8] about twenty-five miles from Honolulu. By 1844 Sarah's health had so improved that she was able to ride horseback again.

Asa and Sarah never had any children of their own. Following the death of Mr. and Mrs. Edwin Locke, also missionaries to the Islands, in 1842 and 1843, the Smiths took into their home the three Locke girls, Lucy, Martha, and Mary. Later, after returning to the States, they adopted the two older girls. The youngest was placed in the home of a relative.

After encircling the globe, the Smiths arrived back in the States with the three Locke girls on May 5, 1846. Asa and Sarah had been away for eight years, three of which were spent in Oregon, nearly four in the Hawaiian Islands, and the rest of the time at sea. They settled first at Amherst, Massachusetts, where Smith accepted a call to be pastor of a Congregational church. In March, 1848, they moved to Buckland in the same state where the frail Sarah died "of consumption" on May 27, 1855, at the age of forty-one.

THE SEED TAKES ROOT

Because of the Whitman massacre, the American Board was obliged to abandon the Nez Perce and Spokane fields along with the work among the Cayuses. However, the Christian seed had been planted and had taken root. Even though deprived of their Christian teachers,

---

8 The author visited Waialua in Dec., 1959. A large stone church building is still being used by a native congregation at that place.

many of the natives, especially among the Nez Perces, kept alive the Christian faith. In 1871, twenty-three years after he left Lapwai, Spalding was able to return to the Nez Perces as an appointee of the Presbyterian Board of Foreign Missions. With him was an associate, the Reverend Henry T. Cowley. They initiated a great revival which lasted for about three years, and which resulted in the baptism of about one thousand of the Nez Perces and Spokanes.

Henry H. Spalding died on August 3, 1874, at his old mission site at Lapwai. Present at the time of his death was Sue McBeth, also a missionary of the Presbyterian Church, who had arrived on the field in the fall of 1873 to carry on the work that Spalding and his associates had started. Sue was joined by her sister Kate, in the fall of 1879. In 1908 Kate published her *The Nez Perces since Lewis and Clark* in which she told of the accomplishments of the training school established by her sister Sue at Kamiah, and which was later moved to Lapwai. Out of this school came fourteen Nez Perces who were ordained to the gospel ministry by the Presbyterian Church.

When Sue McBeth began her work at Kamiah, many of the Nez Perces were still living who remembered the Smiths. In her book, Kate wrote: "Mrs. Smith was a delicate woman, whom the Indians called 'the weeping one'." [9] On March 10, 1882, Asa Smith, then living at Rocky Hill, Connecticut, wrote a kindly letter of inquiry to Kate McBeth asking about the work at Kamiah. "Those whom I knew as children 40 years ago," he wrote, "are now the men & women you have to do with."[10] He made reference to several including "James, the Lawyer's son," whom he remembered "as a little fellow practicing with his little bow & arrow in his father's lodge." Archie, another son of Lawyer, was ordained in 1881. Another of the students of Sue McBeth to be ordained was James Hines, who remembered how as a boy he had ridden one of Smith's four horses used while plowing. He said that he also helped in taking care of the Smith's cow. Thus the work started by Spalding and Smith linked in with the latter work of the McBeth sisters.

One of the most significant statements in the Smith letter of March 10, 1882, was this: "Please remember me kindly to them & also to Ims-tom-wai-kim if he still lives." Perhaps Smith was referring to Utes-sen-ma-le-kin, one of the ringleaders who ordered him and his wife to leave Kamiah in the fall of 1840. Even as Smith wished to be remembered kindly to those among whom he and his wife had lived for nearly two years, so likewise they were long remembered with appreciation by many of the natives who regretted their departure.

[9] *Op. cit.*, p. 60.

[10] Original letter in archives of San Francisco Theological Seminary. Printed in Drury, *Diaries of Spalding and Smith*, 221.